The Politics of Women's Interests

T0352652

Women have interests in common. They also have interests in conflict. This book explores some of the points at which women's interests coincide and considers how they can be aggregated in order to shape political discourses, rules and institutions.

Each of the studies in this volume considers the controversial question: What are 'women's interests'? The book begins with a systematic conceptual analysis and follows with examples of feminist engagement with key political institutions – both local and global – to show why this concept is important and useful in feminist politics today.

The book covers a range of institutional arenas – electoral systems, state-level bureaucracies, civil society, the EU, the UN and the International Criminal Court – in order to illuminate the ways in which women's interests shape and are shaped in these settings. The collected authors suggest that, while coalitions between women will always be fragile due to deep differences between them, it is strategically vital to retain 'women's interests' as a political category.

Looking at experiences in the US, UK, Australia, Canada, and New Zealand, this book will be of great interest to students and researchers in the fields of gender studies, political science, and comparative politics.

Louise Chappell is Senior Lecturer in the School of Economics and Political Science at the University of Sydney, NSW, Australia. **Lisa Hill** is a Senior Research Fellow in Politics at the University of Adelaide, SA, Australia.

Routledge research in comparative politics

The Politics of Women's Interests

New comparative perspectives

Edited by Louise Chappell and Lisa Hill

Routledge
Taylor & Francis Group

LONDON AND NEW YORK

First published 2006
by Routledge
2 Park Square, Milton Park, Abingdon, Oxon, OX14 4RN

Simultaneously published in the USA and Canada
by Routledge
711 Third Avenue, New York NY 10017

Routledge is an imprint of the Taylor & Francis Group, an informa business

First issued in paperback 2016

Transferred to Digital Printing 2008

Typeset in Baskerville by Wearset Ltd, Boldon, Tyne and Wear

British Library Cataloguing in Publication Data
A catalogue record for this book is available from the British Library

Library of Congress Cataloging in Publication Data
A catalog record for this book has been requested

ISBN13: 978-0-415-36834-6 (hbk)
ISBN13: 978-1-138-97864-5 (pbk)

To James and Julian

Contents

Figures

Tables

Contributors

Rosie Campbell is a lecturer in research methods in the School of Politics and Sociology, Birkbeck College, University of London. Her research focuses on gender and politics in Britain. Recent research projects include a co-authored study of gender and political participation in Britain. She was part of the British Representation Study team who surveyed all of the candidates for the 2005 British general election.

Louise Chappell is a senior lecturer in government and international relations at the University of Sydney where she teaches and researches in the fields of human rights and gender and politics. Louise's publications include *Gendering Government: Feminist Engagement with the State in Australia and Canada* (2002), which was awarded the 2003 American Political Science Association's Victoria Schuck Prize for the best book published in the field of women and politics. Amongst Louise's other publications are articles in the *International Feminist Journal of Politics*, *Parliamentary Affairs*, and the *Australian Journal of Political Science*. Louise's current research projects include an assessment of the implementation of the Rome Statute of the International Criminal Court as well as the development and implementation of the UN protocol to prevent the trafficking of women and children.

Jennifer Curtin is a lecturer in politics in the School of Political and Social Inquiry at Monash University, Melbourne. Her current research interests include the descriptive and substantive representation of women and their 'interests', with a particular emphasis on candidate gender quotas. She has published numerous chapters and articles on women's trade unionism and parliamentary representation and she is the author of *Women and Trade Unions: A Comparative Perspective* (1999), and co-author of *Rebels with a Cause: Independents in Australian Politics* (2004).

Roberta Guerrina is lecturer in politics in the Department of Political, International and Policy Studies at the University of Surrey. She is author of *Mothering the Union: The Politics of Gender in the European Union* (2005) and *Europe: History, Ideas, Ideologies* (2002). She is a specialist in

European Union gender politics and social policies. She also has an interest in feminist theories of international relations and human rights. She is an active member of the British International Studies Association's 'Gendering International Relations' Working Group and has published in a number of international journals.

Lisa Hill has been a senior research fellow in politics at the University of Adelaide since 2001. Prior to that she was a five-year fellow in political science at the Research School of Social Sciences, ANU. Her current areas of interest are political theory, intellectual history and issues in electoral law. She is the author of *The Passionate Society: The Social, Political and Moral Science of Adam Ferguson* (2006), and has recently published articles in *Journal of Theoretical Politics*, *European Journal of the History of Economic Thought*, *Federal Law Review*, and *Australian Journal of Political Science*.

Benita Roth is an associate professor of sociology and women's studies at the State University of New York, Binghamton. She has published *Separate Roads to Feminism: Black, Chicana, and White Feminist Movements in America's Second Wave* (2004). In her current research, she continues to look at how women situated in extra-institutional and institutional settings make political decisions and formulate strategies given intersecting structural inequalities like class, race/ethnicity, and sexuality.

Marian Sawer is currently leading the Democratic Audit of Australia, in the Political Science Program, Research School of Social Sciences, Australian National University. She has been the rapporteur for two UN Expert Group meetings on national machineries for women, in Santiago de Chilé in 1998 and in Rome in 2004. Recent books include *The Ethical State? Social Liberalism in Australia* (2003), *Us and Them: Anti-Elitism in Australia* (edited with Barry Hindess, 2004) and *Representing Women in Parliament: A Comparative Study* (edited with Manon Tremblay and Linda Trimble, forthcoming from Routledge).

Merryn L. Smith is currently a Ph.D. candidate with the School of Government at the University of Tasmania, researching the impact of international norms of gender equality on the political participation of women in Timor-Leste. She is also affiliated with the school's Democratization and Citizenship Research Unit, which aims at advancing and promoting the study of democracy, democratization and citizenship globally and within the East Asian region. Her research interests include citizenship, feminist International Relations, and normative politics. She also engages in feminist activism to promote and protect women's human rights through Amnesty International.

Katherine Teghtsoonian is associate professor in the Studies in Policy and Practice programme at the University of Victoria in British Columbia,

Canada. She has conducted research on a wide range of topics, including child care policy debates, job training policy debates, women's policy agencies in Canada and Aotearoa/New Zealand, gender analysis mainstreaming initiatives, and the manner in which developments in these various empirical arenas have been shaped by neoliberalism. Her most recent research has involved a comparative analysis of the (now-former) Ministry of Women's Equality in the Canadian province of British Columbia and the Ministry of Women's Affairs in Aotearoa/New Zealand. She has published articles in a number of journals, including the *Australian Journal of Political Science*, the *Canadian Journal of Political Science*, and *Feminist Studies*.

Jill Vickers is a fellow of the Royal Society of Canada and chancellor's professor of political science at Carleton University in Ottawa. Active in the women's movement, she was parliamentary chair of the National Action Committee on the Status of Women, president of the Canadian Research Association for the Advancement of Women, and president of the Canadian Association of University Teachers. She is the author of a dozen books and many articles and reports to government about women in politics. The Canadian Political Science Association recently created the 'Jill Vickers Prize', to be awarded annually, in recognition of her founding role in feminist political science. Recent works include *The Politics of Race – Canada, Australia and the United States* (2002), *Gender, Race and Nation: A Global Perspective* (with Vanaja Druhvarajan, 2002), *Reinventing Political Science: A Feminist Approach* (1997), *Women and Nationalisms: Canadian Experiences* (with Michèline de Sève, 2000), and *Politics as if Women Mattered* (with Pauline Rankin and Christine Appelle, 1994). She is currently working on a 30-country study of women's involvements with nationalism and nation-building.

Acknowledgement

The editors wish to thank Nicole Vincent for her able assistance in preparing the final draft of this book.

Glossary

ACT Australian Capital Territory.

ALAC Australian Labor Advisory Council.

ALP Australian Labor Party.

ANOVA Analysis of variance, a test used to compare means (averages) between groups.

ASEAN Association of South East Asian Nations.

BC British Columbia, one of the provinces in the Canadian federal system. Provinces in Canada are analogous to states in the Australian or United States federal systems.

BC CEDAW group A coalition of women's groups in British Columbia that prepared and presented a submission to the United Nations Committee on the Elimination of Discrimination Against Women in early 2003, for consideration during CEDAW's review of the Fifth Report presented to it by the Government of Canada.

BES British Election Study.

CAWS Ministry of Community, Aboriginal and Women's Services, a ministry in the provincial government of British Columbia established following the 2001 election.

CEDAW The Convention on the Elimination of all Forms of Discrimination Against Women.

Chi-square test A test of association for two qualitative variables.

Confirmatory factor analysis Factor analysis that tests a specified relationship between the variables.

Correlation coefficient A test of association for two quantitative variables.

Cronbach's Alpha Coefficient A test for the internal reliability of a scale. Values close to one indicate nearly perfect reliability.

CSW UN Commission on the Status of Women.

DACOWITS Defense Advisory Committee on Women in the Services (United States).

DAW United Nations Division for the Advancement of Women.

District magnitude In proportional representation systems the districts are multi-member. In Chapter 5 district magnitude does not refer to the geographical size of the district, but the number of members that can be elected from a particular district.

EC European Community.

ECHR European Convention on Human Rights.

ECJ European Court of Justice.

ECOSOC Economic and Social Council.

EMILY's List A national organization (Australia) that promotes the election to Parliament of progressive Labor women through financial, training and mentoring assistance to endorsed candidates at both the State and Federal levels.

EOC Elements of Crimes Document.

ERA Equal Rights Amendment.

EU European Union.

Euratom European Atomic Energy Community.

EWL European Women's Lobby.

Factor analysis A test for common factors between a number of variables.

FAO Food and Agriculture Organization.

Femocrat Feminist bureaucrat.

FFQ Quebec Federation of Women/Federation des Femmes de Quebec.

First-past-the-post An electoral system, usually used in conjunction with single-member districts, where the person with the most votes wins the seat, irrespective of how many votes they receive. In other words, there is no requirement to obtain a majority of votes.

FTE Full-time equivalent position.

FWCW Fourth World Conference on Women (Beijing).

GAD Gender and development.

Gender quota A rule which aims to increase the legislative presence of women. Gender quotas can be categorized into three broad strategies: as reserved seats for women; as national legislative quotas; or as political party quotas. Some initiatives have been enshrined in law, with financial penalties applied to parties that do not abide; while others have been voluntarily adopted by (usually) left-leaning parties.

Hare-Clark The Hare-Clark electoral system is a single transferable vote (STV, see below) method of proportional representation used in multi-member electorates. It is named after Thomas Hare (1806–1891), who wrote on proportional representation, and Andrew Inglis Clark (1848–1907), a Tasmanian Attorney-General, who introduced proportional representation into State law (Australian Capital Territory Electoral Commission). Hare-Clark differs from other STV methods in several ways: there is a technical difference in the way votes are transferred from candidates elected on the first count and candidates eliminated; it is usually used in conjunction with Robson Rotation; and casual vacancies are filled by a recount rather than a casual vacancy.

Histadrut Umbrella labour union in pre-state Israel (Palestine).

ICC International Criminal Court.

ICCPR International Covenant on Civil and Political Rights.

ICESCR International Covenant on Economic, Social and Cultural Rights.

ICJ International Court of Justice.

ICTR International Criminal Tribunal for Rwanda.

ICTY International Criminal Tribunal for Yugoslavia.

IDEA Institute for Democracy and Electoral Assistance.

IGO Intergovernmental Organization.

ILO International Labour Organization.

IMF International Monetary Fund.

Interpol International Criminal Police Commission.

IOM International Organization for Migration.

IPU Inter-parliamentary Union.

IUCN World Conservation Union.

IWHRC International Women's Human Rights Law Clinic.

IWY International Women's Year.

LEAF Legal Education and Action Fund. An organization which presents test cases on women's rights and gender issues.

Majoritarian A system that requires the winning candidate to receive a majority (more than half) of the vote to ensure election.

MCFD Ministry of Children and Family Development. A ministry in the provincial government of British Columbia; formerly the Ministry for Children and Families, established by the New Democratic Party government in 1996.

Mixed member proportional (MMP) A representation system that provides electors with two votes. One is used to elect an electorate representative by means of a simple plurality system and the second to elect representatives from a party list.

MSF Médecins Sans Frontieres.

MSP Medical Services Plan. A provincial government programme through which eligible, medically necessary services are insured in the province of British Columbia. Administration of the programme was contracted out to the private sector in early 2005.

MWA Ministry of Women's Affairs, a ministry in the government of Aotearoa/New Zealand, established following the 1984 election.

MWE Ministry of Women's Equality, a ministry in the provincial government of British Columbia established after the 1991 provincial election and dismantled following the 2001 provincial election.

NAC National Action Committee on the Status of Women, an umbrella organization formed in 1972 which aggregates the views of over 600 feminist groups in Canada. Currently inactive.

NCBW National Congress of Black Women.

NDP New Democratic Party, a provincial political party on the centre-left of the political spectrum that formed the government in British Columbia 1991–2001.

NGO Non-governmental organization.

NOW The National Organization of Women, a chapter-based, hierarchical organization (USA).

NPM New public management.

NWPC National Women's Political Caucus.

OAS Organization of American States.

OECD Organization for Economic Cooperation and Development.

OPEC Organization of Petroleum Exporting Countries.

PACs Political Action Committees.

Party list A proportional system in which each party puts up a list of candidates. Voters indicate their preference for a particular party and the parties then receive seats in proportion to their share of the vote. Districts are usually quite large in this system. There are two broad types of list systems: closed and open. In a closed list system the party fixes the order in which the candidates are listed and elected, and the voter simply casts a vote for the party as a whole. The open list approach allows voters to express a preference for particular candidates, not just parties.

PrepCom Preparatory Committee.

Proportional representation An electoral system in which legislators are elected in multi-member districts, meaning there are a number of winning candidates in each district. Each elected candidate represents the same proportion of voters as every other elected candidate.

Robson Rotation A modification that ensures that the names of candidates are printed in different orders on consecutive ballot papers. This is done so that no candidate appears in the same position on every ballot paper. Electoral systems experts consider the top and bottom positions to be the most favourable positions for candidates. The use of Robson Rotation also reduces the influence of political parties by impeding them from directing voters to list candidates in a particular order (Australian Capital Territory Electoral Commission).

RPE Rules of Procedures and Evidence.

Sainte-Lague formula One of a number of formulae that can be used to allocate seats under party list systems. The outcome tends to favour minor parties over major parties in that it is harder for major parties to win each additional seat (for details of the formula see G. Newman (1996) 'New Zealand's new electoral system: From FPP to MMP', Research Note 6, Canberra: Department of the Parliamentary Library).

SAP Structural Adjustment Plan.

STV Single transferable vote. A proportional system in which voters are required to rank individual candidates according to their preference. A candidate must receive the calculated threshold quota in order to be elected. Any candidates whose first preference votes equal or exceed the quota are declared elected. Votes surplus to the quota cast for successful candidates are transferred amongst the remaining candidates according to the second preferences recorded by the voter.

TEC Treaty Establishing the European Community.

TEU Treaty on the European Union.

Threshold quota The minimum percentage of votes that a candidate requires in order to be elected. In some systems this quota is fixed at 5 per cent (e.g. in New Zealand). In others it is based on a more complex calculation. For example in the Australian Senate the threshold quota is arrived at by dividing the total number of formal ballot papers by one more than the number of vacancies, and then adding one to the result.

ToA Treaty of Amsterdam.

ToM Treaty of Maastricht.

UDHR Universal Declaration of Human Rights.

UK United Kingdom.

UN United Nations.

UNCHR United Nations Commission on Human Rights.

UNDP United Nations Development Programme.

UNESCO United Nations Educational, Scientific and Cultural Organization.

UNGA United Nations General Assembly.

UNHCR United Nations High Commissioner for Refugees.

UNICEF United Nations Children's Fund.

UNIFEM United Nations Development Fund for Women.

UNSC United Nations Security Council.

VAP Voting age population.

WCGJ Women's Caucus for Gender Justice.

WEAL Women's Equity Action League.

WEL Women's Electoral Lobby.

WHO World Health Organization.

WID Women in Development.

WIJG Women's Initiatives for Gender Justice.

WNC Women's National Coalition.

WTO World Trade Organization.

WWC Women Workers' Council. A women's caucus within the *Histadrut.*

1 Introduction

The politics of women's interests

Lisa Hill and Louise Chappell

Women have interests in common. They also have interests in conflict. In this book we are interested in exploring some of those points at which women's interests coincide and how they can be aggregated in such a way as to be able to shape the way in which political discourses, rules and institutions affect women. The chapters are mainly comparative in nature, drawing on experiences internationally as well as in Australia, Canada, New Zealand, the US, and the United Kingdom. We take a broad view of political institutions to include the bureaucracy, parliament, legal structures, civil society and electoral institutions, as well as regional and international political institutions such as the European Union and the United Nations. The concept of 'interest' is understood to consist of two related aspects: 'the form aspect' which denotes the demand for involvement and control over politics and public affairs and the 'content or result aspect' relating to the issue of the substantive values 'that politics puts into effect and distributes' (Jónasdóttir 1988: 40).

Each author, either implicitly or explicitly, explores the question of whether or not it is proper to speak of women as having specific interests distinct from those of men. We are well aware that assuming there is a definable women's interest necessitates a successful navigation between what Jodi Dean has described as the Scylla of 'essentialist exclusion' and the Charybdis of 'constructivist de-politicization'. It is important to acknowledge 'the richness and complexity of women's experiences' without sacrificing a capacity to theorize 'the conditions for and possibilities of feminism as a political movement' (Dean 1997: 2).

For many years, feminists in the West made the mistake of assuming that women shared all interests in common – constructing and imposing a notion of universal womanhood. A strong critique was developed in response to this over-generalization. Women from post-colonial states joined with others in the West experiencing inequalities based on racial, sexual, and ethnic difference, to argue that women's lives were far too disparate and diverse to speak of a common interest between them. As the pendulum swung away from similarities to differences, the notion of 'women's politics' was replaced with 'gender politics', which focused more on discursive practices than on the importance (and use) of power within political institutions. But this created a new set of problems. As Jill Vickers notes in this volume, 'unrelieved difference is as unrealistic as undivided commonality'. Further, the shift towards difference became paralysing for the development of new ideas and strategies about how women engage in politics, leaving men comfortably in control of the institutions that shape women's lives and gender practices.

Finding a way to cut through this 'either similar or different' approach to women's interests has become imperative at a point in history where the feminist movement itself is under attack from a number of directions. This becomes clear when reading Marian Sawer's account of the apparent abeyance of the feminist movement in recent years and it holds equally in western liberal states, such as the US, Canada, Britain, Australia, and New Zealand as it does in other contexts. The rise of neo-liberal (and, in some cases, socially conservative) governments has led to the retreat of the state in favour of market forces. This trend has, in turn, enabled, if not encouraged, a reassertion of individual over collective interests (see Sawer in this volume and 2003). The combination of these broader ideological shifts, which are reflected in the policies and practices of political institutions, and the emphasis on *difference* by some feminist theorists and activists, has led to the neglect of many of the inequities shared by women as a group. Left uncontested are such issues as women's low rates of political representation, low incomes and a significant wages gender gap, as well as the limited (and dwindling) provision of childcare, health and social services. Also left unaddressed is the persisting emphasis in neo-liberal and conservative policies and discourse on women's 'appropriate' or 'natural' gender roles as mothers and wives.

This book represents an attempt to bridge the gap between 'sameness' and 'difference' approaches to women's interests. The contributing authors work from the assumption that women do share some political interests, but they also accept that important differences exist between women as a group. Through delicate and mutable alliances, women may adopt a 'strategic essentialism' (Spivak 1995; Jhappan 1996) that enables them to work for a period of time toward a single objective but this does not mean that they will automatically share other interests in all political spaces. Positing the existence of specific gender interests does not preclude the possibility that there may be specific cultural interests; moreover, neither does it mean that there can be no general human interests.

Jill Vickers takes up this first point in Chapter 2 where she argues that 'although common interests *may* exist, it is more likely that *any* aggregate of women has both shared and conflicting interests'. Nevertheless, where women do find common ground on specific issues and can articulate shared objectives, the notion of women's interests becomes a necessary and powerful political tool for women's actors.

For Vickers, and other contributors to this volume, women's interests are fragile but also dynamic. They are not fixed but are constructed through political processes over time. Institutional practices and discourses shape the way men and women are conceived and through this process gender stereotypes and expectations are constructed. While historically women and their interests were defined very narrowly, these can alter over time and place. As a number of the following chapters show, this change can occur primarily through the acceptance and construction of new discourses and practices brought about by women's engagement with institutions.

The contributing authors take as given the central importance of political institutions and processes in constructing the nature of women's interests. Accordingly, they adopt a pragmatic and strategic attitude towards women's engagement with these institutions. As Vickers reminds us, avoiding 'public' politics and interaction with the state is not an option for women; to do so leaves the power with those in formal institutions, primarily men, to go on defining women's interests as if they know what they are. Thus in order to pursue any shared interests women must embrace politics and its institutions. But in doing so they are not simply involved in a process of co-option – a point elaborated on by Roth in this volume. It is important to conceive of institutions, whether bureaucratic, legal or representative in nature, as operating in a co-constitutive way with those seeking institutional engagement. On the one hand, institutions play a role in shaping (and constraining) social identities, including those of women, while on the other, social groups, including women, help to shape the institutions.

Chapters in this book point to examples where, through their engagement with political institutions, women's activists have had some success in expanding conceptions of women and their interests. The ability of feminist actors to refine the prevailing conception of women's interests at the supra-national level (see Guerrina Chapter 9, Smith Chapter 10, and Chappell Chapter 11), through the bureaucracy (see Sawer Chapter 6, Teghtsoonian Chapter 7, and Roth Chapter 8) and through electoral politics (see Campbell Chapter 3, Hill Chapter 4, and Curtin Chapter 5) gives empirical support to the wisdom of women's continuing and proactive involvement in 'mainstream' politics.

Accepting that women's engagement in political institutions makes a difference in terms of expanding public conceptions of women and their interests is not an evasion of the fact that there are often serious limitations to these interventions. As Benita Roth suggests, 'feminist fading' can occur even in the most 'friendly' of institutions. In relation to the EU Roberta Guerrina and Merryn Smith show how problematic engagement can be when women's interests are included in policy debates but are constructed too narrowly.

The examples we highlight of successes and limitations of efforts to aggregate and articulate politically women's interests point to some important lessons for future feminist organizing. Hill's chapter underlines how increasingly vital is the women's vote to the success or failure of political parties; Curtin reminds us that proportional electoral systems are not a 'cure-all' for women's representation in electoral politics but that these electoral processes will only make a difference when they are combined with a concern by political parties for deep and systemic improvements to the representation of women. Sawer, Roth, Teghtsoonian and Chappell all emphasize the importance of having both *insider* and *outsider* activists working together to push for the advancement of new conceptions of women's interests.

While it is important to recognize the success of some women in using political institutions to advance their objectives, it would be unwise to assume that these positive developments are permanent or predictable, particularly in light of the shift toward neo-liberalism and, in some instances, (neo) conservatism in the comparative settings included in this volume. Because political institutions, whether at a domestic or international level, still tend to be dominated by men and male-centered thinking and practice, women's efforts to express and re-define what is understood to be their 'interests' will continue to meet with resistance. The chapters that follow are written with this sobering reality in mind, and in some cases look for ways of overcoming it.

References

Dean, J. (1997) 'Feminist solidarity, reflective solidarity: theorizing connections after identity politics', *Women and Politics*, 18(4): 1–26.

Jhappan, R. (1996) 'Post-modern race and gender essentialism or a post-mortem of scholarship', *Studies in Political Economy*, 51: 15–63.

Jónasdóttir, A.G. (1988) 'On the concept of interest, women's interests, and the limitations of interest theory', in K.B. Jones and A.G. Jónasdóttir (eds) *The Political Interests of Gender*, Sage: London.

Sawer, M. (2003) *The Ethical State? Social Liberalism in Australia*, Melbourne: Melbourne University Press.

Spivak, G. (1995) 'Subaltern studies: deconstructing historiography', in D. Landry and G. MacLean (eds), *The Spivak Reader: Selected Works of Gayatri Spivak*, New York: Routledge.

2   The problem with interests

Making political claims for 'women'

Jill Vickers

Formal politics, which involves decision-making by governments and international organizations, has been marked, historically, by women's virtual absence; despite a few women presidents and prime ministers, governing is an activity dominated by men. Since the mid nineteenth century, however, some women have made claims, especially about rights of access, on behalf of all women. Early women's movements demanded citizenship and access to education and civil rights to enter into contracts, assemble freely and marry according to personal choice. These movements emerged globally, moreover, and were not limited to 'the West'. Some were independent; others developed within mixed-sex movements led by men. Through this process, women developed capacities for self-organization: formulating and pursuing projects over time. In this chapter, I explore the bases on which women's movements formulated and expressed political claims, drawing many into 'women's politics' in both *formal* and *informal* political arenas. Still others did the political work of challenging male-centred discourses. Although some women joined projects focused on class or national liberation, enough mobilized around 'women's politics' to advance gender justice.[1] 'Women's politics' encompassed the varied grounds activists used in asserting claims, demanding policies, resources, and changes in social and political institutions in the interests of 'women'.

The idea of 'women's politics' relating to formal politics seems irrelevant, almost improper, to many contemporary feminists. In this chapter, I explore why, in current feminist scholarship, the idea of 'a politics of women's interests' is rarely used. And why, when most feminists now use only *gender*, we also use 'women' to represent collective political actors; and why – when most feminists focus on the politics of difference and identity – we are reformulating the idea of 'a politics of women's interests' which includes both commonalities and differences.

In earlier activism, claims purportedly 'in the interests of women' invoked a universal woman whose interests were self-evident and shared by anyone with the equipment to bear and feed children. This understanding is no longer tenable, especially in a globalized environment. The idea that 'women' everywhere share a common interest properly has been repudiated, along with the universalism of feminist ideology that constructs an essential 'woman' as equally oppressed by the same forces everywhere. Women's lives are as much shaped by the 'development gap' (Vickers 2002a) between rich and poor countries, by nationalisms, and by class, sexual orientation, 'race' or caste divisions within countries, as by gender and reproductive capacity. Whether 'women' can be constructed as a group with any interests in common is the subject of intense debate, in 'the West' where post-modern relativism challenges any universalism; and in the 'two-thirds world' where white, Euro-American women's claims to leadership increasingly are challenged. Women in the global south and minority women within 'western' countries challenge both false universalism and assumptions of superiority and claims to leadership. But why were 'women's interests' rejected as a basis for feminist politics? The idea was rejected partly because the idea of 'interests' was associated with a liberal willingness to work inside existing political systems. But it also involved a confusion between 'women' as a political category and 'woman' as an ontological category.[2] In my discussion, I address the effects of both sets of difficulties.

When debates emerged within political science about 'gender' and 'difference' the weakness of feminist scholarship in the discipline led to a premature abandonment of the concept of 'women's interests'.[3] The texts in this volume demonstrate our need to understand the relationship of *organized* women to governments and quasi-governmental international institutions. This is because if some women do not aggregate and articulate accounts of women's collective interests to decision-makers, directly or via conveyers like political parties, the men who still dominate all major institutions will do so for them. In each arena explored in this volume, 'women's politics' involve struggles between men's efforts in dominant institutions to determine what 'women's interests' will be; and accounts by women who constitute an *organized interest* to express a consensus about 'women's interests' constructed through some deliberative process.[4] Refusing to acknowledge that 'women' have interests *both* in common and in conflict reinforces the delusion that political power organized in institutions can be ignored with impunity, especially when neo-liberal policies restructure decision-making so that it occurs further and further away from where most women live. Democracies, however flawed, remain the best arena for women's citizenship. And, however critical we may be of democratic governments, we need the understanding of 'interests' and 'power' that feminist political scientists can now provide to balance the critiques of theorists.

This chapter has three main parts. First, I explore why the concept of 'women' is needed in addition to 'gender' by feminist political scientists exploring women's experiences of politics. There is a role for gender analysis in exploring women's political activism, but relationships with state and quasi-governmental international institutions which command or involve *coercive* power also require the idea of 'women' as collective actors. This does not mean that we should see 'women' as an essential or ontological category. Initially, I use 'women' to denote the organized interests and 'woman' to denote the ontological category. 'Women' does not mean that a common interest exists by theoretical fiat, even within a specific country or group, *unless one can be demonstrated to exist empirically.* My methodological assumption is that, although common interests *may* exist, it is more likely that *any* aggregate of women has both shared and conflicting interests (Vickers 1997; Vickers 2002a). 'Women' as an organized interest involves some women constructing a solidarity around a specific issue or issues by foregrounding shared interests, goals or identity. If women aggregate their issues and goals within a coalition, or more permanently in an organization, and articulate their projects in the name of women, they may become an *organized interest.* Using the strategy of 'strategic essentialism' (see Jhappan 1996; building on Spivak 1995), they can advance a shared, constructed position despite differences they choose to ignore (or do not yet recognize) to 'do politics' within state-focused or international institutions. Alternately, dominant women within organizations may represent their interests and goals as if they were shared by all, or else not even realize they are not shared. But if ignored for too long or often, minorities withdraw and form their own organizations. Where 'women' constitutes a mutually agreed-on political banner, it can be used to pursue access to formal politics. The rubric also is used by elite men commanding political institutions, however, usually in an imposed essentialism so that what they consider to be appropriate behaviour for women will be embodied in laws and policies, and backed up by courts or with force. It is this competition to represent 'women's interests' which this volume explores.

In the second part of the chapter, I explore why the concept of 'women's interests', and linked ideas like the *general interest* and *organized interests,* also are needed by feminist political scientists to explain how groups of women facing various political regimes construct and advance their claims to formal political institutions. In the third section, I explore women's experiences with organizing 'interests' in both nation-state and trans-national arenas. I examine several organizations women developed in western democracies to sustain solidarities and make coalitions more enduring. This emphasis on feminist *praxis* in organizations is different from the small consensus-based groups usually associated with second-wave activism. In the former, the central problem is how to hold responsible those making claims on behalf of 'women'. The persistence of debates about the acceptability of organizing 'women's interests' and asserting them in formal politics reveals the potency of, and dangers in, claims based on 'strategic essentialism'. Failing to insert claims determined by women into formal politics is also dangerous, however, because it leaves men's accounts unchallenged. To make these issues more concrete, I briefly explore three cases: (1) the National Action Committee on the Status of Women (NAC) – an umbrella organization aggregating the views of over 600 feminist groups – which represented Canadian 'women' for three decades; (2) The National Organization of Women (NOW) which struggled to become an organized interest articulating women's claims to the US Congress, thereby provoking internal conflicts; and (3) conflicts over how 'women's interests' are constructed in international arenas.

Why 'women'?

The emergence of organized women's movements contesting men's power to determine what is 'in the interests of women' marked a critical change in state-focused and in international politics. For 'women' to intervene in the politics of nation-states, they first had to develop and articulate a collective voice formed issue by issue, or in longer-term solidarities facilitated by organizations. They had to learn to insert claims into decision-making processes which required developing receptive listeners (even allies) since male decision-makers rarely understood what 'women' wanted without considerable help. Even when women entered decision-making positions, their exceptional status often meant they too had to be 'cultivated' to understand what organized women were advocating. In the various 'waves' of activism over more than a century, organized women approached these challenges differently. Some women concluded state-focused activism was not productive, but many tried to gain access or articulate their views as individual voters, party or union members, through mixed-sex lobbies and movements, but especially through *autonomous* women's groups and movements. The capacity for self-organization is probably as important as gaining citizenship rights for women to advance gender justice in democratic systems. Recently, however, many women in western democracies have abandoned the project of interacting with governments, believing that representation of collective interests is impossible; or that after access (e.g. the vote) was won, women no longer shared any interests in common.

Since the 1980s, the 'challenge of difference' (Druhvarajan and Vickers 2002) has fragmented feminist movements and often destroyed organizations built by earlier activists – experiences frequently used to explain why the idea of women's political interests has fallen into disrepute. The globalization of discourse after the collapse of cold war categories ('first world', 'third world') also demands that we re-assess western feminist views on interest-based analysis. It has become urgent especially to determine how 'women's interests' can be asserted in international arenas and transnational systems like the EU. Again, the elite men who still dominate these institutions are eager to define 'women's interests' and roles. Some organized women have found space in international politics for their activism, such as in the International Criminal Court and the UN as discussed in this volume. Such activism may only promote leadership by women in neo/imperialist states who will determine what interests will be represented. As within nation-states, the most advantaged women often shape the collective voice that is advanced. How much more dangerous is operationalizing a collective voice in international arenas. Nonetheless, if networks of organized women do not assert some shared understandings of 'women's interests' the elite men making decisions at the United Nations (UN), World Bank, International Monetary Fund (IMF), the International Criminal Court or in non-governmental organizations (NGOs) surely will. So while complex and open to western dominance, it is urgent that organized women pursue the project both at home and internationally.

Many feminists in 'the West' believe a politics of 'women's interests' necessarily involves essentialist understandings of women's experiences; an approach no longer tenable. Consequently, they replace understandings of politics which include both formal (state) and informal (civil society and the private realm) spheres with post-modern ideas of fluid and multiple identities in which 'gender' replaces 'women' and 'politics' is diffused throughout society and discourse. This trend challenges the category of the political as a differentiated activity. As Anne Phillips observes, the idea that feminism provides 'an alternate conception of politics' which rejects 'the distinctiveness of [formal] politics from other practices in our social life' is 'a near-consensus' (1998: 11). While this broader conception of the political has had positive results in understanding the complex nature of male dominance and the perpetuation of patriarchal power, 'politics' 'was subjected to such devastating criticism that it threatened to dissolve as a distinct category of analysis' (Phillips 1998: 4). This 'depoliticizing of politics' is what feminists working in political science address by re-conceptualizing feminist accounts of 'politics' again to include states and the politics of interests. 'The personal is political' de-legitimized engagement with formal decision-making to the point where specialized concepts to explain state politics were deemed unnecessary.[5] While not discounting the importance of representations of masculinity and femininity, or the politics of the family and civil society, the feminist project within political science assumes formal politics and state-based decision-making *are* specialized behaviours needing specialized analytic tools, if only because of their monopoly over legitimate uses of force.

Where women do not articulate a common voice to decision-makers, allies, or receptive listeners, democracies cannot be deepened by the feminist project. Where women do develop collective demands, and especially where they develop allies and receptive listeners, many women's circumstances can be enhanced. The texts in this volume focus mostly on 'the politics of women's interests' in western democracies. But the importance of the concepts extends to all democratic regimes. Reclaiming them for feminist political science should also shed new light on the potential of a politics of 'women's interests' for deepening women's experiences of democracy.

'Women' and early 'waves' of feminist activism

Early activists made claims on behalf of 'women' as a sex because all women experienced the same legal disabilities such as being denied the legal status of political citizenship and social adulthood entitling them to civil rights. Hence in Iran or Saudi Arabia women still are engaged in 'first wave' struggles while they seek these rights. Women in countries without effective democracy struggle for meaningful citizenship when they risk their lives to oust dictators and re/establish democracy. These struggles are about women wanting citizenship so they can define their own life opportunities instead of having roles, laws and policies made by men who control state decision-making imposed on them because of their sex. Some women even oppose campaigns for suffrage, experiencing little disability because of their wealth, standing or because they have gained from alliances with men in power. Nonetheless, first-wave activists formulated their demands as in the interests of 'women' because all women potentially could benefit from access to citizenship and civil rights.[6]

In subsequent 'waves' of activism, universal claims also were made in the name of 'women' as a sex, especially for the right to control their own bodies regarding sexual access and reproduction. Unlike the logic of first-wave claims, which drew women into political systems managed by male-dominated institutions, these claims involved women using self-organization and citizenship to achieve objectives that varied according to their location in society (Rankin and Vickers 2001). In both periods, women struggled to achieve first-class citizenship by deepening democracy and gaining greater access to decision-making sites where mostly elite men still defined 'women's interests'. 'Western' feminists focused on the 'public/private' divide which marked a public zone where 'women' could be (almost) equal as citizens from a private zone where they are constructed (usually unequally) as men's wives and children's mothers. Leagues of women voters, national councils, women's action committees and electoral lobbies all initiated *electoral projects* using women's votes to expand the scope of their equality and remove disabilities in pursuit of gender justice. The idea of a voting bloc of women – now captured in the *gender gap* – was basic to that project. Discussions of the gender gap are provided in this volume by Campbell (Chapter 3) and Hill (Chapter 4).

In many western democracies, women's electoral projects were hampered because women's citizenship was long delayed (to the mid or late twentieth century, such as in France or Switzerland). Where democracy was based on male citizenship for many decades, men's constructions of 'women's' interests and women's exclusion were justified by elaborate theories. This made it hard for many women, especially in powerful post-imperial states, to see state-focused politics as anything other than male-dominated and implicated in patriarchy. To them, the result of engagement most likely would be co-option. Where most women gained citizenship before 1939, they voted and lobbied for reforms, from prohibition to the creation or expansion of welfare state programmes. They also worked to *transform* electoral and legislative systems to deepen democracy and enhance women's participation.[7] Women of dominant groups led, benefiting from privileges of 'race', class and the affluence made possible by their location in global empires: a story now better understood through 'post-colonial' and anti-racist writings. Dominant women claimed to represent other women's interests; but, where they could, dominated women challenged these claims and organized to express their own views. Wherever democracy was established, women had a common interest in gaining and exercising citizenship. But this did not exhaust the issues around which diverse women organized. Many women saw the end of war as an interest shared by their sex, for example, and debate between essentialist and social constructionist explanations of this pacifist 'tendency' persists.

The second 'wave' of women's activism, which began in 'the West' in the 1960s and 1970s, also made universal claims, especially about bodily experiences and power relations within families, accounts challenged by 'race' and other minorities. Many second-wave feminists, especially in post/imperial countries, held negative views about democracy because they saw it as compatible with the oppression of 'women'. Formal politics were seen as saturated with male norms and assumptions legitimizing women's lack of political power and perpetuating the idea that male dominance and privilege were inevitable (Phillips 1998). Often there were not even token women in legislatures, courts, police, and bureaucracies (except as secretaries) in democracies supposedly based on political equality. This provoked two responses: feminist theoretical arguments against *representative* and in favour of *direct* democracy in small consensus-based groups; and Marxist and anarchist arguments against government. Bureaucracy and the military especially were viewed as incompatible with feminist values (see Marian Sawer, Chapter 6 in this volume, on this point). Democratic governments in which women could vote but were never decisions-makers were seen as facilitating men's participation in formal politics through women's unpaid domestic work (Phillips 1998: 6–10; Pateman 1985). Systematic male dominance and female subordination were theorized as *patriarchy,* which many believed was a universal structure capable of explaining women's oppression everywhere and at all times. If states were complicit with patriarchy, liberation meant living in a counter-culture or engaging in *counter-hegemonic* activism, not legitimizing the formal political system by participating in it.

The absence of women from formal and international politics also resulted in new versions of the electoral project to get more women s/elected to decision-making positions. Women did create and run for feminist parties or lists (usually with little success); or pressed to get male-dominated parties to get more women elected, not just run them as 'lost-cause' standard-bearers. As Sawer illustrates in this book, in Australia a *femocrat project* and in Scandinavia *state feminism* were developed to establish agencies within government administrations to advance women's interests. These projects were stimulated elsewhere by international activism, especially at the United Nations. Women worldwide believed their status and condition needed improvement, but they also divided more into ideological camps (as did the world) about the causes of women's oppression and their remedies. Engaging or not with decision-making institutions increasingly was a subject of contention, not a matter in which access implied a shared interest.

The emergence of 'gender'

In the 'third wave' of activism, western feminists, academics and activists often work on different trajectories, especially regarding 'women's' claims vis-à-vis states. Achieving greater access by women to institutions of democratic states, and projects to reform their electoral, legislative and judicial systems to deepen democracy, remain a strong focus of much feminist activism, and of the growing field of feminist political science. Focusing on issues as diverse as what kind of electoral system will best represent 'women' (see for example Jennifer Curtin, Chapter 5 in this volume), or constitutional politics, feminists who focus on formal state and international politics build networks and coalitions around these new issues of access, and around specific issues of concern to variously located women. But 'women' as political actors receded in the academy as a new feminist 'gender project' emerged – symbolized in part by a change in language. 'Women' as the central concept of feminist politics has been replaced by 'gender' but not just as a matter of semantics. Carver asserts that, while the 'lazy' popular usage makes 'gender' synonymous with 'women' and even 'loosely with sex' (1998: 18), 'gender' involves a different understanding of politics based on the belief that sex, sexuality and gender *all* are *discursively produced*.

This differs from the views in this collection in which *sex/gender regimes* are understood as constructed by *both* discourse and social practices, and bodily experiences; and in which 'women' continues to resonate as a political collectivity but with interests both in common and in conflict. In this volume, we explore current issues of access and deepening democracy, in which most women do share interests at some level. For example, the fact that EU policies construct 'women' primarily as workers in protective legislation, allowing them limited space to contest their oppression or exploitation in the domestic sphere, gives most women a common interest in expanding the political space within this new regional political arena (for a discussion see both Guerrina, Chapter 9, and Smith, Chapter 10, in this volume). In most democracies, women still struggle for physical and economic security; access to education; reproductive autonomy and health care; and access to employment, services, responsibilities and resources, all of which suggest that the political claims around 'women's interests' have not lost any currency. Why then has the concept become discredited within the academy?

In this section, I outline the third-wave 'gender' project and explore its implications for feminist political science focused on laws and policies which operate both as discourse and social practice. It is important not to dismiss positive elements in the turn to 'gender', provided power (especially coercive force) as an element in social practices and the body in relation to sex and reproduction also are taken seriously. Nation-states' interest in women has been as much in their bodily power to reproduce populations as in their cultural power to reproduce collective identities. While constructing gender differences through discourse is part of the process of regulating male/female relationships, it is only part of the long history of relationships between state powers and women's bodily and cultural powers of reproduction and men's struggle to control it.[8] First, we need to understand the implications of the turn to 'gender' instead of 'women'. Several recent volumes reveal the trend. In *Gender Politics in Global Governance*, the editors argue that by using 'gender' rather than 'women ... we follow prevailing practice among feminist scholars today'. But they also acknowledge the 'theoretical commitments the term implies' (Prügl and Meyer 1999: 5).

> Gender emerged as a crucial concept of the women's movement, originally replacing the term *sex* (which social scientists had used to describe differences between women and men) but increasingly replacing as well the term *woman*. Feminists insisted that sex differences were not natural and biologically given. Instead, they argued that gender inequalities were the result of pervasive social construction processes ranging from childhood socialization to gender images in the media.
>
> (Prügl and Meyer 1999: 5)

Joan Scott argued that gender was 'a primary way of signifying relations of power' (1986: 1067). Gender divided the world in a binary fashion that provided the means for the articulation and legitimation of power. Like power, gender inhabited social relations including symbols, norms, organizations, institutions and subjective identities (Prügl and Meyer 1999: 5–6).

The differences between men and women previously attributed to nature (sex) are now generally seen as socially constructed. But while this may privilege gender over sex, it is not clear why it privileges 'gender' over 'women'. Indeed, Prügl and Meyer cite those who argue that '[t]he retreat to analyzing gender' results in a *de-politicization* in which a cacophony of many different descriptions of 'women's' local experiences and diverse constructions of 'gender' make '[a]n internationalist "we" unspeakable' (1999: 6). The fragmentation of 'woman' in the face of the assertion of difference, and the postmodern insistence on infinitely fluid identities led to the rejection of 'women'. Yet unrelieved difference is as unrealistic as undivided commonality. Moreover, a key problem in replacing 'women' is the political potency of the term; without it, de-politicization seems inevitable since 'gender forces' lack agency. The authors insist they can retain 'women's' agency without using 'woman'. But is the question correctly posed? Feminist political science needs both *sex* and *gender* as well as a concept of 'women's interests' which does not signify an essential or universal wom*a*n.

Bayes *et al.* (2001) adopt Connell's (1987) concept of *gender regimes.* To Connell *gender* is an 'active process' used to create 'divisions of labour, power and emotions between men and women as well as modes of dress, deportment, and identity' (cited in Bayes *et al.* 2001: 1). Gender regimes are seen as constructed by economic, political and inter-personal practices, not by biological sex differences; but also not by discourse alone. Their focus is on how globalization and democratization affect 'gender regimes'. But they introduce a third force – 'feminization' – which represents 'movement by women into the public arena' and lets them move from 'gender' to 'women' studied as actors in movements. While 'women's' engagements with nation-states are addressed briefly in several essays, the main focus is how women in movements struggle in civil society to respond to globalization and democratization. Consequently, women respond to 'factors' (globalization and democratization) and are constituted by them (feminization), although they do become actors.

In both Bayes *et al.* and Prügl and Meyer, the usage of 'gender' falls into Carver's 'gender' = 'women'-by-another-name category and both groups of editors find ways to re-introduce 'women' where the analysis of politics needs them. Is the gender project any deeper than a new politically correct terminology? In fact, it has more significance than either group suggests. The retreat from bodily sex differences reflects western feminism's anti-natalism and the negative connotations of nature (especially if unmediated by technology) in western thought generally. Many feminists fear that if women are associated with what is 'natural' male dominance will be unchangeable. 'Gender' is also a way of incorporating multiple 'genders' or sexual diversity (Butler 2004) which is believed to require dismantling 'women' as a collective to be oppressed, marginalized or liberated through political action. If 'women' are oppressed as a group, the logic runs, no other group contained within or overlapping with it can also be oppressed. Yet Iris Marion Young (1988) has shown us through her 'multiple faces of oppression' analysis that we can be oppressed and oppressors simultaneously. Or is the real issue the retreat from formal politics and widespread feminist disillusionment with democracy?

I employ an interactionist approach in which social manifestations and discursive constructions of differently located women's sex/gender experiences are the focus of their politics. I follow Gayle Rubin (1975) in using the concept of *sex/gender* which designates a variable relationship between what is influenced by biology (sex) and what is socially constructed (gender).[9] Combined with Connell's notion of gender *regimes*, the hybrid construct I employ is *sex/gender regimes* which is composed of both: (1) *sex/gender arrangements* – social practices through which sex/gender is manifested; and (2) *gender scripts* – discourses through which gender is constructed.

Justice versus transformation?

To many feminist political scientists, the gender project is attractive but problematic. In formal politics, women and men are citizens (or non-citizens) and bearers of rights, not genders. This binary must be modified to integrate exclusions based on 'race' and disabilities and sexuality, and other aspects of personal status affecting people's social location. But 'gender' as a product of discourse relates less clearly to the issues of access which mobilized 'women' collectively in politics over the past century and a half. Recent struggles between feminists, seeking to insert 'gender' to designate women, versus the Vatican allied with other conservative states fighting to entrench 'sex' to represent women in international conventions, show that discourse is relevant. So the knowledge needs of feminist political science transcend an 'either gender or women' framework. Can we choose both?

To put the question differently: is feminism to be a political force? or has 'the political been subsumed by a larger agenda, the relationship between "feminist theory" and social/linguistic/political theories?' (Haste 2001: 21). Each option points to different ideas about how social change is achieved. Haste outlines two projects organized respectively around a 'discourse of power' which challenges social, political and economic power in institutions, laws, policies and practices which exclude or oppress 'women'; and a 'discourse of identity' about 'transforming the meaning of gender … [assuming that] only by destabilizing the meaning of gender … can the institutions be challenged effectively'. The first, modernist, project includes both liberal and liberationist feminists for whom the discourse of power is a search for rational justice. The post-modern project of 'linguistic feminism' forefronts linguistic processes believing 'gender is embedded in language, symbol and culture' (Haste 2000: 22). Feminist political science must draw from both, however, even if we cannot determine definitively if linguistic practice is epiphenomenal or causal.

Valerie Bryson suggests a way to overcome the either/or approach to the women and gender question. She juxtaposes the belief that '[m]any

feminists have tended to see "things" ... low pay, rape, or female foeticide
– as more significant than ... the discursive construction of marginality in
a text or document' with the assertion that '[p]olitics is not the mere
effects of discourse' (2000: 44). Bryson concludes that *both* analysis of
'things', especially power, and 'analysis of how "things" are mediated
through language and discourse can become vital feminist tools, giving
rise to practical political demands'. Real 'flesh and blood women' are
'systematically disadvantaged because of their sex', but what it means to be
a woman is not inherent in biology so the meanings societies give to
'woman' are conveyed in discourse. She believes understanding what
'woman' means in laws and policies in different times and places is a
crucial part of the justice project. Although 'power refuses to disappear
with the wave of a deconstructionist's magical wand' (Jones cited in
Bryson 2000: 44), power does not exist apart from discourse. Dichotomiz-
ing between a power order and a symbolic order cannot work for feminist
political science which must consider both.

To Bryson, law and policy – two key 'products' of formal politics –
operate both as discourse and social practice. The most significant inter-
mingling of them is in institutions. To explain this relationship I find
useful a conceptualization derived from Mary Douglas' image of lichens as
algae and fungi living in symbiosis. In this understanding, institutions
consist of *structures* (well-worn paths created by many repetitions of behaviours) in *symbiosis* with the *ideas* that legitimate them. The structures alone
are insufficient to institutionalize repetitive behaviours. For example, the
structures of free and fair elections are only part of democracy. Democracy also involves legitimizing *ideas*. Indeed, all institutions need constant
interaction between structures and ideas to persist, and institutional
power results from their symbiosis and their ability to form a new equilib-
rium between the two when either changes. *Political* institutions involve
structures established through their monopoly on the use of force. But
without legitimizing ideas the need for coercion would be very high.[10] The
exclusion or marginalization of 'women' as half the adult population constitutes a major *potential* threat to the legitimacy of democratic systems.
Where the promises in discourses of consent, citizenship, and participation and social practices diverge, legitimacy can be challenged. Challenges
also result from the diminished citizenship of those racialized or stigmat-
ized by disability or sexuality. Outsiders have their interests defined by
those in power; insiders can define their own interests.

Organized women's struggles for access to powerful institutions challenge ideas which make their exclusion seem natural. The increase in the
number of women decision-makers has not disrupted this pattern except
where a *critical mass* has been reached in key institutions. Hence, the essays
in this volume retain a focus on feminist strategies for *changing* structures,
like electoral systems which determine what proportion of those elected to
legislatures will be women, or Black, or others marginalized. But chal-

lenges to how discourse constructs 'gender' are also important. While few feminist political scientists see 'gender' as caused by language alone, most realize the importance of analysing the discourse which legitimizes the social practices of power, especially laws and policies. All the authors in this volume, but in particular Teghtsoonian and Sawer, emphasize the importance of language and the metaphors it embeds, especially as legitimizing elements of institutions. But institutions with coercive power have as much solidity in formal politics as discursively constructed sites. Coercive power – from domestic to international – must be centre stage to guide feminist transformation of nation-states and 'women's' participation in international arenas. Democratization and strategies to deepen democracies also require a focus on both dimensions.

Why women's interests?

In this section I explore why the idea of 'women's interests' was abandoned and argue that it was unwise if we are to understand how feminist movements can engage with nation-states and international politics, especially through autonomous feminist organizations. When debates about 'gender' and difference first emerged, there were few feminists working within political science to formulate the difference between treating women as an essentialist category of being and as a political category which groups of women might construct. Indeed 'feminist political science' was rejected as an oxymoron by those developing gender studies. 'Politics' was seen as diffused throughout society, not the subject matter of scholarly expertise. The emergence of organized women's engagements in formal politics world-wide in recent decades, however, demonstrates its value. But we must retool the concepts available to feminist political science by drawing from feminism, from mainstream political science, and especially from self-organized women practising politics from a feminist perspective.

Strategic essentialism and the 'gender debates'

To reclaim 'interests' as part of women's politics, we must retire 'the universal woman' permanently. Women may organize under the banner of 'women's interests', but cannot claim to speak for all women. Moreover, organizing under the banner for one or several issues does not preclude organizing under other banners as well. This is one important meaning of 'strategic essentialism'. Being able to assert what are 'women's' best interests in a particular context enables contestation when men are making laws and allocations or formulating policies based on *their* images of what is good for 'the universal woman'. Regardless of women's differences and alliances with other movements, nation-states have distinctive interests in *women as a sex* because of their power to reproduce collectivities (nations, faiths, 'races', ethnicities, etc.) both physically and culturally. Not all women bear children, but their power to do so makes their relationships with powerful institutions, especially states, different from men's (a point taken up by Smith in Chapter 10 in this volume). Feminists rightly resist translating women's bodily experiences into collective claims unmodified by other interests, differences, alliances and technological interventions. Yet, men's dominance in decision-making means women's experiences are marginalized in state discourses, so their interests are depoliticized. Men's accounts of women prevail in state policy and academic theory. For example, conventional development economics asserts that 'men and women in a family have a fundamental unity of interest' (Nelson and Chowdhury 1994: 5). International organizations like the World Bank, the IMF, and mainstream NGOs, increasingly influential in decision-making, accept such accounts, contrary to most women's experiences. To counter powerful men's representational monopoly, activists must organize women as broadly as possible, usually by addressing shared elements of women's oppression. But many third-wave feminists resist the idea that 'women's interests' can be formulated and represented on the belief that a 'politics of women's interests' will be based on essentialism.

In order to explore a way out of the dilemma of post-modern politics dissolving into an 'interminable difference' Radha Jhappan suggests a *context-dependent* approach she calls 'contextual essentialism' (1996: 53) or 'strategic essentialism'. Conceptualizing how racialized women can act politically in a world that defines them in essentialistic terms, she believes most racialized women retain some measure of essentialism in their politics. Jhappan explains:

> Strategic essentialism … sees identity as a function of context and allows us to stress one or several aspects of our identities according to the axis of oppression at issue in particular situations, without necessarily tying individuals to a specific identity for all times and all purposes.
>
> (1996: 53)

Jhappan draws on feminist political praxis evident in many feminist organizations beyond small-scale, homogenous groups. She shows how activists can address sex/gender issues politically without claiming that each woman's experience is the same, or homogenizing claims or solutions. Self-organized women can aggregate diverse views, provided their organization incorporates women with diverse projects and does not marginalize those not like the majority. They can articulate to decision-makers an account of 'women's interests', if they can reach a 'rough consensus', through lobbying, working through a political party, a union, an allied movement, or a special structure in government (commissions) or bureaucracy (women's bureaus). In this volume both Sawer and Teghtsoonian demonstrate how this has been done through the bureaucracy in Australia, Canada, and New Zealand. But major concerns remain: the possible neglect of minority movements or unpopular causes; alternately the under-representation of those who do not wish to be under the banner of 'women', or especially of feminism. Several examples are raised in Judith Butler's recent work.[11]

The politics of 'women's interests'

Other concepts affect women as citizens of democracies: 'special interests' is a concept used by neo-liberals to discredit claims about disabilities resulting from structural discrimination. The new neo-liberal citizenship regime conceptualizes the good citizen as one who doesn't need support from government, so when feminists make demands on behalf of 'women', they are declared as claiming to be a 'special interest'. The strategy of 'strategic essentialism' suggests formulating a temporary (contextual) consensus about 'women's interests'. Solidarities then will form, fracture and shift; some will disappear. While some solidarities are spontaneous, 'the politics of women's interests' requires organizations which persist over time. How they should function is an issue feminist political science must address. By the rules of democratic process, women's organizations should provide for the expression of diverse voices through open, deliberative processes.

Some feminists rejected mainstream democratic rules favouring direct democracy based on consensus. Both consensus-based and representative organizations involve dangers (see Vickers *et al.* 1993). In representative organizations the 'tyranny of the majority' is a risk. But debating diverse views on issues and reaching a compromise position are ordinary acts of democratic citizenship. Given the incompleteness of women's citizenship,[12] especially in liberal democracies, women are between a rock and a hard place. Political parties are often unresponsive. Organizations which work by consensus have limited utility in formal politics: majority-rule organizations risk majority domination unless safeguards exist specifically to protect minorities. Nonetheless, women must find ways to organize beyond the grassroots, because if they do not male elites will form 'women's wings' of political parties or male-directed 'women's groups' to give them the answers they want. Elite attempts to co-opt women's organizations and leaders or steer their actions through funding policies, are all dangers of democratic self-organization. Some feminist political scientists believe, however, that 'women's interests' may best be represented by *autonomous, women-led* organizations. But even within these organizations issues of accountability arise, especially when majority women are dominant within them.[13]

Refusing to acknowledge that 'women' may have interests in common around which coalitions can be formed reinforces the belief that power in formal political institutions can be ignored with impunity. Privileged, western women often can ignore formal politics without the negative consequences experienced elsewhere, or by minorities. But globalization and neo-liberal restructuring make this more dangerous. Democratic deficits resulting from regionalization (the EU for example) and the increased power of international organizations have weakened some nation-states. But the institutions of formal politics still have great power over women's lives; and in some cases women can access this power. This requires the clearer view of formal politics, interests, and power which feminist political scientists can now provide.

Strengths and weaknesses of interest theory

Reporting on a UNESCO-sponsored study of women's movements under both democratic and non-democratic regimes, Nelson and Chowdhury (1994) believe identifying successful strategies requires systematic comparative analysis using reformulated political science concepts like 'interests', 'interest aggregation' and 'interest articulation'. They noted that feminists in the 43 countries studied used these concepts in ways which transformed, and perhaps transcended, their original meanings (Nelson and Chowdhury 1994: 33). They believe movement activism will remain the central feature of women's politics, and that it is not a temporary phenomenon that will disappear when women and their demands are integrated into formal politics. As women make up half the population in each country, the project of integration is multi-generational and perhaps not achievable in full without profound changes even in democracies. Consequently, women must both organize in movements (informal politics) and participate in formal politics, as well as work to change political systems, to make their participation possible and more effective. Nelson and Chowdhury apply the concepts of 'interests' and 'interest articulation aggregation' to both formal and informal politics, believing this 'offers larger possibilities for understanding women's activism' (1994: 33). Transforming these concepts using experiences from both arenas characterizes feminist political science.[14]

Jónasdóttir explores 'women's interests' partly to uncover how and why 'the same structures of oppression – work, despotic political authority and systems of social stratification – affect women and men *both differently and in the same ways*' (1988: 7, emphasis added). She assumes the answer to 'why differently?' has something 'to do with ... structurally different conditions of women and men' (Jónasdóttir 1988: 7). She insists that sex/gender theory must distinguish among 'different expressions of power – economic, political, sexual and linguistic – [otherwise] power is so dispersed, ubiquitous and fluid that one has no clear notion of what its substance is, or of the norms for determining adequate paths of resistance to it' (Jónasdóttir 1988: 6–7). The thesis that identifying 'women's interests' is required to determine how to resist the powers blocking realization of them is central.

Liberal political science assumes 'the public' (where men dominate) is absolutely distinct from 'the private and personal' (where women were located until recently), so its account of 'interests' is too narrow. It reduces 'claims of conflicting 'interests' to 'conflicts of individual rights' which 'mask[ed] the social forces [such as gender] that structured these claims' (Jónasdóttir 1988: 19).

How can we better understand women's activism through 'women's interests'? Many feminists believe 'women *as women* ... [are] a group with "representable interests"' (Jónasdóttir 1988: 33). Each wave of activism organized electoral projects based on this premise; first to get the vote; then to get more women s/elected, both of which efforts assumed 'women' have enough characteristics and/or experiences in common to be 'represented' by other women. The concept of *critical mass* assumes that when enough women become decision-makers the diversity of their experiences becomes represented substantively. When a few token women are expected to represent half the population only a symbolic presence is possible. Post-modern feminists challenge the possibility of representation, especially of substantive representation. Most feminist political scientists assume it is possible with a critical mass, without downplaying the difficulty of achieving it.

Gender gap politics also assumes women and men may share experiences which shape their political attitudes and how they vote. The fact that gender gaps differ in nature in different countries (and for different groups within countries), do not exist everywhere and change over time, must dispel any idea that they reflect essential differences (a point made by Hill in this volume). The discourse of 'interests' does not require universals. Using the concept of interests does not mean assuming that women (or men for that matter) have universal or essential interests. Claims that any interest is shared require empirical substantiation in this retooled framework; feminists who reject interests completely may be rejecting the idea that women have *objective* interests. But women can have subjective 'interests' which motivate their political behaviour in specific contexts. Let us revisit a classic debate in 1981 between US feminist political scientists Virginia Sapiro (1981) and Irene Diamond and Nancy Hartsock (1981). Sapiro wondered if, in her time and place, women had representable *political* interests as women. Diamond and Hartsock rejected her focus on 'interests'. They advanced a theory of needs, promoting a collective order in which 'interests' were (inappropriately) self-interested and individualistic. Many women's 'interests', however, reflect their families' needs because they act 'in the interests' of the children, elders, sick and disabled kin for whom societies expect them to provide care. While feminist political scientists reject the theoretical fiat of development economics that women and men in families have identical interests, the entanglement of needs and interests within families makes assumptions about individualism in 'interests' questionable.

These early insights are useful for understanding the role women's movements played in persuading women they had 'interests' to assert while a rigidly enforced private/public divide excluded domestic issues from formal politics. Hernes (1984), Jacquette (1974) and others struggled to make the democratic theory of interests relevant for women still largely relegated to the private sphere. How could women in this context conceptualize that they had interests to express as citizens, a chicken/egg problem since citizenship in liberal democracies was defined by what existing citizens did.[15] As Jones writes: 'citizenship is delimited conceptually by falsely universalizing one particular group's practice of it' (Jones 1998: 223). Just as our understanding of work changed because of feminist studies of 'women's work', 'feminist studies of women's political participation (understood as both implicit and explicit feminist practice) provide the basis for an alternate discourse on citizenship' (Jones 1998: 223). But to subvert political meanings based on the activities of elite white men, we need alternate political practices. Jónasdóttir observed: 'we need a shift from viewing women and women's organizations ... as a source of power for men to a view that acknowledges women's resources and women's organizations as a power basis of their own' (1988: 34). Women's practices in their autonomous political organizations are one source. But women-friendly polities are another, as this volume shows.[16]

Can the interests/rights framework of analysis be adapted for 'women's' (changing) specificity? Generally, feminist political scientists assumed some interests were representable. But whether women share *objective interests* is more complex. Dahlerup (1987) believed the vote was an objective interest, without resurrecting 'the universal woman'. Arguing that women may share objective interests requires we provide evidence and make a reasoned argument for the claim. We can make it a rule of methodology to assume that women will have *both* interests in common *and* interests in conflict unless there is persuasive evidence to the contrary (Vickers 1997; Vickers 2002a). Understanding 'interests' as substantially socially constructed within specific contexts, coalitions and organizations is less likely to lead to false claims of objective or common interests. Where peak organizations, feminist parties or lists exist which are designed to act as 'parliaments of women' they should have conventions to protect the rights of minorities to dissent.

Feminist theorists of democracy have yet to give us an understanding of how majority/minority rights can be worked out in feminist organizations. Fears of essentialism are as disabling to women's politics as unwarranted assumptions about a universal woman or stereotyped categories. Even when women were excluded from formal democratic politics, they created autonomous organizations to act first in defence of the interests of others, but increasingly in their own right creating a parallel sphere of informal politics. For women to emerge as full-fledged political actors, we must reformulate the theory of interests, citizenship and democracy as informed by feminist praxis. In politics we are what we do.

Reframing interest theory for feminist analysis

Jónasdóttir believes the concept of 'interests' can be useful if redefined to transcend its male-centred, utilitarian meaning. She also wishes to transcend the needs/interests dichotomy, arguing that, *politically,* feminist demands involve a fixed component (needs) and a dynamic, changing one (interests) (Jónasdóttir 1988: 35). Are these objective and subjective interests in another guise? To assert that women have representable 'interests' is to claim they are fully citizens with a stake in the political process, even if the issues they wish decision-makers to consider originate in the domestic sphere. Instead of decision-makers (mostly men still) formulating their interests, many women claim the right to organize, debate, assert and be in conflict about their interests. But Jónasdóttir would also have us ask: 'Can we claim that women have certain objective interests regardless of what women themselves think?' (1988: 36). Part of the equation is whether demanding (and perhaps gaining) something claimed to be an objective interest of all women could actually harm some women. While it is hard to imagine how winning the vote for all women (regardless of the views of female anti-feminists) has harmed them, we cannot say the same about demands to be included in the military or even for the Equal Rights Amendment (ERA). To refurbish this framework, we need not believe 'women' have objective interests. But we do have to accept the framework of rights and interests as the existing political system under regimes of representative democracy and (less securely) regarding international institutions. To the extent that decisions are based on claims made by organized interests and constructed by women themselves, not by experts[17] or bureaucrats, the framework of interests and rights honours the right of social adults to be self-governing.

Belonging to an interest group means taking part in the process of aggregating views of needs and wants. Interest aggregation in mainstream political science usually is a function of political parties. But there is significant evidence that many parties mainly represent men's interests. Where parties have integrated women and represented their interests, autonomous women's organizations to perform these functions may not exist. Here, I explore the roles of structures other than parties for articulating women's views. Commissions, legislative committees, state feminist structures, media and various international agencies and conferences also can play this role. But my main interest here is *self-organization* in aggregating 'women's interests' and to assert the importance of women's organizations to democratic politics in order to make women equal to other social interests, class interests, group interests and private interests, in all of which individual women also may have an interest. Jaquette recently argued that the effect of political participation by women on democratic political systems is a major historic force: 'The trajectory of women's movements and the vitality of women's organizations are important indicators of how well democratic institutions are working on the ground' (2001: 111). Where women reject the idea that they need to organize as women to explore their shared interests, or formulate a shared conception of the common good, democracy may be in trouble. Where women lack the capacity or inclination for self-organization, or are prevented from it, the feminist project will not succeed. But this does not negate the important criticisms made by feminists of representative democracies. Rather it suggests that critics should promote the deepening of existing democracies because it is only in democracies that women can eventually be first-class citizens.

'Interest' originates in the Latin *inter esse*, to be among or between (Jónasdóttir 1988: 39). When women assert an interest, they claim the right to *be among* state decision-makers and *be listened to* when making political demands. Having an interest acknowledged marks the difference between citizens and non-citizens; and between first-class and marginalized citizens. All women have an objective interest in expanding the presence of women among decision-makers because only thus can all kinds of women be heard. Democratic theory makes decision-makers accountable to citizens (as experts and bureaucrats are not) so women as a group have an interest in the conduct of elections and in electoral system design, especially where they were designed to create legislative majorities artificially.[18] As bearers of rights and interests, women citizens must monitor state politics but rarely have the power to do so. Women's organizations are rarely integrated into state systems, so they can adopt any norms women choose. Women legitimately want more from political systems than they are getting, so some turn away from formal politics. But women's struggle around the world to gain democracy is a wake-up call for women privileged within stable democracies. Integrating women into existing political systems while working to transform them is the best way to deepen existing democracies and implement feminist agendas, provided women have their own, autonomous organizations too. Real democracy is our goal, however critical we are of actual democracies.

Becoming citizens does not guarantee women representation of their interests, nor protection of their rights in western democracies. For this they need to engage in electoral projects and gender gap strategies, and to work to transform political systems and political discourse. Some try to reform parties to represent women's interests. Others construct organizations to gather, debate and express women's diverse views. I explore several examples below. The international sphere is also available to organized women as an arena for political activity and as a gallery where examples of the effects of competing strategies can be seen. As discussed in Smith's chapter, women's activity in the UN system responds largely to UN initiatives to draw organized women into its various arenas, beginning with the Decade for Women, which in turn stimulated the formation of women's organizations in many countries. But the politics of identity and difference makes the construction and expression of 'women's interests' far more complicated and spurious universal claims more likely. This is because the politics of identity constructs an apartheid concept of difference: that is, it usually assumes those who are 'different' share no interests in common whereas the empirical situation is an untidy pattern of shared and conflicting interests out of which politics must make an agenda. I suggest methodological guidelines to ensure incorporation of the diverse dimensions of women's lives, urging against an apartheid interpretation of 'difference' that ignores the possibility of commonalities (see Vickers 2002a). Anne Phillips argues for tolerance but warns that it is most effective where power is 'relatively evenly distributed' (1999: 126). She acknowledges that this is uncommon, especially in international arenas. Shared contexts may allow women to meet 'the challenge of difference' and transcend identity-based conflicts. Possibilities for co-operation among organized women to expand the EU's narrow construction of 'women's interests' is one example.

Organized women's interests

In this section, I ground my conceptual discussion in several concrete cases, first exploring women's movements' relationship to formal, state politics. I focus on two major feminist organizations – the US National Organization of Women (NOW) and the Canadian National Action Committee on the Status of Women (NAC) – which underwent conflicts over whether they should engage with formal politics and over the mode of engagement, that is, whether to engage with political parties, or to stay outside the electoral arena and lobby as an autonomous, organized interest on women's behalf. Considering the widespread belief among academics that 'gender' should be seen as a principle of social organization, not as a characteristic of persons which could motivate political action (Feree *et al.* 1998), the fact that the main strand of the women's movements in both countries[19] engages with state politics is the first point to note. Most feminist political scientists believe women share a common interest in having a political presence, even when their substantive interests differ along national, 'race', class or other lines. So the second point to note is that NAC and NOW worked to express the views of a wide range of women and construct claims to insert 'the interests of women' into the formal political system.[20]

In her study of NOW and NAC, Lisa Young concludes: '[a] defining characteristic of the contemporary American women's movement is the high priority it places on electoral and partisan politics' (2000: 27). A less open opportunity structure made it more difficult for NAC to engage in partisan politics, although it spent over three decades working to influence governments. Young found the US movement became increasingly involved in getting women elected and less in direct policy intervention, but NOW began by trying to influence Congress indirectly before there were many women legislators and as the judiciary became more conservative. By contrast, NAC became more radical and detached from electoral politics over time. Created in 1972 to push for implementation of recommendations by the Royal Commission on the Status of Women – the movement's blueprint for a decade – its original focus was policy (Vickers *et al.* 1993). Many factors (strict party discipline in Canada's multi-party parliament, a winner-takes-all electoral system and the movement's success in gaining equality provisions in the Charter of Rights (1982) and lobbying for women justices)[21] make electoral politics less attractive for Canadian feminists, despite the presence of around 20 per cent women legislators. In particular, the exhaustion of the agenda provided by the Royal Commission Report meant NAC had to debate priorities and set an agenda. But the opening up of a judicial path to change made aggregating interests and striking compromises seem the more difficult alternative. NAC became increasingly radical as its ability to influence governments declined. Its increasingly radical stance lost it government funding and attracted more radical participants. Eventually, a coalition of Blacks, Asians, Aboriginals, women with disabilities and 'out' lesbian women assumed leadership positions and NAC's access to government decision-makers declined further. Withdrawal of the powerful Quebec Federation of Women (FFQ) weakened NAC's legitimacy as 'a parliament of women', but it played a significant role in constitutional debates in the early 1990s. In the new millennium, organizations like Legal Education and Action Fund (LEAF), which conducts legal challenges to advance 'women's interests', have replaced NAC, along with an informal coalition of about 40 pan-Canadian organizations. By contrast, NOW remains a vital force.

NOW: from social movement to organized interest

First-wave US feminists were also oriented to formal politics but they were more focused on the idea of achieving the common good by importing maternal values into, and cleaning up, party politics. As progressives and reformers, many believed women 'possessed special insights into issues of social justice and social welfare' and that the federal government should aid and protect women and children (Koven and Mitchel 1993: 7). Second-wave feminists initially largely rejected involvement in formal politics, so how was it that NOW leaders persuaded so many women to focus on it? Many organizations created by first-wave feminist activists were still functioning in Washington and both their example and their help in gaining access facilitated NOW's transition. Unlike some British feminists, who believed even the vote 'would pollute women by implicating them in the violent business of wars and empire' (Koven and Mitchel 1993: 11), few US feminists avoided involvement in government because of its growing empire's impact on women elsewhere. The main transformative project on the second wave's agenda was the Equal Rights Amendment (ERA), and reforms to electoral or legislative processes were not a focus as they had been for the first wave.

The second-wave movement began with a strong radical strain which appeared to 'rule out engagement with established political parties as a viable strategy' (Young 2000: 31). Writing in 1989, Joyce Gelb concluded that the US movement was characterized by lobbying government as an autonomous interest group rather than integrating into political parties, which she considered a strength. NOW's period as an organized interest group was ended by the growing anti-feminism of Republicans and changes in funding laws which allowed feminist organizations to fund feminist-friendly candidates through Political Action Committees (PACs). This led NOW into the Democratic Party – as the unions, civil rights groups and anti-war activists had gone before them (Young 2000: 29, 39ff). How did a social movement apparently hostile ideologically to engagement with governments become an *organized interest* presenting 'women's interests' to legislators, thereby significantly expanding the federal government's range of interests and involvements to include many issues previously considered private? In a context of seriously disaffected social movements, how did feminists apparently bent on cultural trans-formation develop the structures needed to organize a large, geographi-cally dispersed interest? Two largely compatible explanations appear in the literature: (1) *ideological* – that the movement was never that radical and always contained a majority of liberal feminists willing to engage with the state and parties (Young 2000); (2) *organizational* – that a coalition of older, pre-feminist organizations experienced in lobbying Congress assisted NOW, connecting it with willing listeners early on and providing early policy successes (Costain 1981). The passage of the ERA through Congress and its failure to gain ratification focused NOW on the project of getting women elected at all levels. When Canadian feminists achieved inclusion of equality rights and constitutional sanction for affirmative action programmes, by contrast, the pressure was off NAC, since legal activism was now most fruitful. Opportunities to achieve change through the US courts declined without the federal ERA and because Republican presidents appointed more conservative judges. This put the pressure on NOW to act electorally.

Despite Young's ideological explanation, all social movements face dif-ficulties becoming organized as an interest, lobbying and integrating into parties: indeed, few succeed. Movements allow activists more freedom, involvement and leadership opportunities, so many resist the transition regardless of ideology. Costain (1981) has identified three factors affecting whether movements will gain access to the formal political system, or dissipate: (1) there must be enough change in the external environment to break down members' resistance to organizing to lobby; (2) there must be knowledgeable groups willing to assist in the start-up phase; and (3) 'supportive listeners' must be available, namely, members of Congress willing to help direct early lobbying attempts. NOW faced problems persuading members that 'women' should constitute themselves as a collective voice with 'interests' to represent. The struggle in NOW between grassroots members and leaders showed the importance to many members of non-hierarchical/consensual values and a participatory style. But 'lobbying requires a uniform organizational posture on specific issues and centralized decision-making' (Costain 1981: 104). Members who opposed a professional office in Washington squared off against leaders like Betty Friedan eager for central direction.[22]

NOW is a chapter-based organization with local and state chapters based on individual memberships, a national organization with an office (in Chicago) and professional staff. Lobbying required a professional (and expensive) office in Washington, so chapters angry with the move to a politics of interest tried to halt the project by refusing to pay dues and insisting on keeping the Chicago office open (Costain 1981: 104). Many members believed NOW was becoming too reformist, and run by a small elite of leaders and lawyers. At the 1975 convention 'the entire staff was fired in response to pressure from more politically and organizationally radical NOW members' (Costain 1981: 105). The chasm between radical members and legislative staff is spelled out by one staffer in 1975: 'A number of crazies are trying to end the legislative activity of NOW. Rather than lobbying against abortion laws they want to teach self-abortion' (cited by Costain 1981: 105).

Costain believed the successes NOW and several other feminist movement organizations experienced motivated them to become a more organized interest. When the ERA was passed by the Ninety-Second Congress, NOW was joined by the Women's Equity Action League (WEAL) and the National Women's Political Caucus (NWPC) in Washington to lobby for more legislative change. Two positive changes encouraged the transition, despite resistance from members and local/state chapters committed to a more radical, outsider strategy: (1) rapid, positive changes in public attitudes supporting the movement's more moderate goals; and (2) 'passage of favourable legislation by Congress in several areas of great concern to the movement' (Costain 1981: 105). Congress was receptive and far-reaching results seemed possible. Moreover, these successes showed that NOW could work with established traditional women's organizations to formulate 'women's interests'. By 1984, however, African American women formed a separate organization to express their interests and, led by Democratic party activists, they formed the National Congress of Black Women (NPCBW). By 1988, President Regan had appointed three new conservative justices to the Supreme Court. One NOW activist asserted: '[i]t's time to rethink our strategy, sisters. The belief that "we can always go to court" has been rendered a myth – at least for another generation' (cited by Young 2000: 39).

Choosing strategies to represent 'women's interests'

Different strategies exist which organized US women use to express 'women's interests' to the national government. Acting as an organized lobby was an easy choice because the congressional system opens legislators up to lobbying. Other strategies include: forming coalitions with other movements; integrating into political parties; getting sympathetic legislators elected; influencing the electorate through media and *gender gap* politics in which women's political attitudes and voting behaviour are organized. Strategies to transform the political system are more difficult to achieve. Such strategies include: electoral system reform to represent women more fairly; electoral spending limits to level the playing field; *femocrat* projects of entering the bureaucracy to promote feminist goals; projects to get more women judges appointed, especially to the highest courts; alliances with national projects; and constitutional reform. Strategies chosen reflect movements' assessments of their opportunities given their political system, movement strength, and the availability of allies. NOW's integration into the Democratic Party and its involvement in the electoral project through its Political Action Committee were not available to NAC with Canada's multi-party parliamentary system and strict election spending laws. NOW moved from autonomous lobby to partisan activism following the NWPC. Founded in 1971, NWPC was a bipartisan caucus inspired by Betty Friedan and Bella Abzug, an activist Democrat (Young 2000: 33). Conflicted about bipartisanship and whether to support only women or everyone with feminist commitments, it had considerable impact on the 1972 Democratic convention. Its successes led most of the movement into the Democratic Party as Republicans became more anti-feminist.

The strategies outlined above assume 'women' have 'interest(s)' to be organized and represented. Formulating them was problematic in NOW, especially around the influence of leaders versus local/state chapters. Friedan's 'lavender menace' slur against lesbian 'infiltration' demonstrated her belief that successful lobbying would be difficult if 'out' lesbians were prominent in NOW's leadership. If NOW had had to resolve this issue internally, it could well not have survived. Soon after, however, lesbian rights became part of NOW's account of 'women's interests'. Like the Canadian Royal Commission Report which gave NAC a blueprint which didn't have to be debated for over a decade, a parallel process occurred for NOW. Stimulated by the UN's International Women's year in 1975, the first National Women's Conference in Houston in 1977 shaped NOW's policy agenda and allowed it to avoid a major split over lesbian rights. Alice Rossi (1982), in her detailed study of women who attended the Houston Conference to debate the movement's agenda, reveals how. First the conference allowed feminists to identify 'bottom line', controversial issues (abortion, sexual preference and lesbian rights); and it showed them what the effects of debating them within a feminist organization would be like by embroiling them in bitter conflicts with organized conservative women (Rossi 1982: xiif). This conference removed from NOW's plate the problem of determining whether abortion and lesbian rights were 'in the interest of women'. Although this experience showed political co-operation among NOW, NPCBW and older, pre-feminist organizations was possible, it doomed a bi-partisan approach, as anti-feminist women who lost the debates at Houston turned to the Republican Party to implement their vision.

Jane Jacquette has argued that one of the major challenges facing contemporary feminism is how to overcome 'the anti-state bias of much contemporary feminist theory' (2003: 331). She addresses her critique to first-world feminists for whom 'politics has become "identity", "text" or "performance" and "radical" has come to mean moving beyond "narrow" economic concerns' (Jacquette 2003: 344). She decries the fact that influential feminists attack liberal democracy, dismissing 'rights talk' as selfish and individualistic (Jacquette 2003: 344) while women around the world struggle to gain the advantages of stable democracies, liberal rights and some measure of economic justice. I would suggest that much of our criticism of the normal politics of western democracies exists primarily in academic theory rather than in feminist practice. The examples in this section demonstrate that, despite ideological critiques, major feminist organizations have found ways to engage with formal politics and to express 'women's interests'. Feminist political science focuses on those experiences, without rejecting the critiques of existing democracies out of hand.

'Women's interests' beyond nation-states

Barriers between domestic and international politics have eroded and 'women's interests' are affected by institutions at multiple levels from local government to the European Union (EU), the UN, World Court, World Bank and International Monetary Fund (IMF). Nuket Kardam (2004) believes a global gender equality regime is emerging with norms, principles, legal instruments and compliance mechanisms. For example, the UN Convention on the Elimination of all Forms of Discrimination against Women (CEDAW) was passed by the General Assembly in 1979 and came into force in 1981 when 20 states ratified it. A majority of world states have now signed on, although some with reservations. To the extent that governments honour international commitments, they 'are obliged to ... eliminate obstacles to gender equality in constitutional, legal, political and bureaucratic realms through political and legal reforms' (Kardam 2004: 89). Kardam believes that these international developments occurred because a global women's movement and its associated NGOs 'exercised "structural" and "intellectual" leadership in the codification of gender equality norms' (Kardam 2004: 93). But one problem is whether the majority of women worldwide benefit from having 'women's interests' constructed in terms of gender equality, rather than within a framework of justice stressing a fair distribution of resources among countries of the world, and within countries. International conventions allow western feminists to do an end run around their states, especially where neo-liberal governments have gutted feminist projects established before the turn to economic rationalism and globalization.

Global women's networks, led by women from the 'two-thirds world', work to insert gender justice issues in many areas of international debate. But NGOs funded by western agencies still shape the agenda and deter-mine how 'women's interests' will be interpreted. Lois West's (1999) account of UN women's conferences is revealing. Regarding the 1995 Conference in Beijing she reports that the results were achieved by the combined efforts of 'elite women' active in the UN and international arenas and 'grassroots women working at the local levels' which 'interna-tionalized feminist movements to an unprecedented degree' (West 1999: 182–3). For the first time the feminist coalition faced 'an organized, antifeminist backlash of conservative, traditional, religious movements and states' (West 1999: 183) determined to define 'women's interests' in terms of fixed, reproductive roles. West believes three important develop-ments shaped the politics of the Conference: (1) recognition from UN reports that women's situation globally was not improving (millions more now live in absolute poverty); (2) that activists had inserted 'women's issues' into UN Conferences, thereby mainstreaming their concerns; and (3) the new information technology and the emergence of many feminist (and some anti-feminist) NGOs had globalized women's networks (1999: 183). The organized opposition forced feminists in the international arena to construct 'women's interests' to counter it. The counter-movement, in opposition to what it considered 'radical feminist ideas', declared the Platform anti-family, unholy and harmful to women. The 1995 Beijing Platform of Action was 'a mainstreamed international femin-ism that subsume[ed] feminist goals under an umbrella of human rights' (West 1999: 189). Western feminists believed 'women's interests' were best defended within a human rights framework. But their ability to dominate this process meant discussions of 'justice' between the world's rich and poor countries and women were marginalized. Nonetheless, NGO plat-forms constituted alternate arenas for feminist politics and allowed women from diverse contexts to voice their accounts, which helped elite women connect with issues and interpretations of grassroots women. Despite western women's dominance, this interaction between elite and grassroots women allowed a feminist account of 'women's interests' to be articulated against conservative attempts to roll back feminist gains.

Activism in UN arenas highlights the importance of open, democratic processes to feminist politics. Where there is no space for democratic participation, it is much harder for organized women to influence how 'experts' construct their interests and conceptualize their roles. Consequently, feminist political scientists are concerned about *democratic deficits* in influential international institutions. Where experts and bureaucrats determine what is 'in women's interests', organized women often have no option except to protest against the generally negative results, as many women have against the World Trade Organization and other agents of globalization. Feminists were able to have violence against women seen as a barrier to development in the UN system, but could do little to change gender-blind, neo-liberal assumptions in the World Bank and International Monetary Fund resulting in structural adjustment plans (SAPs) which devastated women's lives in many countries. In this volume, Louise Chappell explores these issues in relation to the International Criminal Court (Chapter 11) and Merryn Smith does so in relation to the United Nations (Chapter 10).

Conclusion

The concept of 'the politics of women's interests' used in this volume is useful because it focuses our attention on the importance of democracy to women's citizenship and achievement of feminist agendas. Through 'the politics of women's interests' women can learn to organize with others, learn what they have in common, how to disagree and how to construct a consensus on what represents 'women's interests' in various contexts. But the concept has dangers to which we must be alert. Majority women too often will represent their claims as good for all women; the 'universal woman' we object to when experts, bureaucrats and other decision-makers conjure her up hides behind many feminist accounts despite claims to respect difference. Academic feminists too often assume our expertise lets us speak for all women. We have yet to develop widely accepted protocols such as, for example, that feminist scholarship must assume 'women's interests' differ unless proven otherwise. Nowhere is this clearer than in the assumption that what women want is merely equality with men. For many women gender justice also requires more equity between rich and poor countries and between rich and poor women. In political practice, we lack structures to hold women accountable when they claim to represent other women's interests. This is partly because feminist theorists focus largely on critiques of democracy, rather than on developing theories of democratic behaviour when women run their own organizations. This becomes especially problematic when western feminists get to define meanings in international documents with little sense of how their definitions will affect women elsewhere.

Despite these and other dangers, it is important to reject the view that 'women's politics' is everywhere except in formal political arenas influencing governments. Women's citizenship means working to deepen democracy as much as winning it. Retreating from the formal political arena and seeing only abstract forces as causes of women's circumstances denies the reality that the citizenship women won must be activated, and interests must be debated, aggregated and expressed. Like other citizens, women must work through existing organizations or develop our own. We will experience conflict and, therefore, will need to develop the skills to promote solidarities and to make coalitions that last through organization. To retreat to the study of discourse alone represents both a lost opportunity and a failed political project. This volume reveals some of the many sites, arenas and projects through which women in many democracies are attempting to expand the significance of their citizenship.

Notes

1 By gender justice, I mean the goals which women have shared across time and space: physical and economic security, access to what will achieve that security (e.g. education, civil rights); rights to sexual and reproductive autonomy; and access to citizenship and decision-making power to enable self-determination (Nelson and Chowdhury 1994). Note that this conception incorporates 'equality' but interprets it as something more complex than 'sameness'. For example, women in different contexts may use their reproductive autonomy both to have and to avoid having children.

2 An ontological category invokes man and woman as essential categories of being.

3 This led to confusion between philosophical implications of the fact that not all women share a female experience like pregnancy and political implications of the fact that no men can. Some women adopt a stance of 'strategic essentialism' (Jhappan 1996) to make claims about widely shared experiences. 'Women's politics' are shaped by the fact that while some women cannot or do not bear children, no man can. That not all women share a gendered experience does not make it any less a 'women's' experience if only women can experience it.

4 Umbrella organizations articulating 'women's interests' to the Canadian federal government are represented as 'the parliament of women' – e.g. the first-wave National Council of Women of Canada (NCWC) and the second-wave National Action Committee on the Status of Women (NAC). US organizations like the National Organization of Women (NOW) and the League of Women Voters also have formal decision-making processes for determining what they represent as 'women's interests.

5 I explore the fragile project of feminist political science in *Reinventing Political Science: A Feminist Approach*, Halifax: Fernwood Books (1997). With most feminists appropriating the 'political' to signify *all* power relations as embodied in 'gender', it was difficult for the few feminists working in political science to conceptualize how the formal politics of states differed from 'politics' throughout all of society. The recent emergence of a larger cohort in the field has begun to reverse this trend, as this volume shows.

6 I am aware that the 'wave' metaphor is problematic, especially when 'western'

time periods are imposed elsewhere. It is a convenience in this analysis which focuses mainly on the West.

7 Changes included introduction of direct primaries and initiative/referenda provisions in the US and 'city manager systems' eliminating political parties from local government in the US and Canada. Feminists in both countries were hostile to political parties, which they considered corrupt, but believed women could 'clean up' government through their exercise of citizenship. Prior to the 1960s and decolonization, however, they were whites-only democracies (Vickers 2002b). These 'reforms' entrenched 'white' electoral power. Initially only 'white' women' in these countries could vote.

8 For accounts of the long relationship between state power and women's bodily powers to reproduce populations see Eisenstein, Z. (1981) *The Radical Future of Liberal Feminism*, USA: North Eastern University Press; also Lerner, G. (1986) *The Creation of Patriarchy*, New York: Oxford University Press.

9 The proportion of biological/social is not fixed since technology mediates between them. Technology (and who controls it) determines how much the life options of women are shaped by biology (technologically mediated or unmediated) so this varies. Ortega y Gassett's image of a boat on an ocean shore is helpful in understanding interactionism. As tides rise and fall through the year, the portion of the boat in the water (biological) and on the shore (social) varies. In some contexts, technology mediates so women can choose about reproduction, sexuality, even become 'the opposite sex'; then the boat is barely in the water or is even high and dry. Where technology is not available, or is controlled by men enforcing patriarchal and heterosexual rules, the boat may be largely 'in the water' – so anatomy is destiny, for the moment. An interactionist approach does not require rejection of women as biological entities to conceive of how to achieve change.

10 The distinction made between 'strong' and 'soft states' relates less to structural weaknesses than to inadequate legitimization so that those in charge of state institutions cannot implement their policies/laws without excessive force.

11 Butler was the first major US scholar to assert the gender turn by appropriating 'politics' for cultural work. She writes about the 'New Gender Politics' defined as 'movements concerned with transgender, transexuality, intersex, and their complex relations to feminist and queer theory' (2004: 4). 'Gender' now means more than gender discrimination or abstract forces of analysis; it also means diverse gender identities, and associated movements. Butler believes that 'none of these movements is . . . postfeminist' (2004: 8); so they are consistent with feminism provided it is constructed around 'gender' instead of 'women', with 'gender' understood as historical, socially constructed and 'performative' (2004: 10). Butler admits confusion about 'the status of the term "gender" in relation [both] to feminism . . . and lesbian and gay studies' (2004: 181). Her confusion about international conflict about 'sex' versus 'gender' in how 'women' will be represented in UN conventions and international laws is especially revealing. The Vatican (and allied conservative states) demanded 'gender' be replaced by 'sex' in the NGO Platform on the status of women because they saw 'gender' as 'nothing other than a code for homosexuality' (2004: 181). Women activists resisted, because they believed 'sex' would mandate 'sex' = women = maternity, an essentialism women have struggled to erase in a century of activism. Butler concludes 'no simple definition of gender will suffice' because the term 'has become a site for contest for various interests' (2004: 184). Butler believes feminists use 'gender' as the opposite of sexual difference 'because gender endorses a socially constructivist view of masculinity and femininity, displacing or devaluing the *symbolic* status of sexual difference and the political specificity of the feminine' (2004: 185). Butler shows the importance to

feminist political science of these debates and their significance for different forms of politics. In adopting 'women' and sex/gender as key concepts, we must not ignore debates about 'gender' and 'sexual difference'.

12 Many political scientists work with three main categories of democracy: (1) *electoral democracies* – with competitive and 'free and fair' elections, but under-developed rights, freedoms and organizational infrastructure associated with democracy; (2) *liberal democracies* – with competitive, free and fair' elections plus well established civil and political rights and freedoms and equality of opportunity; and (3) *social or economic democracies* – as in (2) above except with state policies to achieve greater equality of condition. Western democracies fall into categories (2) and (3), although those which have undergone transitions from dictatorships recently (e.g. Spain, Portugal) may not have well established rights and freedoms.

13 Without feminist rules of accountability, it may hard to distinguish between pseudo-interests constructed by male elites; and overstated claims by majority women.

14 Surveying the field is beyond my brief in this paper. Vickers (1997) and Karen Beckwith (2000) provide good starting points.

15 In civic republican traditions, the problem is how women could advance visions of the common good. I am focusing here mainly on the liberal conceptions of citizenship and democratization.

16 Feminist political science emerged mostly in democracies on the fringes of the West; in the successor democracies of the British Empire (New Zealand, Australia, and Canada) and the Nordic countries (Finland, Norway, and Sweden). These states are less powerful and more open to influence by women, who also often 'got in on the ground floor' by becoming citizens when the democracy was founded. Feminists in imperial/post-imperial countries face far more powerful states, less open to influence. Note that femocrat projects and state feminism also originated in these countries.

17 Increasingly state feminist agencies substitute expertise provided by femocrats for claims by organized women's movements. This reflects a general trend to expertise and economic rationality. But it also indicates a vacuum where feminists have refused to engage with decision-makers and the interest-production system in mainstream political parties/lobbies or in autonomous women's organizations.

18 In most of the countries studied in this volume, single-member, first-past-the-post electoral systems make it difficult for new citizen groups to get their own elected, especially those geographically dispersed throughout the territory, as women are. Consequently, electoral reform to more proportionate systems is on feminist agendas in several states. However, as Curtin discusses later in this book, they alone are not a panacea for addressing women's under-representation in legislatures.

19 I limit my analysis mostly to federal level politics. At the state/provincial levels, the picture is more varied. The Franco-Quebec movement enjoys a more positive relationship with the provincial state; whereas in Alberta one-party dominance and right-wing governments led most organized women to focus on local politics and cultural transformation. Right-wing governments can direct feminist energies to alternate parties (e.g. the Democrats in the US), provided they have a chance at power. Canada's multi-party system makes partisan choice more complex; the most women-friendly party, the New Democrats, are a permanent minority federally, but formed governments in four provinces including British Columbia.

20 NAC imitated the first-wave National Council of Women in considering itself 'a parliament of women' (Vickers *et al.* 1993).

21 The Chief Justice currently is a woman and the appointment norms now require three out of nine justices on the court to be women. Representational issues are more evident on the Canadian Supreme Court because a minimum number of justices trained in the Quebec Civil Code is always required. The first few women justices appointed were clearly feminist in orientation and a strong cadre of feminist lawyers and judges has played an important role in re-directing feminist political energy toward a legal strategy.

22 A similar conflict happened when President (1982–1984) Doris Anderson determined to move the NAC office to Ottawa. Her failure signalled a decline in NAC's influence on governments.

References

Bayes, J.H., Hawkesworth, M.E., and Kelly, R.M. (2001) 'Globalization, democrat-ization, and gender regimes', in R.M. Kelly, J.H. Bayes, M.E. Hawkesworth, and B. Young (eds) *Gender, Globalization and Democratization*, Lanham: Rowman and Littlefield.

Beckwith, K. (2000) 'Beyond compare? Women's movements in comparative perspective', *European Journal of Political Research* 37(4): 431–68.

Butler, J. (2004) *Undoing Gender*, London: Routledge.

Bryson, V. (2000) 'Feminist challenges to "common sense"', in A. Bull, H. Diamond, and R. Marsh (eds) *Feminisms and Women's Movements in Contemporary Europe*, Basingstoke: Macmillan.

Carver, T. (1998) 'A political theory of gender: perspectives on the "universal subject"', in V. Randall and G. Waylen (eds) *Gender, Politics and the State*, London and New York: Routledge.

Castro, G. (1999) *American Feminism: A Contemporary History*, New York: New York University Press.

Connell, R.W. (1987) *Gender and Power: Society, the Person and Sexual Politics*, Stan-ford: Stanford University Press.

Costain, A. (1981) 'Representing women: the transition from social movement to interest group', *The Western Political Quarterly – Special issue on women and politics*, 34(1): 100–13.

Dahlerup, D. (1987) 'Confusing concepts – confusing reality: a theoretical discus-sion of [the] patriarchal state', A. Showstack-Sasoon (ed.) *Women and the State: The Shifting Boundaries of Public and Private*, Tiptree: Hutchinson.

Diamond, I. and Hartsock, N. (1981) 'Beyond interests in politics: a comment on Virginia Sapiro's "When are interests interesting? The problem of political representation of women"', *The American Political Science Review*, 75(3): 717–21; reprinted in *Feminism and Politics* (1998), Oxford and New York: Oxford University Press.

Eisenstein, Z. (1981) *The Radical Future of Liberal Feminism*, USA: North Eastern University Press

Druhvarajan, V. and Vickers, J. (2002) *Gender, Race and Nation: A Global Perspective*, Toronto, Buffalo, and London: University of Toronto Press.

Epstein, C.F. (1981) 'Women and power: the roles of women in politics in the United States', in C.F. Epstein and R.L. Coser (eds) *Access to Power: Cross-national Studies of Women and Elites*, London: Allen and Unwin.

Feree, M., Lorber, B., and Hess, B.B. (1998) *Revisioning Gender*, London: Sage.

Gelb, J. (1989) *Feminism and Politics: A Comparative Approach*, Berkeley: University of California Press.

Haste, H. (2001) 'Sexual metaphor and current feminisms', in A. Bull, H. Diamond, and R. Marsh (eds) *Feminisms and Women's Movements in Contemporary Europe*, New York: St Martin's Press.

Hernes, H.M. (1984) 'Women and the Welfare State: the transition from private to public dependence', in H. Holter (ed.) *Patriarchy in a Welfare Society*, Oslo: Universitetsforlaget.

Hoskyns, C. (1999a) 'Gender and transnational democracy: the case of the European Union', in M. Meyer and E. Prügl (eds) *Gender Politics in Global Governance*, Lanham, Boulder, New York, and Oxford: Rowman and Littlefield.

—— (1999b) *Integrating Gender: Women, Law and Politics in the European Union*, London and New York: Verso.

Jacquette, J.S. (1974) *Women in Politics*, New York: Wiley.

—— (2001) 'Women and democracy: regional differences and contrasting views', *Journal of Democracy*, 12(3): 111–26.

—— (2003) 'Feminism and the challenges of the "post-Cold War" world', *International Feminist Journal of Politics*, 5(3): 331–54.

Jhappan, R. (1996) 'Post-modern race and gender essentialism or a post-mortem of scholarship', *Studies in Political Economy*, 51(Fall): 15–63.

Jónasdóttir, A.G. (1988) 'On the concept of interest, women's interest, and the limitations of interest theory', in K.B. Jones and A.G. Jónasdóttir (eds) *The Political Interests of Gender: Developing Theory and Research with a Feminist Face*, London, Newbury Park, and New Delhi: Sage.

Jones, K.B. (1998) 'Citizenship in a woman-friendly polity', in S. Gershon (ed.) *The Citizenship Debates*, Minneapolis: University of Minnesota Press.

Kardam, N. (2004) 'The emerging global gender equality regime from neoliberal and constructivist perspectives in international relations', *International Feminist Journal of Politics*, 6(1): 85–109.

Koven, S. and Mitchel, S. (1993) *Mothers of a New World: Maternalist Politics and the Origins of Welfare States*, New York: Routledge.

Lerner, G. (1986) *The Creation of Patriarchy*, New York: Oxford University Press.

Lombardo, E. (2003) 'EU gender policy: trapped in the "Wollstonecraft dilemma"?', *The European Journal of Women's Studies*, 10(2): 159–80.

Meyer, M.K. and Prügl, E. (1999) *Gender Politics in Global Governance*, Lanham, Boulder, New York, and Oxford: Rowman and Littlefield.

Molyneux, M. (1986) 'Mobilization without emancipation? Women's interests, state and revolution', in R.R. Fagen, C.D. Deere, and J.L. Coraggio (eds) *Transition and Development: Problems of Third World Socialism*, Boston: Monthly Review Press.

Nelson, B. and Chowdhury, N. (eds) (1994) *Women in Politics Worldwide*, New Haven and London: Yale University Press.

Pateman, C. (1985) 'Feminist critiques of the public/private dichotomy', in S.L. Benn and G.F. Gaus (eds) *Private and Public in Social Life*, London: Croom Helm.

Phillips, A. (1998) *Feminism and Politics*, Oxford and New York: Oxford University Press.

—— (1999) 'The politicisation of difference', in J. Horton and S. Mendus (eds) *Toleration, Identity and Difference*, Basingstoke: Macmillan.

Prügl, E. and Meyer, M.K. (1999) 'Gender politics in global governance', in M.K. Meyer and E. Prügl (eds) *Gender Politics in Global Governance*, Lanham, Boulder, New York, and Oxford: Rowman and Littlefield.

Rankin, L.P. and Vickers, J. (2001) *Women's Movements and State Feminism: Integrating Diversity into Public Policy*, Ottawa: Status of Women. Online. Available at: www.swc-ctc.qc.ca/research/01 0606–066 265 7756–e.html (accessed 2 March 2005).

Rossi, A. (1982) *Feminists in Politics*, New York: Academic Press.

Rubin, G. (1975) 'The traffic in women: notes on the political economy of sex', in R.R. Reiter (ed.) *Toward an Anthropology of Women*, New York: Monthly Review Press.

Sapiro, V. (1981) 'When are interests interesting? The problem of political representation of women', *The American Political Science Review*, 75(3): 701–16; reprinted in *Feminism and Politics* (1998), Oxford and New York: Oxford University Press.

Scott, J.W. (1986) 'Gender: a useful category', *American Historical Review*, 91(Dec.): 1053–75.

Spivak, G. (1995) 'Subaltern studies: deconstructing historiography', in D. Landry and G. MacLean (eds) *The Spivak Reader: Selected Works of Gayatri Spivak*, New York: Routledge.

West, L. (1999) 'UN women's conferences and feminist politics', in M.K. Meyer and E. Prügl (eds) *Gender Politics in Global Governance*, Lanham, Boulder, New York, and Oxford: Rowman and Littlefield.

Vickers, J. (1997) *Reinventing Political Science: A Feminist Approach*, Halifax, Nova Scotia: Fernwood Books.

—— (2002a) 'Methodologies for scholarship about women', in V. Druhvarajan and J. Vickers (eds) *Gender, Race and Nation: A Global Perspective*, Toronto, Buffalo, and London: University of Toronto Press.

—— (2002b) *The Politics of 'Race': Canada, Australia and the United States*, Ottawa: Golden Dog Press.

—— and Rankin, P.L. (1998) 'Locating women's politics', in M. Tremblay and C. Andrew (eds) *Women and Political Representation in Canada*, Ottawa: University of Ottawa Press.

——, Rankin, P., and Appelle, C. (1993) *Politics as if Women Mattered: A Political Analysis of the National Action Committee on the Status of Women*, Toronto: University of Toronto Press.

Young, I.M. (1988) 'Five faces of oppression', *Philosophical Forum*, 24(4): 270–90.

Young, L. (2000) *Feminists and Party Politics*, Vancouver: UBC Press.

3 Is there such a thing as a political women's interest in Britain?[1]

Rosie Campbell

This chapter is intended to ascertain whether there is any evidence to suggest that men and women might think about politics in different ways. If there are differences in men's and women's political priorities or between the priorities of sub-groups of men and women then there is some basis to claim that a 'women's' interest exists, albeit in a nascent or unarticulated form. This chapter conceives of women's interests as context and group specific and not essentialist in nature. Thus, it takes seriously Jill Vickers' contention that the term 'women' does not mean that common interests exist by theoretical fiat, even within a specific country or group, unless one can be demonstrated to exist empirically.

Do men and women organize their political views in the same way?

This chapter is concerned with the ways that men's and women's political views could differ. Men and women may hold different views about political issues. For example, men may be more likely to support military intervention than women. Alternatively, men and women may have differing political priorities. There may be no observable difference in the position men and women take on issues but they may view them as being more or less important. For example, women may prioritize spending on education, whilst men might be more likely to prioritize tax cuts (Box-Steffensmeir *et al.* 1997; Chaney *et al.* 1998; Kornhauser 1987, 1997).

Testing for these two possible locations of difference, or similarity, requires different methods of analysis. Issue location is relatively easy to assess with readily available national datasets. A simple test would be to compare the mean responses of the sexes to issue related questions. Issue preference is more difficult to measure. Ideally, issue preference should be accessed by direct questions asking respondents to rank issues in an order of priority. The British Election Study (BES) has asked respondents to do this on two occasions since its inception. An alternative approach is to use statistical tests to measure the impact of specific issues on vote choice. This chapter does not attempt to provide a comprehensive model

of voting by sex, but uses vote choice as a means to identify issue preference. There have been comprehensive studies that compare the attitude
positions of the sexes over a vast range of issues. This chapter focuses
specifically on measures of ideology and issues which have been theorised
to be of special significance to women (Shapiro and Mahajan 1986).

The discussion will proceed by examining issue preference expressed
in responses to an ordered question in the 2001 BES by sex and sex/age.
The analysis then moves to issue location; mean differences between the
sexes are compared for different measures of political ideology. Ideology
is conceived as an underlying mechanism through which attitudes are
framed. Ideology is commonly measured by a respondent's left–right position. Finally, issue preference is re-examined by assessing which measures
have the most impact on the vote choice of respondents by sex and generation. There is variation in the questions asked throughout the British
Election Study series and, due to availability of suitable questions, the last
two stages of the analysis are conducted on the 1997 BES and not the 2001
BES.

Gender differences in ideology: pointers from the gender gap literature

Having identified the two possible locations of gender difference in ideology it is necessary to consider two more important questions. Why should
we be interested in gender differences in ideology and what reasons are
there for theorizing that they might exist? The answers to these questions
stem from two sources: feminist theory and feminist empirical research. A
brief précis of the two approaches is presented below.

From the theoretical perspective this study is partially designed to test
whether there is evidence to support Anne Phillips's arguments for fairer
representation of women in parliament (Phillips 1994, 1995). Phillips is a
proponent of quota systems, which ensure that political parties choose
female candidates. It is her contention that women's interests cannot be
sufficiently articulated through patriarchal political systems. She claims
that there are 'women's issues', or experiences particular to women,
which can only be addressed by women themselves, because until the
debate is located in the public arena, and policies initiated by female
politicians, the issues themselves will not be clearly defined.

For Phillips's argument to be sustained, I contend that there should, at
the very least, be some evidence to suggest heterogeneity between the
political priorities of the sexes. Differences between the sexes within sub-
sectors of the population would be sufficient to support the Phillips case.
They might be theorized to exist because of the cross-cutting nature of the
sex variable, which interacts with all other demographic factors. Thus we
might not expect the interests of middle class and working class women,
for example, to be identical, but we might expect them to be different

from middle class and working class men, respectively. Such an approach encourages what Vickers describes as 'a politics of women's interests' which includes both commonalities and differences. Whilst this study seeks to address a specific feature of arguments about the representation of women, it also attempts to test elements of Norris's gender generation gap theory (Norris 1999). Norris has demonstrated that the traditional gender gap, where women were more likely than men to vote for the Conservative Party in Britain, has reversed in generations born since the Second World War. Thus, in generations born prior to the Second World War the traditional gap holds, but women born after the Second World War are more likely to vote for the Labour Party than men of the same generations. Norris and Inglehart suggest that the gender generation gap is an international phenomenon and is part of a global developmental pattern where women are becoming more left-leaning than men (Inglehart and Norris 2000).

In the United States the modern gender gap in vote choice has been apparent at the aggregate level, with more women than men voting for Democratic candidates in presidential elections since 1980 (Norris 2001; also Hill, Chapter 4, this volume). This development has generated some detailed and insightful research into gender and voting patterns. In some cases feminist theories such as Carol Gilligan's ethics of care (Gilligan 1982) have been operationalized to test whether women are more altruistic than men in their motivations for vote choice. From this perspective women are theorized to favour increased taxation and spending on welfare provision, whilst men are theorized to be more likely to be governed by pocket-book voting or income tax levels. The alternative model of gender difference applied in the United States is akin to feminist standpoint theory or, alternatively, rational choice theory. Women are thought to be more inclined to support increased spending on welfare than men because women are more likely to be the beneficiaries of such provision or because of their specific experiences as women (Bendyna and Lake 1994; Box-Steffensmeir *et al.* 1997; Chaney *et al.* 1998; Mueller 1988).

Whether the rational choice or ethics of care approach is preferred, the hypothesis generated is that women will be more likely than men to support political parties that offer increased spending on welfare. If the gender generation gap evident in Britain can be explained by either theory, we would expect attitudes towards welfare provision, particularly health and education, to impact upon the voting choices of younger women. This hypothesis will be tested in the third and final sections of analysis.

However, the model is further complicated by the theoretical explanations for the traditional gender gap in voting, where women, in the past, were more likely to vote for right-leaning political parties than men. In the United States there is a tendency for Southern religious women to be more inclined to vote for the Republican Party than other women. It is possible that the traditional gender gap in voting might be better explained by reference to traditional values or moral conservatism.

Inglehart and Norris attribute global patterns of change in the gender gap to 'long-term structural and cultural trends, that have transformed women's lives and have gradually produced a realignment in women's politics in post-industrial societies' (Inglehart and Norris 2000). Women's location in the home and the influence of religiosity and the church are considered to be likely explanations for the traditional gender gap, hence the emphasis on moral conservatism as a predictor of vote choice. In order to include a measure of moral conservatism in the analysis, Heath *et al.*'s liberal/authoritarian scale is utilized and its impact on the vote choice of the sexes compared (Heath *et al.* 1993).

Evidence of distinctive women's interests?

From a brief reminder of the gender gap literature we can see how left–right ideology and issue preference are theorized to play a crucial role in explaining the vote choices of men and women internationally. This emphasis on ideology warrants an examination of whether the theorized differences in attitude between the sexes are apparent in responses to the British Election Survey (BES).[2]

In her study of the Swedish Riksdag, Wängnerud addresses the very element of Phillips's argument for quota systems that is relevant to this study. Wängnerud utilizes an ordered question to test Phillips's claims (Wängnerud 2000). The question is: 'Thinking about this year's election, is there any issue or issues that is especially important to you when it comes to choosing which party you are going to vote for?' Wängnerud is able to compare the men's and women's responses to this question over time, from 1982 to 1994. She found that 'jobs and the environment were two of the policy areas most frequently mentioned by both the sexes in the period studied ... Family policy is an important area among female voters, but not among male voters ... Social policy and health care is given higher priority by female voters than by male voters ... The economy and taxes are prioritized more highly by male voters than by female voters' (Wängnerud 2000). These findings are similar to those that have been emanating from the United States. From this data analysis Wängnerud concludes that 'the analysis underpins the view that there are grounds for adopting a gender perspective on the political process. We obtain confirmation that the theory of the politics of presence involves pivotal issues in representative democracy' (Wängnerud 2000).

A question asking the respondent to order preferences is available in the 2001 BES. The question asks respondents to specify their most important election issue.[3] In the Swedish voter survey respondents were asked to specify three issues, which led to more illuminating results. The responses to the 2001 BES question, by sex, are outlined in Table 3.1. A Chi-square

Table 3.1 Respondents' most important election issue, by sex, 2001 (%)

Issue	Male	Female
Britain's membership of the European Monetary Union	9.5	6.6
Britain's relations with the European Union	5.0	2.7
Law and order	3.6	2.9
Educational standards	**7.5**	**14.2**
Environment	0.5	1.0
National Health Service	**25.6**	**31.3**
Inflation, prices generally	0.5	0.3
Public transport	0.5	0.7
Taxation	5.3	3.1
State of the economy	**4.7**	**0.8**
Unemployment	0.9	0.7
Respondent's standard of living	1.6	1.2
Price of petrol	1.2	0.5
Foot and mouth disease	0.3	1.2
Immigration/asylum seekers	2.2	1.7
Pensions	2.4	3.5
Other	13.0	9.2
None	5.6	5.1
Don't know	10.2	13.2
Total	100%	100%
	$n = 1,455$	$n = 1,560$

test was conducted and was significant at the 0.001 level. It shows that there is a less than one in 1,000 chance that the variables, sex and most important election issue, are independent of each other. In later analysis the individual issues are considered separately.

In all of the categories there is some difference between the sexes, the most striking involve educational standards, the state of the economy and the National Health Service. Nearly twice as many women as men prioritize education, with 7.5 per cent of men naming education as their top priority compared with 14.2 per cent of women. This represents a gap of 7 per cent. Women were 5 per cent more likely than men to state the NHS as their top priority; 25.6 per cent of men named the NHS as their top priority compared with 31.3 per cent of women. Men were more likely than women, by 3.9 per cent, to state that the economy was the most important election issue, with 4.7 per cent of men prioritizing the economy compared to 0.8 per cent of women. When the respondents who prioritized education and the NHS are combined, 46 per cent of women prioritized one of these issues compared with 34 per cent of men. The interpretation of these results is considerably illuminated when they are broken down by sex and age. The relationship between issue priority age and sex is presented in the form of bar charts in Figures 3.1 to 3.6 below.

An obvious interpretation of Figures 3.1 and 3.2 is that women are more likely to prioritize education when they are of child-bearing age and that

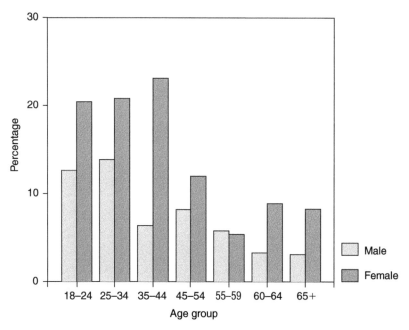

Figure 3.1 Respondents who named educational standards as the most important
election issue, by age and sex (source: BES 2001).

Note
The difference between the sexes is significant at the 0.05 level for the respondents aged
25–34, at the 0.01 level for respondents aged 65+, and at the 0.001 level for the respondents
aged 35–44 (Chi-square test)

they are more likely to emphasize the NHS as they approach pensionable
age.[4] However, further exploration of these two theories is not possible
because the 2001 British Election Study does not contain information on
parenthood. These results have some implications for the gender generation gap theory. We have seen that prioritizing spending on health and
education is linked to votes for Democratic candidates in the US case. In
Britain, however, older women are thought to be more likely to vote for
the Conservative Party than men or young women. If the theory is applicable to both countries we would expect the older women who prioritize the
NHS to vote for the Labour Party. In relation to ideological position, it
might be that the liberal/authoritarian scale is better able to explain the
votes of older women than the left–right scale. Alternatively, there may be
external factors inhibiting the Labour vote amongst older women, such as
a perception that it is a masculine institution. Alternatively they may
believe that the Conservative Party will provide the best healthcare policies.

   Figure 3.3 demonstrates that, on average, European issues are more
important to the vote choices of men than women.

   Figure 3.4 shows that taxation was most important to men aged 25 to

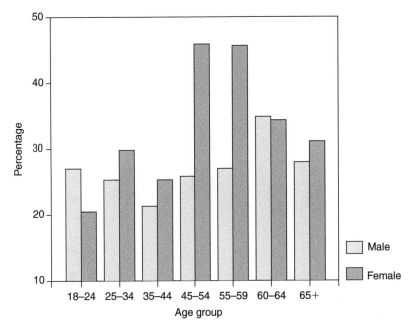

Figure 3.2 Respondents who named the NHS as the most important election issue,
by age and sex (source: BES 2001).

Note
The difference between the sexes is significant at the 0.01 level for the respondents aged
55–59, and at the 0.001 level for respondents aged 45–54 (Chi-square test)

34. This finding supports the gender gap thesis, which suggests that
women will be most interested in welfare provision, whilst men might be
more likely to be governed by pocket-book politics. Figure 3.5 shows that
the economy was more important to men than women in every age group,
except the under-25s, a finding that also supports theories about gender
difference from feminist theory and research in the United States.

Figure 3.6 indicates that immigration or asylum was most important to
men aged 18 to 24, something that was not predicted by feminist theory or
research. Some of the percentage differences represented in Figures 3.1
to 3.6 are relatively small, others are larger, and many of the gaps are statistically significant.

There is evidence to suggest that sex interacts with age or generation to
produce effects on attitude. In order to establish whether these are age or
generation effects it would be necessary to conduct a time series analysis,
which is not possible using the British Election Study, because there are
too few ordered questions. These initial results do not refute the gender
generation gap thesis and the differences are large enough to suggest that
more rigorous research is needed in order to determine true differences
and discount random error.

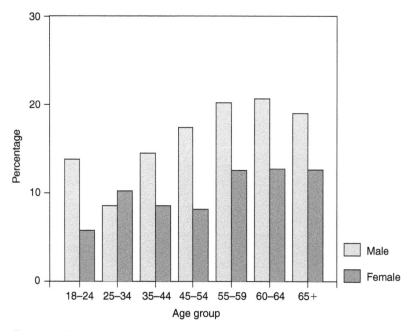

Figure 3.3 Respondents who stated that Britain's relations with the European Union or European Monetary Union was their most important election issue, by age and sex (source: BES 2001).

Note
The difference between the sexes is significant at the 0.05 level for the respondents aged 18–24, 35–44, 55–59 and 65+. The difference is significant at the 0.01 level for the respondents aged 45–54 (Chi-square test)

These findings contribute to the research of Phillips and Wängnerud outlined in the introduction to this chapter. If Wängnerud's claims are accepted, then the gender dimensions of the issue priority scale illustrated in Table 3.1 and Figures 3.1 to 3.6 are sufficient to support Anne Phillips's call for sex quotas in Britain.

Gender and ideology

This section is designed first to assess whether men and women from different sub-sectors hold the same ideological positions, and second, to test whether the measures of ideological position commonly employed in studies of voting behaviour in Britain are equally applicable to both sexes. Previous research has highlighted the potentially gendered nature of attitude positions.

'A single, broadly defined liberal-conservative ideological continuum almost certainly cannot be applied ... to women, if it ever could ... It is possible that men and women – or different generations of them – organize their attitudes and opinions in different ways. Compassion, traditional

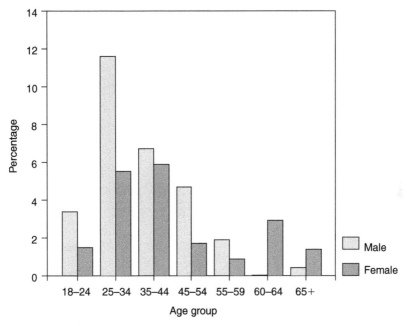

Figure 3.4 Respondents who stated that taxation was their most important election issue, by age and sex (source: BES 2001).

Note
The difference between the sexes is significant at the 0.01 level for the respondents aged 25–34 (Chi-square test)

values, regulation and protection, and force and violence may be the major dimensions that help structure women's attitudes, others may apply to men' (Shapiro and Mahajan 1986).

Shapiro and Mahajan neatly encapsulate the issues that need to be addressed within a study of gender and ideology. The core question, 'whether men and women systematically organize their political views and choices in the same way', is easily transferable to a British context, and the debate about whether electors structure their opinions at all is an international one.

Many studies of the gender gap in voting in the United States found that women will prioritize healthcare and education spending and that such an emphasis can explain why they are more likely than men to vote for the Democratic candidates in presidential elections (Hill, Chapter 4, this volume; Box-Steffensmeir *et al.* 1997; Chaney *et al.* 1998; Kornhauser 1987, 1997). Implicit in the argument about female voting patterns is the assumption that the indicators of the traditional left–right scale might not adequately explain the left-leaning tendencies of women. Thus we might predict that the traditional left–right scale should not have as large an impact on women's voting as men's. Instead, indicators that specifically address health and education should have greater explanatory power in

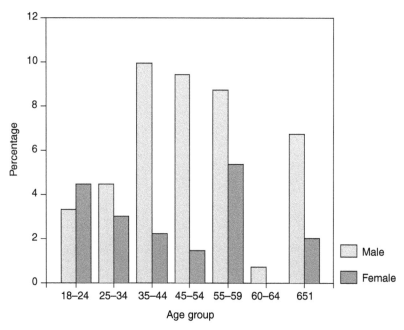

Figure 3.5 Respondents who stated that the economy was their most important
election issue, by age and sex (source: BES 2001).

Note
The difference between the sexes is significant at the 0.001 level for respondents aged 35–54,
and at the 0.05 level for respondents aged 65+ (Chi-square test)

regard to the voting choice of women. The prediction outlined above is
refined by the introduction of the liberal/authoritarian scale. The
research from the United States, which indicates that women prioritize
healthcare and education, contains a parallel dimension. Where Southern
religious women are more likely to affiliate with the Republican Party,
their motivations are thought to be based in moral conservatism rather
than left–right position. This brings us to a second hypothesis, that older
and/or religious women's voting behaviour will be better explained by the
liberal/authoritarian scale than by the left–right scale. Testing the
liberal/authoritarian hypothesis will be relatively straightforward. As well
as applying the standard scales and testing for differences between the
sexes we must ensure that the scales are not themselves gendered. Each
item within the scale must be considered and we must theorize whether
there might be gender implications. So the first step in the analysis is to
assess whether the scales are gendered and the second step is to see
whether their effect on voting behaviour is different for men and women.

The hypothesized ideological differences between the sexes have been
outlined above. In the following section different measures of ideology are
tested for sex and gender relationships.

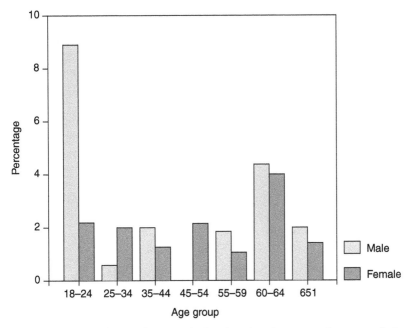

Figure 3.6 Respondents who stated that immigration or asylum was their most important election issue, by age and sex (source: BES 2001).

Note
The difference between the sexes is significant at the 0.05 level for respondents aged 18–24 (Chi-square test)

One method of measuring ideological position is to look at respondents' self-placement on the left–right scale. Table 3.2 contains the mean differences between the sexes on the self-placement left–right scale in the 1983 and 2001 BES. The mean differences are not substantial. In both studies the majority of respondents placed themselves in the middle of the scale, limiting the amount of variation to be explained within any group.

Table 3.2 Mean difference in self-placement on the left–right scale[5]

Year	Birth cohort	Gender gap[6]
1983 BES	1907–1946	–0.06
	1947–1966	+0.09
	Total	–0.03
2001 BES	1907–1946	–0.18
	1947–1986	+0.21**
	Total	+0.01

Note
** Significant at the 0.05 level (one-tailed ANOVA)

However, there is a small but significant difference between the mean values of men and women born between 1947 and 1986 in the 2001 survey, indicating that of the respondents born between these years women placed themselves slightly to the left of men. The direction of the gaps are in line with the gender generation gap theory in each case, although the other gaps are not statistically significant. Thus, there is some evidence to support Norris's gender generation gap thesis, where younger women are predicted to be more left-leaning than younger men. As the results, represented in Table 3.2, provide support for the gender generation gap theory it would be interesting to further the investigation by conducting a rigorous time series analysis of self-placement on the left–right scale. However, because the self-placement variable is not available in every BES, the birth cohorts were simplified to two groups in order to test Pippa Norris's finding that the gender generation gap is evident in post-Second World War birth cohorts.

Socialist/laissez-faire and liberal/authoritarian scales

Self-placement measures of ideology can be problematic because we do not know what respondents understand the left–right scale to be. For such reasons researchers often prefer to calculate ideological position by amalgamating responses to different attitude questions (Sanders 1999).

A set of scales developed by Heath *et al.* (1993) to measure socialist/ laissez-faire and liberal/authoritarian ideology are widely used in studies of voting behaviour research. They provide convincing evidence for the robustness of these scales. However, feminist theory, and especially gender gap theory, suggest that these scales might provoke different responses in the sexes. Heath *et al.*'s bio-dimensional scales are the most recent advances in a long-running academic debate that preceded Converse's study of belief systems in mass publics. As noted above, many studies of the gender gap in voting in the United States suggest that women will prioritize healthcare and education spending and that this emphasis can explain why they are more likely to vote for the Democratic candidates in presidential elections than are men. Implicit within this argument about voter choice is the assumption that the indicators of the traditional left–right scale might not adequately explain the left-leaning tendencies of women. The hypothesis drawn from this model would be that the traditional left–right scale should not have as large an impact on women's voting as men's, but that indicators that specifically address health and education should have greater explanatory power in regard to the voting choice of women. This model is further defined by the introduction of the liberal/authoritarian scale. The research from the United States which supports the argument outlined above contains a parallel dimension, where Southern religious women are more likely to affiliate with the Republican Party, but their motivations are thought to be based in moral conservatism rather than a left–right position. This leads us to a second hypothesis, namely, that older and/or religious women's voting behaviour will be better explained by the liberal/authoritarian scale than by the left–right scale.

As well as applying the standard scales, a gender perspective requires us to test the scale for gender dimensions. This will require us to look at each item within the scale and theorize whether there might be gender implications. The hypotheses considered thus far have been generated by reference to the literature from the United States. The aggregate gender gap evident in the United States is not apparent in Britain, although there is some evidence that this gap might be evident within age groups. It is important therefore to consider the implications of the context. It may be that in Britain factors such as class interact with sex to produce gendered effects within subgroups.

There has been a large body of research responding to Converse's study of belief systems in mass publics (Converse 1964). Converse tested what he described as 'issue constraint'. He compared intercorrelations on issues assuming that high correlation coefficients supported the notion that a single liberal/conservative scale underlay attitude structures. He found a close relationship between different issue preferences in political elites but no such strong correlation was evident in the mass public. In the 1980s there was a spate of articles in which confirmatory factor analysis was used to test whether issues hung together in liberal/conservative scales (Conover 1980; Feldman 1988; Fleishman 1988; Judd *et al.* 1981; Judd and Milburn 1980). The literature suggests that individual's responses to certain issues are related and that it should be possible to predict an individual's attitudes toward, say, nationalization using their attitudes toward the redistribution of wealth. Possibly, the lack of structure evident in Converse's analysis can be attributed to the fact that values are at least bi-dimensional. The employment of confirmatory factor analysis (Structural Equation Modelling or SEM) allowed researchers to specify latent factors, such as left–right positions. These factors could be defined as the underlying causal explanation for particular variables, i.e. attitudes to nationalization. Thus researchers were able to avoid the problem of data dredging, where the results of exploratory factor analysis may be produced by correlated measurement errors and therefore be spurious. SEM provided researchers with a method of coherent hypothesis testing. Using the LISREL programme, Fleishman found strong indications of a bi-dimensional attitude structure within the American public. In Britain, Heath *et al.* (1993) have developed stable and robust liberal/authoritarian and socialist/laissez-faire scales, which support the contention that the belief structures in mass publics are at least bi-dimensional or are best explained by the use of two scales. Such scales are often employed in studies of voting behaviour in Britain and if gender differences are found within the scales this will impact on our understanding of British electoral behaviour.

An analysis of whether responses to Heath *et al.*'s scales are patterned by gender will be undertaken in the next section. First, the components of the scale will be outlined and discussed. Second, analysis is undertaken in Table 3.3 to determine whether Heath *et al.*'s scales are equally applicable to men and women and men and women from different birth cohorts. Finally, the analysis in Table 3.4 attempts to test whether there are substantive gender differences in location on Heath *et al.*'s scales.

In addition to the theories already outlined Jelen *et al.* (1994) suggest that women are more liberal than men and that this is not specifically addressed in the literature. They state that the gender gap is typically the largest on questions of war and peace and environmental issues, and weaker on economic issues. They cite Gilligan's model as a possible reason for the higher levels of sympathy for the disadvantaged found among women. They also suggest that there might be a more self-interested motivation because women tend to be more socio-economically disadvantaged than men. However, Jelen *et al.*'s research locates no significant differences on the left–right scale between men and women in the UK, Germany and the Netherlands. Women were found to be more right wing in Italy and France. But they do find a tendency for women to be more 'dovish' or pacifistic in four out of the six countries examined. Economic issues were only significant in Britain and the Netherlands. In the UK these issues were very specific with, for example, women less likely than men to believe in the importance of trade unions. Dutch women were much less likely than Dutch men to believe that the unemployed were lazy. Overall, women were found to be less likely than men to support nuclear power. Jelen *et al.* question why, when they have found these differences, was there no gender gap in ideology or positioning on the left–right scale? One might suggest in response that the traditional left–right scale might be inadequate here. Jelen *et al.* (1994) suggest that the left–right scale might mean different things to men and women. Alternatively, one might theorize that the difference between men and women will be evident within subgroups and not necessarily at an aggregate level. Norris's gender generation gap theory

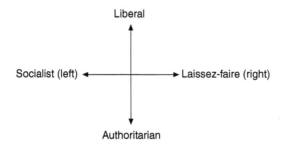

Figure 3.7 Testing the robustness of Heath *et al.*'s scales by sex: bidimensional attitude structure

suggests that women should be more left leaning than men in generations born since the Second World War and the reverse should apply to prior generations. This highlights how subgroup differences can cancel each other out at an aggregate level. The analysis in Table 3.4 attempts to test whether the left–right scale means different things to men and women.

The items in Heath *et al.*'s socialist/laissez-faire scale are:

- Ordinary people get their fair share of the nation's wealth.
- There is one law for the rich and one for the poor.
- There is no need for strong trade unions to protect employees' working conditions and wages.
- It is government's responsibility to provide a job for everyone who wants one.
- Private enterprise is the best way to solve Britain's economic problems.
- Major public services and industries ought to be in state ownership.

The items in Heath *et al.*'s liberal/authoritarian scale are:

- Young people today don't have enough respect for traditional British values.
- Censorship of films and magazines is necessary to uphold moral standards.
- People in Britain should be more tolerant of those who lead unconventional lives.
- Homosexual relations are always wrong.
- People should be allowed to organize public meetings to protest against the government.
- Even political parties that wish to overthrow democracy should not be banned.

Examination of the items above allows us to make some predictions about how they should apply to the sexes in Britain. If left-leaning ideological positions amongst women are concerned chiefly with the Welfare State, we would expect questions about public or private provision of services as well as trade unions to be less significant in their vote choice than those which specifically address education, health and benefits. A scale that is designed to tap into the theoretical priorities of women might contain items such as: 'would you support tax increases for spending on healthcare and/or education?' A question of this type is available in the 1997 BES.[5] All of the items in Heath *et al.*'s two scales are available in the mail-back component of the 1992 and 1997 BES.[6] The availability of a question that asks respondents to choose reduced taxation or increased government spending on health and social services in the 1997 BES makes it more suitable for this chapter's central research questions and therefore the 1997 BES is used in all subsequent analysis.

When the six socialist/laissez-faire items are summed into a scale, the range of actual scores is 6 to 28, the mean is 15.3 and the standard deviation

Table 3.3 Descriptive statistics and scale reliability for Heath *et al.*'s socialist/laissez-faire and liberal/authoritarian scales in the 1997 BES

Scale	Birth cohort	Sex	Cronbach's alpha	Mean	Standard deviation	Range
Socialist/	1907–1946	Men	0.69	15.4	4.2	6–27
laissez-faire		Women	0.68	15.7	3.8	6–28
	1947–1976*	Men	0.67	15.5	3.7	6–28
		Women	0.63	14.8	3.3	7–26
	All	Men	0.67	15.4	3.7	6–28
		Women	0.66	15.2	3.8	6–28
		All	0.67	15.3	3.6	6–28
Liberal/						
authoritarian	1907–1946	Men	0.52	20.3	3.3	9–30
		Women	0.47	20.4	2.9	10–30
	1947–1976	Men	0.62	17.9	3.6	7–27
		Women	0.54	17.9	3.1	6–28
	All	Men	0.62	18.9	3.6	7–30
		Women	0.58	18.9	3.3	6–30
		All	0.59	18.9	3.4	6–30

Note
*The mean difference between the sexes was significant at the 0.01 level.

is 3.6 (*n*=2,399). The Cronbach's Alpha Coefficient of the scale is 0.67, indicating that it is internally reliable.[7] The Cronbach's Alpha Coefficient for the male respondents was 0.67 and 0.66 for the female respondents. The Cronbach's Alpha Coefficient for those born between 1907 and 1946 was 0.69 for men and 0.68 for women. The Cronbach's Alpha Coefficient for respondents born between 1947 and 1976 was 0.67 for men and 0.63 for women. These figures suggest that the scale was marginally less reliable for the younger women than for the rest of the sample. However, the values are all above 0.6 and therefore are acceptable. The only significant mean difference between the sexes was among the respondents born between 1947 and 1976 where British women were slightly left of men on the scale.

The liberal/authoritarian scale is less reliable than the socialist/laissez-faire scale. The Cronbach's Alpha Coefficient was 0.47 for women born between 1907 and 1946 and 0.62 for all men. The most significant mean differences are between the age groups and not the sexes. Overall, there is little difference between the sexes in Britain in the reliability of either scale, suggesting that they are suitable measures for men and women, and for different generations of men and women.

There is some evidence to support the gender generation gap thesis as women born after the Second World War were slightly more left-leaning then men of the same generations. Correlation coefficients were calculated between the socialist/laissez-faire scale and the self-placement left–right scale. There were no significant differences between the sexes or sex/generation, hence the scales are appropriate for both sexes.

The analysis thus far has focused on sex and sex and age or birth cohort. Gender is a term which is designed to capture the relationship of the sex variable to social context. Sex cross-cuts all other demographic factors and women from different groups may not share the same priorities. It is therefore necessary to analyse the measures of ideology by sex within sub-groups. Table 3.4 contains all of the sub-sectors analysed by Pippa Norris in her article on the gender gap in the United States (Norris 2001). The table is replicated here, but instead of examining the gender gap in voting, the mean difference between the sexes' responses to Heath *et al.*'s socialist/laissez-faire and liberal/authoritarian scales are presented. There are no significant differences between men and women's responses to the socialist/laissez-faire scale within age groups, but there are significant differences by birth cohort.[8] Women born between 1957 and 1976 are slightly more left-leaning than men of the same generations. Women with a Certificate of Secondary Education (CSE) or equivalent are more right-leaning than men with the same qualifications; whilst women with A levels or a degree are slightly to the left of men with the same qualifications. The evidence suggests that it is possible that education has a different impact on the ideological preferences of men and women. There is a significant difference in the mean position of non-white men and women on the socialist/laissez-faire scale, but the small sample size undermines any further extrapolation. Within the Salariat, women are slightly more left-leaning than men, indicating that occupational class may also have a different impact on the ideological preferences of men and women. Within the liberal/authoritarian scale, there are some significant mean differences between the sexes.[9] Roman Catholic women give slightly more liberal responses than Roman Catholic men. There are other significant differences that were not predicted and are not easy to interpret. For example, women aged between 45 and 54 are slightly more liberal than men of the same age, but this pattern was not continued in those over 54. Overall, there is some evidence to support the gender generation gap in left–right position and some evidence to suggest that education and occupational class might interact with sex to produce different ideological positions.

Alternative measures of ideology

In the introduction to the section on ideology it was mentioned that questions asking respondents to state their position on tax versus spending on welfare provision might be more appropriate measures of the left–right position of women than the traditional measures. A question of this type is available in the 1997 BES. Respondents were asked to choose between one of these three options:

1   Reduce taxes and spend less on health, education and social benefits.
2   Keep taxes and spending on these services at the same level as now.
3   Increase taxes and spend more on health, education, and social benefits.

Table 3.4 Mean difference in ideological position between the sexes in the 1997 BES

Sub-group		Socialist/laissez-faire (Gender gap)	Liberal/authoritarian (Gender gap)
Age	18–24	0.66	0.36
	25–34	0.45	−0.03
	35–44	0.47	−0.03
	45–54	0.07	0.58**
	55–59	0.06	−0.83
	60–64	−0.42	−0.67
	65+	−0.52	0.11
Birth cohort	1967–1976	0.71**	−0.38
	1957–1966	0.69**	0.10
	1947–1956	0.35	0.45
	1937–1946	−0.52	−0.29
	1927–1936	−0.16	0.05
	1917–1926	−0.68	0.14
Marital status	Married	0.11	0.07
	Not married	0.16	−0.17
Education	No qualification	−0.09	0.39
	CSE or equivalent	−1.8***	0.56
	O level or equivalent	0.06	0.11
	A level or equivalent	1.14***	0.01
	Higher education below degree	0.27	0.23
	Degree	1.66***	−0.6
Race*	White	0.09	−0.08
	Not white	1.58**	2.91***
Goldthorpe-Heath class	Working class	−0.44	0.45
	Supervisors and manual foreman	−0.14	−0.56
	Petty bourgeoisie	−0.39	0.02
	Routine non-manual	0.40	−1.65***
	Salariat	0.94***	0.14
Household income (quartiles)	Lowest	−0.62	0.30
	Second	0.22	0.16
	Third	0.67**	0.52
	Highest	0.56	−0.21
Religion	C of E/Anglican	−0.09	−0.06
	Roman Catholic	0.53	1.29***
	Other Christian	0.31	0.37
	Non-Christian	0.59	2.0
	No religion	0.33	0.37
Total		0.16	0.05

Notes
* The sample size for these categories was less than 50.
** Significant at the 0.05 level.
***Significant at the 0.01 level.

Of the respondents, 72.6 per cent selected increased taxation and spending, 24.6 per cent opted to keep taxes and spending at the same level and only 2.8 per cent of respondents stated that taxes and spending should be reduced. When the data are broken down by sex 73.8 per cent of women and 71.2 per cent of men opted for increased taxation and spending. Of respondents born between 1947 and 1976, 76 per cent of women and 70 per cent of men selected increased taxation and spending. There is therefore a small percentage difference between the two, with 6 per cent more women than men opting for increased taxation and spending on welfare in post-Second World War generations. The data are heavily skewed, restricting further analysis because there is little variation to be explained. The tendency to answer in the affirmative is repeated in questions asking whether more money should be invested in health and education. The response patterns support the contention that ordered questions are the most successful way of accessing issue priority or preference because when asked to respondent to a single issue statement the majority of respondents tend to answer the same way.

Another suggested explanation for the gender generation gap is the rise in post-materialist values. Inglehart's post-materialist theory claims that the generations born since the Second World War have enjoyed more financial security than previous generations and have therefore begun to prioritize non-material political issues, such as reproductive rights, sexual harassment in the workplace and equal opportunities (Inglehart 1977). Norris claims that: 'If this process has influenced the gender gap, support for post-materialist values should be closely associated with left-wing female voting patterns' (Norris 1999: 155). Furthermore, Evans *et al.* note that the post-materialist measurement instrument does not yield clear results. They argue:

> In the most frequently employed version of Inglehart's measure, respondents are asked 'If you had to choose from among the items on this card, which are the *two* that seem most desirable to you? Maintaining order in the nation, giving people more say in important political decisions, fighting rising prices, protecting freedom of speech.' People who select 'maintaining order' and 'fighting rising prices' as their two priorities are defined as materialists. People who select 'more say' and 'freedom of speech' are defined as post materialists. The remainder (the majority of the samples) are defined as mixed cases.
>
> (Evans *et al.* 1996: 100)

The post-materialist measure is available in the 1997 BES. As highlighted by Evans *et al.*, the majority of respondents are described as mixed, with 58.9 per cent of the valid responses to the 1997 BES falling into this category. Only 29.6 per cent of respondents could be described as materialist and only 11.5 per cent fell into the post-materialist category. When the responses were broken down by sex and sex/generation there were no significant differences. The skewed nature of responses to the post-materialist scale seriously limits any explanatory power it might be predicted to have.

Some of the attitudes described by Inglehart as post-materialist are specifically feminist. An alternative to using the post-materialist scale might be to use measures of feminist attitudes. For example, one could use responses to the statement 'equal opportunities for women in Britain have gone too far'.

Bernadette Hayes tested the impact of feminist orientation on vote choice and found that feminist attitudes can be used to predict votes for the Labour Party; that these attitudes can be possessed by both men and women; and that sex/gender has no direct effect on vote (Hayes 1997). Hayes conducted her analysis on the 1992 BES, using three variables to measure feminist orientations. The first asks whether women are given too few opportunities within political parties, the second whether women should have an equal role with men in running business, industry or government and the third whether equal opportunities for women in Britain have gone too far. The first question is not available in the 1997 BES. This could be problematic because perceptions of parties' attitudes to feminist concerns are cited by Hayes as explaining the link between feminist attitudes and support for the Labour Party.

In Table 3.5 the largest gap between the sexes occurs in those respondents who were born after 1947, where 15.8 per cent more women than men stated that equal opportunities for women had not gone far enough. Hayes found that feminist attitudes predicted Labour Party votes of men and women equally well. Thus, if more younger women than younger men possess feminist attitudes we have a possible explanation of the gender generation gap.

Table 3.5 Responses to whether equal opportunities for women in Britain have gone too far, in the 1997 BES (percentages)

Group	Sex	Too far	About right	Not far enough	Total*
All	Male	8.7	54.6	35.7	100
	Female	9.3	42.6	46.2	100
Born 1907–1946	Male	8.6	54.5	35.3	100
	Female	13.0	46.5	37.6	100
Born 1947–1976	Male	9.2	53.3	37.1	100
	Female	6.9	39.2	53.4	100

Note
*The total includes the percentage of missing values.

Table 3.6 Mean responses to the statement 'women should have an equal role with men in running business, industry, or government, or women should stay in the home'

Group	Gender gap or mean difference
All	0.26***
Born 1907–1946	0.04
Born 1947–1976	0.40***

Note
*** Significant at the 0.01 level. ANOVA one-tailed test.

The patterns evident in Table 3.5 are more pronounced in Table 3.6. There was no significant gap between men and women born prior to the Second World War, but there was a significant gap between the sexes in the post-Second World War generations, with women agreeing more strongly than men with the statement 'women should have an equal role with men in running business, industry or government.'

The analysis in this chapter thus far has considered issue preference in ordered questions, using the 2001 BES, and issue-scale location, using the 1997 BES. An alternative method to assess issue preference is to test what measures have the largest effect on vote choice. An attempt to establish whether issues have a differential impact on the vote choices of men and women is complicated by the responses to issue questions. As outlined above, many of the questions of interest tend to provoke affirmative answers in the majority of respondents, limiting their use in regression analysis. However, it is worth attempting some preliminary regression. The logistic regression coefficients, standard errors and Exp(B)s for six logistic regressions are presented in Table 3.7.

The dependent variable is vote choice; whether the respondent claimed to have voted for the Conservative or Labour party. The first regression was conducted on men only and the second on women only, and the results are reported in the section entitled Group/All of Table 3.7.[10] The third and fourth regressions were conducted on respondents who were born between 1907 and 1946, analysing men and women separately.[11] Two regressions were conducted on respondents born between 1947 and 1976, also analysing men and women separately.[12] Post-materialism did not have any significant effects on vote within any of the groups analysed other than women born between 1947 and 1976, where, contrary to theory, post-materialism increased the likelihood of voting for the Conservative Party. The findings may be the result of the ineffectiveness of the measure employed. In all of the generations, the tax/spend on welfare variable had a larger impact on the vote choice of women than men. In the whole sample women who chose increased taxation and spending on welfare were five and a half times more likely to vote for the Labour Party

Table 3.7 Logistic regression on vote in the 1997 general election

Group	Independent variables	Sex	B	S. E.	Exp(B)
All	Post-materialism	Male	0.518	0.775	1.678
(n=956)		Female	−0.863	0.729	0.422
	Liberal/	Male	−0.099**	0.049	0.905
	authoritarian	Female	−0.131**	0.059	0.878
	Socialist/	Male	−0.395***	0.055	0.673
	laissez-faire	Female	−0.518***	0.073	0.596
	Self-placement	Male	−0.511***	0.099	0.600
	left/right	Female	−0.817***	0.122	0.442
	Taxes and spending	Male	0.924***	0.345	2.521
	on welfare	Female	1.729***	0.447	5.634
	Equal opportunities	Male	−0.074	0.319	0.929
	for women scale	Female	0.416	0.361	1.516
Born	Post-materialism	Male	−0.298	1.285	0.743
between		Female	0.175	1.191	1.191
1907 and	Liberal/	Male	−0.055	0.074	0.946
1946	authoritarian	Female	−0.117	0.108	0.890
(n=428)	Socialist/	Male	−0.432***	0.083	0.649
	laissez-faire	Female	−0.454***	0.108	0.635
	Self-placement	Male	−0.556***	0.154	0.573
	left/right	Female	−0.784***	0.166	0.457
	Taxes and spending	Male	1.415**	0.530	4.116
	on welfare	Female	2.084**	0.731	8.038
	Equal opportunities	Male	−0.842	0.525	0.431
	for women scale	Female	−0.329	0.574	0.719
Born	Post-materialism	Male	0.763	1.020	2.145
between		Female	−2.025**	1.027	0.132
1947 and	Liberal/authoritarian	Male	−0.166**	0.071	0.847
1976		Female	−0.122	0.080	0.885
(n=507)	Socialist/laisezz-faire	Male	−0.362***	0.078	0.696
		Female	−0.611***	0.117	0.543
	Self-placement	Male	−0.653***	0.158	0.521
	left/right scale	Female	−0.983***	0.203	0.374
	Taxes and spending	Male	0.569	0.492	1.766
	on welfare	Female	1.725**	0.682	5.611
	Equal opportunities	Male	0.230	0.436	3.272
	for women scale	Female	1.185**	0.548	1.338

Notes
*Significant at the 0.10 level.
**Significant at the 0.05 level.
***Significant at the 0.01 level.

than those who did not, whilst men who chose increased taxation and spending on welfare were two and a half times more likely to vote for the Labour Party than those who did not'. Amongst the respondents born between 1907 and 1946, women who chose taxation were eight times more likely to vote for the Labour Party than those who did not and men who chose taxation were four times more likely to vote for the Labour Party than those who did not. In the group born between 1947 and 1976 the tax and spend question did not have a significant effect on the vote choices of men, but had a significant effect on the vote choices of women, with women who chose taxation five and a half times as likely to vote for Labour than those who did not.[13]

The socialist/laissez-faire and self-placement left/right position scales had roughly the same effect on the vote choices of men and women in all groups. The gender differences in the impact of the tax/spend variable on vote supports the contention that welfare provision is likely to be especially important to women. Among the respondents born between 1947 and 1976 the liberal/authoritarian scale had a significant effect on the vote choice of men but not women. With each step up the authoritarian scale men became 15 per cent less likely to vote for the Labour Party. The significance of the relationship between liberal/authoritarian position and vote amongst men was not predicted by feminist theory or gender gap theory. The effect is echoed by the number of young male respondents who prioritized asylum or immigration in the 2001 general election – a result that warrants further investigation. The measure of feminist orientation employed had a significant effect on the vote choice of women born between 1947 and 1976. Women who felt that equal opportunities for women in Britain had not gone far enough were 34 per cent more likely to vote for the Labour Party than those women who did not.

Conclusion

The research presented in this chapter has demonstrated that there are differences between men and women (and especially different generations of men and women) in issue preference and location. It is apparent from analysis of the 2001 BES that women are more likely to prioritize education and healthcare issues and men are more likely to select the economy as their most important election issue. The differences between the sexes are most interesting when they are broken down by age, with younger women more likely to prioritize education and older women more likely to prioritize healthcare. Men aged between 55 and 59 were twice as likely than the rest of the sample to be most concerned about the European Union. These sub-group differences highlight the necessity of integrating the study of sex differences with other demographic factors, to avoid making essentialist claims about the nature of the sexes and to analyse rigorously the impact of the sex variable on political attitudes. The sex difference in issue priority presented in this chapter provides support for Anne Phillips's claims for gender quotas in Britain because there is evidence that men and women might want slightly different things from the political system and these differences need to be represented. Furthermore, the evidence presented in this chapter supports Vickers' claim that a politics of women's interests is required because there are differences both among women and between women and men.

There is evidence in the 1997 and 2001 British Election Studies to support the existence of an ideological gender generation gap, which underpins Norris's gender generation gap theory of vote choice. Women born after the Second World War were significantly to the left of men on the self-placement left–right scale. Women born after 1957 were significantly more left-leaning on Heath *et al.*'s socialist/laissez-faire scale than men. The two findings support Inglehart and Norris's modern gender gap theory (2000).

No evidence was found that Heath *et al.*'s measures of ideology were less valid for women, or women of different generations, than men. This study has demonstrated that women born after the Second World War in Britain are significantly more feminist than men of the same generations, and this has a significant effect on vote choice. No evidence was found to suggest that post-materialist values affected the vote choices of men and women in different ways. However, such insignificant effects may be a result of the weakness of the measurement instruments used and some more analysis with questions designed specifically for this task would be helpful.

The analysis in this chapter has been descriptive and not causal, but there is some evidence to suggest that education and occupation might have different effects on the ideological position of men and women. Women who had A levels or a degree were significantly more left-leaning than men with the same qualifications. Female members of the Salariat were also more left-leaning than male members.

The scope of this chapter is limited by its dependency on secondary data analysis. The questions used were not designed for the study's purpose and were not available in a continuous time series. The lack of key information, for example whether the respondent was a mother, prohibits a thorough investigation of whether feminist standpoint theory, rational choice theory or an ethics of care can provide the best account of the gender differences outlined in this chapter. The gender differences in issue preference and ideology presented here suggest evidence of women's interests that are distinct from men's in small but significant areas.

Notes

1 A version of this chapter was first published in the *British Journal of Political Science.* See Campbell, R. (2004) 'Gender, ideology and issue preference: is there such a thing as a political women's interest in Britain?', *British Journal of Politics and International Relations*, 6: 20–46. I would like to express my thanks to Blackwell for permitting republication in this volume. I am extremely grateful to Joni Lovenduski and Peter John for all their comments and support and to all those who commented upon earlier versions of this chapter.

2 The British Election Study has been conducted since 1964. The 2001 study was funded by the Economic and Social Research Council (ESRC) and directed by David Sanders and Paul Whiteley, the University of Essex, and Harold Clarke and Marianne Stewart from the University of Texas at Dallas.

3 The BES 2001 cross-section variable name is 'bisssum' and is the summary of the respondents' self-stated most important issue.
4 There is a sharp increase in the number of respondents reporting pensions as the most important election issue in the over 65s. In order to gain more detailed information about respondents' issue preferences it would be useful to ask them for a number of key election issues.
5 The self-placement on the left–right scale was coded 0 left to 10 right. This was recoded –5 left, 0 middle, and 5 right. The 1963, 1964 and 1966 British Election Studies asked respondents about their location on the left–right scale. First a filter question was asked: 'Do you ever think of yourself as being to the left, the centre, or the right in politics, or don't you think of yourself that way?' In 1963, 68 per cent of respondents stated that they did 'not see themselves that way'. This figure was 62.4 per cent in the 1964 survey and 64.6 per cent in the 1966 survey. In each of these studies those respondents who replied to the filter question in the affirmative were then asked to place themselves on the left–right scale. The low response rate to the filter question means that any further analysis of the self-selection left–right variable will be seriously undermined because there is unlikely to be a representative sample of responses to the question. This low response rate may also be an indictment of forced self-selection left–right questions, where respondents are asked to place themselves on a scale without an opt out. These findings reinforce the strategy utilized in this chapter, where left–right position is measured by a battery of items and tested for internal reliability and compared to self-placement on the left–right scale. In the 1970, 1974 February and October, 1979, 1987, 1992 and 1997 BES respondents were not asked to place themselves on the left–right scale. In the 1983, 1997 and 2001 BES the self-placement left–right scale question was asked without a filter. In 1983 valid responses were coded from –10 for left, to +10 for right, and 87.9 per cent of the respondents answered this question. In 2001 valid responses were coded from 0 for left, to +10 right, and 83.2 per cent of respondents answered the question.
6 Half of the scales are coded in reverse order, i.e. from right to left instead of left to right. In order to create a scale these items are reversed.
7 The Cronbach's alpha test for reliability was used by Heath *et al.* and its use here permits a replication of Heath *et al.* The replication is followed by tests to establish whether the scales are equally reliable when applied to men and women and different groups of men and women.
8 In this case the gender gap is the mean value of the male responses minus the mean value of the female responses. The significance of the difference is calculated using ANOVA.
9 This lower reliability is reported by Heath *et al.*
10 Men Nagelkerke R Square = 0.622. Women Nagelkerke R Square = 0.770.
11 Men Nagelkerke R Square = 0.672. Women Nagelkerke R Square = 0.752.
12 Men Nagelkerke R Square = 0.618. Women Nagelkerke R Square = 0.798.
13 Interaction terms suggest that the difference between the sexes is insignificant, with a significance level of 0.08. However, cross tabulations suggest that there is a bivariate relationship.

References

Bendyna, M. and Lake, C. (1994) 'Gender and voting in the 92 presidential elections', in C. Wilcox (ed.) *The Year of the Woman: Myths and Realities*, Boulder, San Francisco, and Oxford: Westview Press.

Box-Steffensmeir, J., DeBoef, S., and Lin, T.M. (1997) 'Microideology, macropartisanship and the gender gap', paper presented at American Political Science Association, Washington, September.

Campbell, R. (2004) 'Gender, ideology and issue preference: is there such a thing as a political women's interest in Britain?', *British Journal of Politics and International Relations*, 6: 20–46.

Chaney, C., Alvarez, M.R., and Nagler, J. (1998) 'Explaining the gender gap in US Presidential elections', *Political Research Quarterly*, 51(2): 311–39.

Conover, P. (1980) 'Comment: Rejoinder to Judd and Milburn', *American Sociological Review*, 45(4): 644–6.

Converse, P. (1964) 'The nature of belief systems in mass publics', in D. Apter (ed.) *Ideology and Discontent*, New York: Free Press.

Evans, G., Heath, A., and Lalljee, M. (1996) 'Measuring left–right and libertarian–authoritarian values in the British electorate', *British Journal of Political Science*, 47(1): 94–112.

Feldman, S. (1988) 'Structure and consistency in public opinion: the role of core beliefs and values', *American Journal of Political Science*, 32(2): 416–40.

Fleishman, J. (1988) 'Attitude organisation in the general public: Evidence for a biodimensional structure', *Social Forces*, 67(1): 159–84.

Gilligan, C. (1982) *In a Different Voice: Psychological Theory and Women's Development*, Cambridge, Massachusetts: Harvard University Press.

Hayes, B. (1997) 'Gender, feminism and electoral behaviour in Britain', *Electoral Studies*, 16(2): 203–16.

Heath, A., Evans, G., and Martin, J. (1993) 'The measurement of core beliefs and values: The development of balanced socialist/laissez-faire and libertarian/authoritarian scales', *British Journal of Political Science*, 24: 115–58.

Inglehart, R. (1977) *The Silent Revolution: Changing Values and Political Styles among Western Publics*, Princeton: Princeton University Press.

—— and Norris, P. (2000) 'The developmental theory of the gender gap: women and men's voting behaviour in global perspective', *International Political Science Review*, 21(4): 441–62.

Jelen, T., Thomas, S., and Wilcox, C. (1994) 'The gender gap in comparative perspective: gender differences in abstract ideology and concrete issues in Western Europe', *European Journal of Political Research*, 25: 171–86.

Judd, C., and Milburn, M. (1980) 'The structure of attitude systems in the general public: Comparisons of a structural equation model', *American Sociological Review*, 45(4): 627–43.

Judd, C., Krosnick, J., and Milburn, M. (1981) 'Political involvement and attitude structure in the general public', *American Sociological Review*, 46(5): 660–9.

Kornhauser, M. (1987) 'The rhetoric of the anti-progressive income tax movement: a typical male reaction', *Michigan Law Review*, 86: 465–523.

—— (1997) 'What do women want? Feminism and the progressive income tax', *American University Law Review*, 47: 151–63.

Mueller, C. (1988) *The Politics of the Gender Gap*, Beverly Hills: Sage.

Norris, P. (1999) 'Gender: a gender-generation gap?', in P. Norris (ed.) *Critical Elections: British Parties and Voters in Long-Term Perspective*, London: Sage.

—— (2001) 'The gender gap: old challenges, new approaches', in S. Carroll (ed.) *Women and American Politics: Agenda Setting for the 21st Century*, Oxford: Oxford University Press.

Phillips, A. (1994) 'The case for gender parity, or why should it matter who our representatives are?' *The Swiss Yearbook of Political Science.*
—— (1995) *The Politics of Presence,* Oxford: Oxford University Press.
Sanders, D. (1999) 'The impact of left–right ideology', in P. Norris (ed.) *Critical Elections: British Voters and Parties in Long-Term Perspective,* London: Sage.
Shapiro, R., and Mahajan, H. (1986) 'Gender differences in policy preferences: a summary of trends from the 1960s to the 1980s', *Public Opinion Quarterly,* 50: 42–61.
Wängnerud, L. (2000) 'Testing the politics of presence: women's representation in the Swedish Riksdag', *Scandinavian Political Studies,* 23(1): 67–91.

4 Women's interests and political orientations

The gender voting gap in three industrialized settings[1]

Lisa Hill

Voting is, arguably, the most important, even the *defining*, act of democratic citizenship because the right to vote is the sovereign right that protects all other rights and freedoms enjoyed by inhabitants of democratic orders. Yet it is acknowledged that representative institutions empowered by voters in the settings under consideration here are imperfect mechanisms of representation due to their dominance by white, middle class, middle-aged, educated men. The conduct of parliamentary affairs, as well as the electoral process that confers legitimacy upon them, remains deeply masculinist in both tone and substance. Nevertheless, as Jill Vickers suggests in Chapter 2 of this volume, this does not give grounds for a turning away by women from such powerful institutions; they have proved to be extremely resilient and will continue to operate regardless. If women refuse to 'aggregate and articulate accounts' of their 'collective interests to decision-makers ... the men who still dominate all major institutions will do so for them' (Vickers, Chapter 2, this volume). It seems wise to assume, therefore, that democracy can only be deepened, and women's interests advanced, by understanding, infiltrating and changing the major institutions of political power.

Understanding how and why people vote the way they do can tell us a lot about the democratic culture in question and how well it is performing in terms of representation. Such knowledge also helps parties understand how best to represent any potential constituency. Voting is known to be something of a bloc affair; voting preferences are not generally random or individualized but tend to form patterns along socio-demographic lines. Class, ethnicity, age, religiosity, and gender are among the many relevant cleavages that may correlate with particular voting preferences. Mindful that it cannot usefully or appropriately be treated as an essential or ontological category, this chapter explores 'women' as a meaningful category in understanding voting behaviour, focusing specifically on a phenomenon known as the 'gender gap'.

In the study of electoral behaviour the term 'gender gap' is used to denote a number of related phenomena, namely: gender differences in voting preferences, gender differences in party identification, gender differences in mass participation,[2] and gender differences in political and ideological opinions (Conover 1994: 51). The term may be culturally specific; for example, in North America it is generally used to describe women's stronger preference for left of centre parties whereas in Britain and Australia it can denote any gender differences in political attitudes or voting choices. This chapter is mainly concerned with gender differences in voting habits[3] though it also deals with the other aspects mentioned. Understanding the gender voting gap is extremely important because even small variations in women's voting preferences can have an enormous influence on party fortunes (Norris 1996a: 336).[4] Further, establishing and recognizing that women do have distinct political preferences underlines the importance of promoting women's political 'presence' (Phillips 1995) in representative institutions.

Drawing on a wide body of existing data, the discussion compares the 'gender gap' in three settings: Britain, Australia, and the United States. Comparisons are enabled by the fact that all three countries share in common a number of important features: all are well-established democracies with fully industrialized economies, in all three women won the right to vote relatively early[5] and all have witnessed proactive feminist movements. Further, in spite of enjoying such apparently auspicious circumstances, all three share in common the additional characteristic of women's under-representation in legislatures (Studlar *et al.* 1998: 781).[6]

Considerable attention is devoted here to competing explanations of political gender differences in an effort to account for the similarities between the British and Australian cases and their differences with the American. A perplexing riddle presents itself: why was America's 'traditional' (conservative) gender gap superseded so readily by a 'modern' (liberal) gender gap while in Australia and Britain the traditional gender gap retained its resilience? The discussion also explores the more general question of whether it is possible to speak of a distinctive women's perspective when it comes to elections. It is argued that women may indeed have a distinct political voice but that this voice may be being stifled or masked by limited electoral choices and moribund party systems that fail to capture and give full expression to it. The picture is further complicated by the facts that: many women's interests overlap with or are synonymous with those of men's (for example, within families and between feminist men and women); some women's interests may conflict with those of other women (for example, between feminist and non-feminist women, single and partnered women, heterosexual and homosexual women, white women and women of colour, poor and prosperous women, or religious and secular women); and women's social position is still taking shape. All sets of dynamics will have a tendency to render less distinct any separate interests women might have from men. The chapter concludes with a reflection on future prospects for the gender gap in each case.

Background

As women living in liberal democracies gradually became enfranchised in the early part of the twentieth century, it was anticipated that they would vote as a powerful bloc of swing voters, thereby effecting 'radical change in party fortunes'. This did not happen. Instead women in places like Britain, the United States, Australia, France, Italy and Germany tended to lean towards the centre-right, a tendency that was originally labelled the 'gender gap' but which should now be thought of as 'the *traditional* gender gap' (Norris 1999). The body of literature that emerged to explain this gap referred to structural factors such as women's greater longevity and greater religiosity relative to men and their exclusion from the paid workforce and concomitant non-membership of trade unions (Norris 1999: 149). Women's lower mass participation was attributed to similar causes as well as their 'restricted access to ... education and income' (Welch 1977; Mueller 1988: 23).

But, in the second half of the twentieth century, women's participation levels began to approach those of men's and their political differences were thought to be declining. This was interpreted to be a result of changes to women's social location, such as their greater participation in the workforce and higher levels of trade union membership, and cultural factors, such as the increasing secularization of society and the expansion and influence of the women's movement (Lipset 1960). Accordingly, the convergence thesis became commonplace. On this view, the increasing similarity between men's and women's social location would cause their objective interests, and hence their political preferences, to converge. Because in a number of important respects women's lives and interests had become more like those of men, it was no longer commonplace to think of women as having a distinctive political voice or perspective.

But by the 1980s the explanatory power of the convergence thesis came under question as new and, in some cases, multiple fractures between the sexes began to emerge. One important change was the emergence of a 'modern generation gap' detected by Pippa Norris and Ronald Inglehart in a major study of the gender gap in almost 60 countries. Overall, they found that the traditional gender gap of women's greater conservatism had been displaced by the 1990s by either convergence[7] or a significant shift to the left of men. This new gap was understood to be less a function of women's altered social location than of attitudinal shifts 'towards more egalitarian attitudes associated with post-materialism and feminism' (Inglehart and Norris 2000: 454; see also Studlar *et al.* 1998).

Because the new patterns and varieties were not uniform between countries and across other social cleavages the reinvigorated divergence thesis (or *modern* generation gap) did not entirely replace, but rather began to compete with, the convergence thesis.[8] As a result, contemporary studies of the phenomenon often conflict over the nature, extent and even existence of a gender gap. It would not be an over-statement to say that the gender gap has become a somewhat complex and mystifying phenomenon to track and study. This enterprise has been stymied by the lack of reliable longitudinal data (Christy 1994: 28; Leithner 1997: 30) as well as an implicit bias by which male political patterns are taken to be the norm from which women either diverge or converge. Nevertheless it is still possible to build up a picture of a women's political perspective that is distinguished by its instability and flexibility on some axes and its stable left-of-centre leanings on others.

The United States

Probably the best place to start when looking for political gender differences is the United States because the existence and nature of its gender gap is generally uncontroverted. Though a clear gender gap pattern is discernible, (i.e. a confirmation of the divergence thesis), explanations for this gap are various.

The development of the gender gap in the United States is characterized by three distinct phases. Although it is often claimed that the (modern) gender gap in the United States was first detectable in the Reagan years, it was, in fact, present as early as 1964. Before 1964 it favoured the Republican Party, after which it shifted in favour of the Democrats, resulting in a gap of between five and seven percentage points from 1964 to 1988. During the 1990s the gap widened and is now of such a magnitude as to constitute a major predictor of voting choice and party identification (Kaufman and Petrocik 1999: 870).

Bill Clinton's re-election in 1996 was largely due to the women's vote. Fifty-four per cent of women voted for Clinton compared to 43 per cent of men, thus generating a 'gender canyon' of 11 points (EMILY's List 1997; Greenberg 1998: 2). Women's preference for Clinton cut across age, class and ethnic cleavages. Among women under 30, the so-called 'soccer moms', there was a gender gap of 20 points in Clinton's favour (Lawrence 2000b: 2).[9] At the presidential election of 2000, 54 per cent of women backed Al Gore, compared to 43 per cent of men. If women's votes alone had been counted 'Gore would have won by a landslide' (Center for Policy Alternatives 2000a). In the most recent (2004) presidential election exit polls indicated that 55 per cent of men voted Republican while 44 per cent voted Democrat. Of women, 48 per cent voted Republican and 51 per cent voted Democrat. The gap is much wider when broken down by race.[10] Notwithstanding the outcome of that particular – and, in many ways, exceptional – election, women's consistent preference for the Democrats seems to be increasing over time (Trevor 1999: 62).[11]

In terms of mass participation, it is also worth noting that American women now represent the majority of registered, potential and actual voters (Center for Policy Alternatives 2000b).[12] Although they voted at considerably lower rates than men after suffrage, over time their turnout rates converged with and eventually overtook those of men. By 1984, women comprised 53 per cent of voters.[13] Because young women vote at a higher rate than young men it is anticipated that the turnout gap will continue to widen (Kenski 1988: 58).

Another kind of gender gap detectable in the United States is the 'independence gap' whereby men appear to be more softly committed to parties than are women; in other words, they are more likely to identify themselves as political independents, whereas women are more likely to identify with a political party.[14] This gap, which is estimated to have existed for 'at least 40 years', has been detected across almost all major social cleavages such as age, education, race, region, marital status, and religion.[15] Authoritative explanations for the phenomenon are elusive, though it has been suggested that the answer may lie in the fact that women rate parties more highly than men and have lower educational levels (being college-educated correlates with non-partisanship in the US).

Voting gap explanations

How can the phenomenon of the gender gap be explained? Responses to this puzzle have varied but the most authoritative of them will now be rehearsed.

Men's behaviour

One obvious and yet often overlooked explanation for the gender gap may be found in changes to *men's* political preferences. On this view, it is men's reaction to feminist agendas played out within the Democratic Party that has caused them to defect in greater numbers than women to the Republican camp, hence the gender gap (Wirls 1986; Greenberg 2000). It has even been suggested that it was women's preferences that remained static while men's shifted (Kaufman and Petrocik 1999: 865). Thought to have begun in the mid 1960s, men's preference for the Republicans first came to notice in the 1970s and had become entrenched by 1992 (Kaufman and Petrocik 1999: 865; Norrander 1999: 566).

The issues gap

One of the major causes thought to underlie women's divergent political preferences is found in another gender gap: the issues gap.[16] There are significant differences between men's and women's attitudes on a number of fundamental social and economic issues, differences that feed directly into voting choices (Seltzer *et al.* 1997). Whereas women tend to be more oriented toward issues like education and health, men show more concern for fiscal matters. Republican pollster Bill McInturff sums up the gap in this way: 'We talk about taxes, crime, welfare and the economy. These issues register much more with men. If you look at women, it is Medicare, health care, education, the environment. [Women] have a very different issues agenda' (cited in Greenberg 1998: 3).

Compassion issues generate considerable differences. American women favour more government intervention and social spending than men (Di Vall 1996; Erie and Rein 1988; Deitch 1988; Greenberg 2000) and exhibit less support for the use of force in foreign affairs (Kaufmann and Petrocik 1999: 876). American men exhibit considerably more conservatism on issues about homosexuality (Herek 2002) and more optimism about the economy (Kaufmann and Petrocik 1999: 875–6).[17] Patriotism and 'traditional family values' are also thought to be more important to American men (Greenberg 2000: 15). The strongest gender differences are generated by feminist women. Feminist women are much more strongly anti-war and anti-involvement than either men or non-feminist women. But even non-feminist women exhibit differences with men on domestic issues like unemployment benefits and policies affecting the elderly (e.g. Medicare). Thus, both non-feminist and feminist women contribute to the issues gender gap, but the contribution of the feminist women is by far the greater of the two (Conover 1994: 57).

In the United States religion provides a major issue cleavage: the more religious a woman is, the more likely she is to support a Republican. For example, in the Presidential race between Dole and Clinton, secular women had a 0.80 probability of supporting Clinton, while weekly churchgoers only had a 0.64 chance of supporting him. Women who classified themselves as 'homemakers' were also less likely to support Clinton over Dole (by about 8 points). Religious homemakers were 20 points less likely than secular homemakers to vote for Clinton, though religiosity had a much weaker effect on the propensity for African American women to support Clinton (Greenberg 1998). Thus, other social cleavages like religion and ethnicity can exert a fragmenting effect on the gender cleavage.

As men's and women's divergent interests have crystallized in the United States, the major political parties have become increasingly polarized. Issues affecting women that were once seen as peripheral (such as those relating to gender roles, reproduction, childcare and sexual mores) are now central to the policy debates (Freeman 1994: 80). American parties have been able to reflect and mobilize women's interests, giving rise, in turn, to a discernible gender gap. This polarization has also captured and reflected men's increasing conservatism.

A different ethic?

While not necessarily discounting structural factors, a number of authors have attributed the gender gap to a distinctively feminine ethic (sometimes referred to as 'the care ethic').[18] Specifically, women's moral psychology is posited as fundamentally different from men's; more embedded, more mindful of relationships and more compassionate.[19] On this view (commonly mistaken to be essentialist), the sexual division of labour has produced fundamental differences in perspectives between the sexes, with women tending to be more compassionate and more concerned with preserving human life than men (Chodorow 1974; Gilligan 1982). Even though there are many issues on which men and women agree, there are a number which generate significant differences, especially where disadvantaged members of society are concerned. This points to the possible existence of 'a distinctive women's perspective characterized by an ethic of caring' (Conover 1994: 57–8). Thus the care ethic is sometimes thought to underlie women's distinctive attitude to foreign policy, violence, and social spending (Frankovic 1982) though it should be noted that the underlying source of this distinct perspective may be somewhat more complex than it initially appears (see below).

Objective interests

There are also a number of structural reasons why women will be more likely to support a party that emphasizes the social safety net. The most obvious of these is that women are generally poorer than men. In the US an escalating divorce rate has increased the levels of single motherhood, hence the feminization of poverty. Single mother families now comprise roughly 60 per cent of poor families in the United States (Goldberg and Kremen 1994: 136–7). Divorce rates are having an interesting effect on the gender gap. Among middle-income voters in states where the divorce rate is rising, there is increasing support for the Democrats among women and declining support for Democrats among men. Women are less likely to vote for the Democrats after marriage and more inclined to do so after divorce.[20] Thus, the rise in divorce and its effect on women's prosperity 'seems to be pushing them to the left' (Koretz 2002).

Such findings about the correlation between women's social location and political preferences are reiterated in European studies of the gender gap. For example, Jelen *et al.* suggest that the issues gender gap may not be a function of women's greater compassion but may be related to their socio-economic disadvantage relative to men. Women's greater longevity means that many of them end their lives in poverty. In addition, single women earn lower wages than single men while divorced women experience a lower standard of living relative to men. Thus, it may be that women's preference for social spending is not born of altruism so much as self-interest. Similarly, women's opposition to 'military adventurism' may be less an artefact of their greater sensitivity to suffering so much as a pragmatic 'butter, not guns' utility calculation (Jelen *et al.* 1994: 172). Alternatively, it is quite possible that the gender gap is produced by a combination of self-interested and altruistic orientations. The fact that the gender gap cuts across class lines could also mean that even though some women do not experience the same economic hardships as others, they may nevertheless *identify* with the hardships of others and vote against their own class interests out of a gendered group altruism.

Another structural explanation for America's gender gap may lie in the fact that many women are state sector employees, the sector most threatened by Republican government cutbacks. Such employees have tended to be the most politicized of women voters and more politically active than rank-and-file female workers. For example, the turnout rate at national elections of state sector women employees is usually around 15–20 points higher than it is for other women. Threats to their own jobs appears to have sensitized such women to the problems of poorer women, creating a new and critical political force on the American scene. According to Erie and Rein, 'it is no accident that the discovery of the "feminization of poverty" by middle and upper income women who dominated the women's movement came precisely at the time when the jobs of middle class women were jeopardized' (1988: 189).

The autonomy explanation

Another explanation for the US gender gap is proposed by Susan Carroll. The 'autonomy explanation' suggests that the gender gap is a function of women's increasing economic and psychological independence from men. On this view, the gender gap always existed in a latent form but became manifest as a result of the feminist movement. Carroll's 1980s study of women voters found that women who were economically independent of men were far less likely to vote for Reagan. In addition, the greater the level of economic dependence on men, the higher the approval rating of Reagan's performance (Carroll 1988: 246).[21]

The autonomy explanation does fit with the fact that the emergence of a modern gender gap correlates historically with changes to women's relationship with men. As women's opportunities have broadened and more women have moved into professional and managerial positions, more women have also become divorced or chosen to remain single. Thus, women's economic and psychological independence from men has been consolidating over time (Carroll 1988: 255) and with it, their political independence. Reagan's woman-unfriendly agenda[22] was presented to the American public at the same time that important structural changes were taking place in American society. A modern gender gap seems to have been the natural result of this complex concatenation of social and political circumstances.

The autonomy explanation is persuasive because it fits with other research findings. For example, it can explain why the gender gap cuts across class lines. Though the class cleavage gives rise to many objective differences in the life circumstances of women, nevertheless both economic independence from individual men and the political gender gap exist across classes. In addition, the autonomy explanation explains the strong correlation found in previous studies between marital status and party choice (Carroll 1988: 255–7; see also Miller and Malanchuk 1983; Plissner 1983).

Britain

For most of the twentieth century Britain has seen a clear pattern of women's conservatism in voting habits (Hayes and McAllister 1997: 5). According to Lovenduski and Randall (1993: 160) if women's votes had not been counted, the Conservatives would have been out of power between 1945 and 1979. When British women were first enfranchised, the obverse trend was expected. Male politicians were so worried that the women's vote would 'radicalize politics' that they introduced women's suffrage in stages.[23] Such worries were, of course, unfounded. Though women's greater political conservatism was a global phenomenon during this time, it was greater and more deeply embedded in Britain (Short 1996: 17). During the 1970s the 'traditional' gender gap ranged from between 11 to 17 percentage points. The 1980s witnessed a narrowing of the gap to the point of negligibility but it re-emerged at the 1992 General Election. In 1992 women's larger vote for the Conservatives generated a gap of 6 percentage points. (Norris 1996b: 335). Up until the 1992 British general election, and in spite of Labour's best efforts to attract the women's vote, the Conservatives still retained a lead of between 4–8 percentage points among women voters.[24]

Things had changed dramatically by the 1997 British general election. In Labour's landslide victory, 46 per cent of women voted Labour, the highest since 1966 (Curtin 1997: 14). Eleven per cent of women swung to Labour compared to 8 per cent of men, thereby closing the traditional gender gap (Lawrence 2000b: 2) and possibly suggesting the emergence of a new (i.e. modern) one. In 2001 the gap in Conservative voting was so small (1 point) as to be negligible. Further, both men and women are now more, and equally, likely to vote Labour than Conservative (42 per cent). The figures for the Liberal Democrats were also very close (men, 18 per cent and women, 19 per cent). Because the gap has been so small in recent years, most commentators on the British scene have concluded that gender has faded as an important electoral cleavage (e.g. Rose and McAllister 1990: 5; Welch and Thomas 1988: 33).[25] Labour's attempt to attract women to the party has not, so far, been enough to generate a consistent 'modern' gap similar to that which prevails in the US (Norris 1999: 161–2).

According to Bernadette Hayes, although it can no longer be said that gender exerts any effect on party preferences, being feminist does. Thus 'as a group, feminist women are neither more or less likely to cast their vote for any one particular party than feminist men'. Feminist men and feminist women are significantly more likely to vote for either Labour or the Liberal Democrats than for the Conservative Party (Hayes 1997: 203). This relationship held even after other socio-demographic variables like age and class were controlled for (Hayes 1997: 211). It should be noted, however, that the same study found that women were much more likely to express feminist sentiments than men. For example, they were more likely to say that women were more disadvantaged than men and were more likely to blame political parties for the lack of political gains for women (Hayes 1997: 207).

Despite the apparent closing of the voting gap there is little dispute about the existence of an issues gap in Britain. Though there appear to be only small gaps between men and women on such compassion issues as alleviating poverty and welfare benefits, other topics give rise to more substantial gaps. Specifically, women's views on foreign affairs and the use of violence and force differ markedly from those of men. Women are far less in favour of allowing US nuclear weapons into Britain and significantly less approving of the death penalty. The greatest gap (a 17 point difference) is generated by the question of whether or not troops should be withdrawn from Northern Ireland.[26] There is also a generation effect here, particularly on the issue of social welfare spending. Whereas younger women tend to be more liberal than their male counterparts, older women tend to be more conservative than their male counterparts. It is also noteworthy that marital status appeared to have some bearing on welfare issues with divorced, single and widowed women far more supportive of pensions and the National Health Service than their male counterparts.[27]

Given this gap, there is a question about why women's greater liberalism on some key issues does not translate into more votes for the Labour Party. One explanation may lie in Joni Lovenduski's observation that the party has not been successful in shaking off its masculinist structure and style. Though the Labour Party has recently begun to address the problem of under-representation, for the period 1945 to 1992 the success rates of women candidates decreased rather than improved (Lovenduski 1996: 6–7). In 1997, the number of women MPs doubled due to the party's use of all-women shortlists. This mechanism for achieving gender equity was later declared illegal and in the 2001 general election the number of women MPs dropped slightly (Squires and Wickham-Jones 2002: 59). Nevertheless, since the Blair government appears to be seriously committed to the promotion of women's interests, it may be successful in retaining and/or converting younger cohorts of women voters in the future.[28]

One potentially misleading aspect of the British case is the existence of what Pippa Norris has labelled 'the gender generation gap'. Because of this gap, researchers often interpret the available data as indicating that the gender gap has closed. But closer scrutiny reveals that this is a methodological error known as the ecological fallacy, whereby potentially misleading conclusions about individual behaviour are derived from aggregate data.

In Norris's study of British voting by gender between 1945 and 1993 she found a pattern that is starting to emerge all over Europe: namely, a reversal of the gender gap by generations whereby older women vote more conservatively than their male counterparts and younger women (under 30) are more liberal than both their male counterparts and older women. Young women thus appear to constitute the most liberal voting bloc in the electorate.[29] Because older women are the most conservative and younger women the most liberal voters, the combined data has a cancelling out effect thereby giving the impression that the gender gap has closed. In fact, a more accurate picture shows the existence of two gender gaps (the traditional and modern) operating simultaneously and parallel to each other.[30]

According to Norris, this development is not a new one but has been detected since 1964 and was strongest during the period from 1970 to October 1974. Since young women's liberalism has been a consistent trend over time Norris suggests that short-term explanations (such as the effect of political leaders or topical issues particular to an election) will not be appropriate in accounting for the gender generation gap (Norris 1996b: 336). Instead, we should anticipate a long-term cohort effect of gender de-alignment, produced, she suspects, by the effects of the second wave of feminism and a more general 'social revolution in sex roles' and 'cultural values' which began in the 1960s and has gained momentum over time. Thus, as older voters die and are replaced by a different generation, it is likely that in the long term the majority of women will become more left-wing in their political preferences (Norris 1999: 161).

Australia

In many ways, Australian patterns follow those detected in Britain. Despite the lack of longitudinal survey data (Leithner 1997: 30) most researchers have been satisfied that there existed a traditional gender gap in Australia from the advent of female suffrage and for most of the twentieth century (Aitken 1977; Renfrow 1994; McAllister 1992; Norris 1996a; Lawrence 2000a; Curtin 1997).[31] While many predicted that the closing of the gender gap was imminent due to changes in women's social location (McAllister 1992; De Vaus and McAllister 1989) others argued that neither convergence nor divergence was likely but rather that the traditional gender gap would persist for some time (Renfrow 1994; Leithner 1997).

For most of this century Australian women were predominantly conservative, a trend that remained strong until the late 1990s. Whereas 44 per cent of women identified with the conservative Liberal/National

Coalition Party in 1993, only 37 per cent of men did (a gender gap of approximately seven points) (Renfrow 1994: 130). By 1996, although younger men and women were less likely to support the Coalition than older cohorts, nevertheless in every age group, the ALP (Australian Labor Party) garnered less support amongst women than men. Female support for the ALP was between three and five percentage points below that of males across all age groups (Lawrence 2000a: 5). But by 1998, there were signs that this gap had begun to close. A poll conducted by EMILY's List prior to the 1998 election suggested that the traditional gender gap had disappeared due to a substantial defection of younger women to Labor (Lawrence 2000a: 6). A secondary gender gap, whereby more women than men tended to vote for the Australian Democrats, also disappeared in 1998 (Curtin 2001: 1). This pattern was repeated and consolidated in the national election of 2001 where equal numbers of men and women (37 per cent) voted for the ALP while slightly fewer women (45 per cent) voted for the Coalition than did men (48 per cent). Women were significantly more likely to vote for the Democrats (7:4) and slightly more likely to vote for the Greens (6:5) (Bean and McAllister 2002).[32]

As with the British case, though, the picture becomes more interesting on closer inspection. Again, it is important to break down the data by age in order to avoid the ecological fallacy, the commission of which tends to obscure the real picture. In 1993, support for the Coalition was much weaker among younger voters: whereas 34 per cent of younger men and 41 per cent of younger women supported the Coalition party, 44 per cent and 50 per cent of older voters respectively gave it their support (Renfrow 1994: 122). Further, young women were the least willing to transfer their preferences to the Coalition, preferring to pass them onto the Democrats and Greens (Gow and Renfrow 1996).

Though Patty Renfrow insisted in 1994 that such patterns would be unlikely to develop into either a long-term convergence or divergence effect due to the persistence of a substantial (7 point) traditional gap between young men and women (Renfrow 1994: 122–3), by the 1998 election the gap had narrowed to two points.[33] It should be stressed, however, that the cohort change story may not yet be over, since another gap, one which could potentially resolve itself into electoral change further down the track, has been detected in Australia.

Voting gap explanations

The issues gap

As with the US and British cases, in Australia an issues gap between men and women is evident. Though Renfrow found no gender differences on economic issues (even those which tested for attitudes on spending trade-offs between reduced taxed and social spending) and only minor differences on social issues (Renfrow 1994: 123–5), Hayes and Bean report a different story (and one more like that of the US) in their study of married Australian women. Rather than being more conservative than their husbands, they found Australian women to be more liberal in their political and social attitudes. They were less likely to favour 'economic conservatism' or cuts to social spending, had greater objections to wage inequality and capital punishment and were more supportive of environmental protection and equal employment opportunities for women (Hayes and Bean 1994: 73).[34] At the 1990 federal election, when it came to allocating second preferences 'gender was strongly predictive of attitudes toward green issues like uranium mining, logging of forests and the greenhouse effect' with women more likely to take a pro-environment line.[35] Women are much more likely than men to report that equal opportunities for women have not improved sufficiently and are also far more likely to agree that government should seek to increase women's work opportunities (Renfrow 1994: 124–5). Since parties of the left have historically been more proactive about furthering women's economic equality rights, it is puzzling that this has not translated into votes for the Labor Party in Australia (to be discussed further).

Significantly, the strongest and most consistent gender gap detected in Australia is that women are far more likely than men to indicate that they 'did not know which of the two major parties best represented their views' (Gow and Renfrow 1996).[36] The 'don't know' gender gap is largest on economic issues (averaging ten points) while a four point gap was generated for the question that tested for which party was thought to best represent women's views on social issues (Renfrow 1994: 126–7).

These findings fit somewhat with the fact that women in Australia are more likely to be softly committed voters than are Australian men. A 1995 poll conducted by the *Sydney Morning Herald* found that women comprised 65 per cent of the 'don't knows'. The 'don't knows' were particularly concentrated among women over 55. Labor polls conducted prior to the 1996 and 1998 elections yielded similar results, with women twice as likely as men to indicate that 'they didn't make up their minds until the day of the election or a couple of days previously' (Lawrence 2000a: 6–7).[37] One problematic feature of defining the gender gap in Australia is the apparent volatility of the women's vote. Whereas the men's vote has been fairly static over time, women's voting patterns have been in flux (Robb 1996: 133). This apparent volatility has been attributed to the massive social changes that have affected women's life circumstances and therefore their political allegiances. Further, because some women's lives are more complicated than others, their electoral behaviour is more labile that than of other women. For example, women in the 25–34 age groups are more stressed and time-poor because many of them have children, hold down part time or full time paid work and run households. Such women are seen to be extremely risk-averse at election time and are wary of any party that promises change that might be perceived as disruptive. It has also been suggested that, because they are highly stressed, women in this group 'don't read a lot of newspapers' making it 'difficult' for party strategists to communicate with them.[38] Another volatile – because risk-averse – group is women in the over 55 age group, who, because of their economic vulnerability, are more sensitive to negative campaigning about potentially disruptive policies (Robb 1996: 134).

At first sight then, the notion of a definable political voice seems elusive. By the same token, the existence of a discernible *issues* gap, its failure to translate into votes for the more progressive party (Labor) and the fact that women are less able to identify a party that best represents their divergent views from men, suggest that there is more to this story than meets the eye. While Renfrow suggests that it is possible that 'women's issues are not dominant or even salient in the formulation of party preferences' (Renfrow 1994: 131), others point to a transformation in party allegiance patterns whereby social group cleavages like class and gender are gradually being displaced by issue group cleavages like environmentalism (Papadakis 1993: 173). Since it is true that women are less inclined to identify with a political party, this probably makes them more open to persuasion about such issues at election time (Lawrence 2000a: 6), but whether it means that gender is no longer a meaningful political category is debatable.

Labour force segregation

One explanation for women's resistance to the Labor Party may lie, as Christian Leithner has suggested, in the nature of the kind of paid work they perform. Australia's work force is highly segregated, with men concentrated in large-scale industrial firms, characterized by high levels of formal bureaucracy, 'organizational and physical separation of management and employee' (and thus potentially antagonistic labour relations) and high levels of trade union membership (Leithner 1997: 36–7). By contrast women are located predominantly in large numbers of small firms (including households) with high levels of interaction between management and workers, 'paternalistic patterns of labour relations' and low to non-existent levels of trade union membership (Leithner 1997: 37). According to Leithner, this pattern of sex-based segregation 'facilitates the development of sex-specific value systems and flows of information in the workplace'. Men's longstanding association with trade unions will tend to predispose them towards collectivism and an antagonism towards management, which is reinforced by daily face-to-face interactions with like-minded workers, hence their predisposition to the ALP. From the trade union side, the preponderance of male members may have led to a neglect of women's interests and concerns, thus reinforcing and perpetuating its masculinist profile (Leithner 1997: 36, 44–5). This fits with other findings that trade unionism is one of the few issues on which women are more conservative than men (Hayes and Bean 1994: 60). Thus, the nature of women's work, coupled with their limited experience of trade unions, could be either perpetuating a system that neglects women's interests or else obscuring the reality that it is in women's objective interests to support trade unionism. Perhaps both dynamics are operating simultaneously.

The nature of parties?

An alternative explanation is that the major parties do not provide enough meaningful choice for women. Thus existing party structures and styles may be masking some gender effects. Policy and attitude differences between men and women will be immaterial unless political parties find ways of mobilizing such differences 'into partisan support' (Renfrow 1994: 125). In order for an issue opinion to have an effect women would have to perceive one or other of the parties as best representing their position on that issue (Lawrence 2000a: 10). This is clearly not happening. While it seems that more of the progressive women's votes are up for grabs, the ALP is failing to capture them. It may not simply be a function of the fact that women's social location is undergoing change, but also that parties have not been able to keep up with, embrace and connect to such changes (Goot 1996). Some signs of the veracity of this argument have been given. For example, the gender gap reversal in 1998 may have resulted from the ALP's increased efforts to align itself with the women's agenda (Lawrence 2000b: 7).[39] Similarly, women's historically greater support for the Democrats (an extremely woman-friendly party whose leaders have been mainly women); their greater tendency to direct second preferences to the Greens; the fact that the populist One Nation Party had mainly male support (Sawer 2002b: 10); the fact that women are more likely to be softly committed voters; and the fact that the first group of women who moved to support the Democrats were women defecting from Labor (Sawer and Simms 1993) all suggest that, contrary to the mooted default conservatism of Australian women, what they are really doing is casting about for acceptable left alternatives to the major parties, especially Labor.

It may be the case that the Labor Party has failed to mobilize fully and capture the issue differences between men and women 'by articulating and communicating effectively policies and candidates that appeal to women' (Renfrow 1994: 131). Labor's recent attempt to 'modernize' is indicative of its fecklessness in relation to women. In 2002, two former high profile leaders of the ALP (Bob Hawke and Neville Wran) were asked to conduct a review of the ALP in light of its disastrous performance in the 2001 federal election. The authors of the Hawke–Wran Review are widely regarded as two of the most masculinist and aggressive of former

Labor leaders. Their report was strongly criticized by women within the ALP. Joan Kirner, convenor of the Labor women's lobby group EMILY's List, reports that she had been assured that the report would recommend an increase in guaranteed parliamentary seats for women (from 35 per cent to 45 per cent). Instead, the status quo was endorsed. According to Kirner: 'Many Labor women are angry and dismayed that yet again women have been used as a bargaining chip; that men can horse-trade our rights for their power' (AM Radio transcript 2002).[40]

At the federal election of 2001, Marian Sawer noted that '[t]here was little for women in terms of policy offerings. Some failed to notice the conservative Liberal/National Coalition had a women's policy, as the word "women" did not appear in its title' (Sawer 2002a). A telling example is that neither of the major parties offered desirable childcare options (Killick 2002). After the most recent federal election of 2004 (which returned the conservative Coalition government) the number of women in ministerial positions did not increase, while the number of women appointed to Labor's front bench increased by only one. Further, the 2005 election saw the number of women elected to the House of Representatives fall for the first time since 1993 (Parliamentary Library 2005: 42). Australian parliamentary politics has never been a woman-friendly enterprise. In 1972 women comprised only 2 per cent of the members of Parliament. Though this has improved over time, by 2005 the average level of representation in Australian parliaments is still only 25 per cent (Parliamentary Library 2005: 42).

In general, then, it is undoubtedly an error to think of women's votes as 'monolithic' because much of their political behaviour and attitudes converges with that of men's; moreover, there are variations according to 'age, workforce participation, income and education' (Lawrence 2000a: 11). But, on the other hand, the existence of a substantial issues gap, and the consistent finding that women find it more difficult to designate a party that reflects their particular concerns, suggests that there is a distinctive women's agenda that has not as yet found adequate expression within existing party choices.

The likelihood of long-term political change in terms of the gender gap was for some time discounted on the basis of a number of substantial studies.[41] Nevertheless, the last two elections point to convergence as a long-term prospect and if the ALP were able to tap into the issues gap, divergence could be a real possibility. The fact that young women are the group least willing to transfer their preferences to the Coalition, preferring to pass them onto the Democrats and Greens (Gow and Renfrow 1996) suggests there is a growing constituency of progressively minded women capable of being mobilized by a suitably reconstructed Labor Party, a Green Party with broader appeal, a revitalized Australian Democrat Party or even a new women's interest party.

Comparisons and conclusions

Although other cleavages are apt to fragment the woman's vote, we have
seen that in all three settings it does appear that the political perspective
of women is distinguishable (though not always strongly) from that of
men, particularly where social spending, equal rights for women and
other minorities, and the use of force is concerned. More importantly, in
all settings women's *objective* interests are distinct insofar as it is consistently the case that women are poorer than men. Why, then, has the
gender gap been more discernible, consistent and especially more liberal
in the United States than it has in either Britain or Australia? A number of
potentially authoritative explanations present themselves.

According to Pippa Norris, relative to women elsewhere 'women in the
United States have higher expectations of gender equality while experiencing considerable inequalities in the objective conditions of their lives'.
She suggests that these contradictions may have caused American women
to be more conscious of the 'relative deprivation experienced by women
as a group' (1988: 233).

Other, more concrete differences offer further and likely clues. Most
notable are those related to party structure and style. Left of centre parties
in Britain and Australia may have appeared less woman-friendly due to
their strong associations with the trade union movement. By contrast, the
US Democrats have no such affiliation. Furthermore, in the last two
decades the major parties in Britain and Australia have become increasingly centrist and catch-all, whereas parties in the US became more polarized over the same period. The gender gap came to prominence in the
Reagan years, a period in which pro-choice and pro-public sector spending women became increasingly politicized, active and influential. Unlike
Britain or Australia, Republicans have, and continue to mobilize, a large
Christian constituency, a fact that has contributed to the polarization of
parties and helped to define women's interests and therefore partisanship. By contrast, none of the major British or Australian parties have, for
example, an official abortion policy, an issue, that in the US has been a
major battleground for the parties.[42]

In the US there are no viable third parties to court softly committed
women or women whose social location is undergoing change. Thus the
(US) Democrats were able to capture this constituency while the existence
of the Australian Democrats and Greens in Australia and the Liberal
Democrats in Britain provided an outlet for women looking for a left
alternative.[43] The funnelling of progressive women into third parties may
have had a deadening effect on the culture and structure of the major
parties, making it more difficult, in turn, for them to recruit more liberal
women.

The gender gap in the United States has also been widened by the
(conservative) movement of men, whereas in Australia and Britain the

men's vote has been more stable. In the US men are also more likely to be softly committed voters, underlining the volatility of their vote relative to women. This is a reversal of the dynamic that prevails in both Britain and Australia.[44]

It is also worth noting that the United States is singular in having particularly well-financed feminist groups in addition to well-organized *anti*-feminist groups (Welch and Thomas 1988: 38). Again, this phenomenon may have exerted a clarifying effect on the emergence of a women's (and, conversely, men's) agenda which parties have been able to capture and mobilize.

At the risk of oversimplifying, while the divergence thesis best fits the United States case, convergence appears to be more appropriate for Britain and Australia. A temporal qualification should be made here, however; for while the US situation seems to be entrenched,[45] the Australian and British ones appear to be in a state of emergence and clarification. While convergence most accurately describes present conditions, because an issues and gender generation gap is detectable in both contexts, divergence (in the direction of a modern gender gap) may be imminent or at least a possibility. Something all three countries have in common, as we have seen, is the existence of an issues gap. In Britain and Australia the discrepancy between the issues gap and voting preferences has been a source of some confusion. While it may simply point to a women's perspective that is just too complicated to capture, it may also be pointing to a failure on the part of parties to recognize, respond to and mobilize women's interests.

And yet 'failure' may be too strong a word, since we have seen that understanding the political perspective of women is beset with many pitfalls. One of these is the apparently mixed nature of their political orientations, so that on many issues they are more liberal than men, and yet on the level of general ideological orientations they are either more conservative or exhibit no differences from men. Jelen *et al.*'s cross-national study of European women found that, as in Britain and Australia, gender differences on concrete issues did not translate 'into a gender gap on general ideological self-placement' (Jelen *et al.* 1994). They concluded that:

> [T]he left–right continuum appears to have a different meaning for men and for women. Women seem much more likely to regard the left–right space as referring to 'preservationist' values of religion and cultural homogeneity, and men conceptualize the left–right space in economic and 'New Politics' terms.
>
> (Jelen *et al.* 1994: 171)

It may be reasonable to generalize this finding to Australian and British women. Assuming that this is the case, existing instruments for testing for differences may be inappropriate, partly because they have been using a male perspective as the norm from which women either depart or approach.[46]

Women may be conservative about issues relating to religion, trade unionism, and the family yet they exhibit more liberal attitudes where violence, the environment, and welfare are concerned. There are also signs that women may be more risk-averse than men on some economic issues and yet more likely to favour social spending on welfare.

An important consideration is that many women's objective interests in relation to men are complex and mutable; it would not be unexpected, for example, to find a heterosexual cohabiting couple agreeing on a social spending issue that materially affects their joint household economy while disagreeing on an issue like military spending. The same couple, once separated, might disagree strongly about the social spending issue and disagree even more strongly about the military spending question. Another factor that must be taken into consideration is the liberalizing effect that a feminist orientation has on both men's and women's electoral preferences. Thus, while the feminist orientation is *about* women, it can equally affect both men's and women's political choices. Finally, there are divisions between women and deep divisions between generations of women; accordingly, mobilizing women's preferences and attitudes into votes may be too complicated an enterprise for parties as they are currently organized and conducted. If democracy is to be deepened in terms of aggregating and articulating women's interests, new political parties may have to be formed while existing parties will need to reassess and reform.

Notes

1 A different version of this argument first appeared in *Policy, Organization and Society* as 'The political gender gap: Australia, Britain and the United States', 22(1), 2003. The author would like to thank the journal for permission to reprint that article.

2 Though less and less so due to the narrowing, and in most cases disappearance, of such gaps.

3 'There are two dimensions to the gender gap or gender differences in voting. The first relates to the gender ratio of each party's support or, in other words, what percentage of conservative voters are women and what percentage are men. The second dimension is the extent to which women as a group split their vote between parties and the extent to which men split their vote. Failure to distinguish these dimensions can lead to a misinterpretation of the gender gap' (Curtin 1997: 2; Leithner 1997: 31–2). This paper is primarily concerned with the gender ratio of party support.

4 This is hardly surprising given that, in any given electorate, women comprise more than half the constituency of eligible voters (Lawrence 2000a: 4).

5 Australia, 1902; Britain, 1928; United States, 1920.

6 Although it should also be noted that Australia and the US are federal systems whereas the British system is unitary. Further, Australia is exceptional in having a compulsory voting regime where turnout consistently hovers in the 85 per

cent (of voting age population) range, as compared to much lower turnouts in Britain and the US.

7 Nevertheless, the traditional gender gap retained its resilience in post-communist and developing nations (Norris 1999: 150). The modern generation gap is more common in industrialized and developed states and is most marked in the United States.

8 'The convergence model suggests that gender has relatively little impact on political attitudes today' whereas the divergence thesis underlines women's electoral distinctiveness. 'The available evidence indicates that during the 1950's women voters in most countries were consistently more conservative than men by a small margin' (Norris 1994: 49).

9 Though it should also be noted that the 'soccer mom' story 'obscured the fact that working class women were more likely than middle class suburban women to support Bill Clinton's re-election bid' (Greenberg 1998: 1).

10 Broken down by race as well as gender, the following pattern is found: white men voted 62 per cent to 37 per cent in favour of Bush, whilst white women were less conservative than their male counterparts, with 55 per cent for Bush and 44 per cent for Kerry. Non-white women are less conservative, with only 24 per cent voting for Bush and 75 per cent for Kerry. Non-white men voted slightly more conservatively than non-white women, with 30 per cent for Bush and 67 per cent for Kerry (CNN 2004). For a discussion of the complicated relationship between gender and race in political attitudes and behaviour see Lien 1998 and Welch and Sigelman 1992. For the US gender gap (1952–1998) broken down by a wide range of socio-demographic cleavages see Norris 2004.

11 Although only presidential elections are canvassed here a similar pattern is found in Congressional elections whereby 'at the aggregate level, sex differences were clearly the most powerful force in shaping the balance of partisan identification'. Furthermore sex is 'an important determinant of partisan identification even after controlling for membership in other social groups' (Mattei and Mattai 1998: 411, 431).

12 Whereas in Britain, men outnumber women in terms of mass participation – 61 per cent and 58 per cent respectively at the 2001 general election – (Butler and Kavanagh 2002: 257). In Australia gender has no impact on turnout, largely due to the effect of compulsory voting.

13 In 2000, 52 per cent of all voters were women and 48 per cent were men. In the 1920s the turnout difference was estimated to be between 30–45 per cent. By the 1950s it had dwindled to 10 per cent, by 1964 to 5 per cent; and by 1969, 4 per cent. It had disappeared by 1976 and had turned around by 1984 (Mueller 1988: 22). African-American women (especially those who are heads of households) have particularly high rates of voting participation. They are 'four percentage points more likely to cast ballots than were African American men of comparable socio-economic status'. Further, 'African American women who were heads of their households were 11 percentage points more likely to exercise the franchise than were white males, after controlling for demographic factors' (Prestage 1994: 40).

14 The American National Election Surveys (ANES) from 1952 to 1996 found a gap of around six percentage points while the General Social Surveys (GSS) from 1972 to 1994 detected a gap of five and a half percentage points. 'The exact location of the independence gap is between the leaning independent category, where more men are located, and the weak partisan classification, which more women choose' (Norrander 1999: 566).

15 Though it is slightly more prevalent among younger, better educated, Jewish, Hispanic and African American citizens (Norrander 1997: 466).

16 According to Studlar *et al.* (1998) the issues and values gap has had far more

influence on the gender gap than either socio-economic status or social location type explanations.

17 Chaney *et al.* (1998) have proposed that this relative pessimism about the economy suggests 'that a part of what has been considered a Republican–Democrat gender gap is really an anti-incumbent bias on the part of women'.

18 This explanation is sometimes referred to as the 'socialization' explanation. For a discussion of differences in perspective between male and female US *legislators* (as opposed to voters) see Kathlene (1989).

19 Though in the US this may be limited to feminist women since Conover found that non-feminist women were just as conservative and lacking in compassion on social issues as were conservative men (Conover 1994).

20 The suggested explanation is that 'some poor men might become a bit richer via divorce but not enough to turn them into Republicans. And affluent single women may be less well off than their married peers, but not enough to spur them to vote Democratic. Working seems to make only middle-income women – not poor or rich women – more likely to support Democrats' (Koretz 2002).

21 For a cross-national exploration of the impact on political preferences of women entering the paid workforce see Iverson and Rosenbluth 2003.

22 '[D]uring the early years of the Reagan administration, women's organizations, the press and many public interest groups generated considerable publicity about Reagan's opposition to the Equal Rights Amendment and abortion and the adverse impact of Reagan's budget cuts and economic policies on women' (Carroll 1988: 255–6).

23 There were two stages. Women 30 years and over got the vote in 1918 but it wasn't until ten years later that women over 21 were enfranchised (Welch and Thomas 1988: 25–6).

24 The Conservatives found their greatest support among older women who 'gave 1.9 million votes to the Conservatives compared with 1.1 million to Labour, a decisive edge' (Norris 1996a: 118).

25 This claim should be tempered by the fact that, in Britain, although there is no gender gap in terms of voting participation, there is a significant gender gap in terms of political activism generally (Norris *et al.* 2004).

26 These differences hold even after employment, age, religion, party affiliation, education, class and marital status have been controlled for: 'In other words, the differences between men and women in these opinions are not artefacts of other demographic characteristics on which men and women differ' (Welch and Thomas 1988: 35).

27 Such differences 'suggest that women not in two adult families do have more need of government assistance in handling care of the aged or other dependents' (Welch and Thomas 1988: 37). Walker found similar points of difference but also points to the fact that, on many issues, even important women's issues like abortion, men and women were roughly even (Walker 1994: 69).

28 For a fuller discussion of British parties and their approach to gender equality in representation see Norris 2000.

29 'In the 1992 general election younger women (those aged under 30) gave a lead to Labour while younger men shifted sharply towards the Conservatives, producing a 14 point gender gap. If we break this down further, the gap is 30 points among the 18–24 age group with young men voting far more conservative (53 per cent) than young women (33 per cent). Among the middle aged the pattern reverses, with women more Conservative than men', with survey results indicating a gender gap of 18 points (Norris 1996a: 333–6).

30 A competing interpretation of generation effects suggests that there is no real

evidence of a traditional gender gap in Britain. It has been argued that the apparent conservatism of British women is largely a 'generational artefact' owing to greater longevity; there are more elderly women than men in the population and this is the group most likely to vote' (Norris 1988: 218).

31 While Leithner acknowledges the apparent existence of the gender gap, he argues that it is a function of non trade union membership (in turn a function of sex segregation in the workforce) rather than gender per se. Thus, because Australia's workforce is likely to remain segregated he expects the pro-coalition gap to persist (Leithner 1997).

32 The figures for the 2004 federal election are as yet unavailable.

33 A gender generation gap was also present. The gap was larger between older (51 per cent) and younger women (36 per cent) than between older (47 per cent) and younger (38 per cent) men (Lawrence 2000a: 3).

34 'Only in relation to trade unions, the Royal Family and attitudes towards communism are Australian wives likely to express a significantly more conservative stance on these political orientations than their husbands' (Hayes and Bean 1994: 60).

35 'These "greener" views may have affected the vote, since fewer women than men moved against the ALP, who were seen by the majority of voters as closer than the Coalition to their views on the environment' (Papadakis 1993; Lawrence 2000a).

36 Except in 1996 when 'they were slightly more likely then men to view the Coalition as closest to their views on the issues of health and education' (Gow and Renfrow 1996).

37 It is worth noting here, though, that women are generally more willing than men to answer 'don't know' in response to survey questions (Norrander 1997: 465).

38 This appears to be true: 'The Labor Party's polling prior to the elections in 1996 and 1998 showed that women comprised a greater proportion of "soft" voters than men and were twice as likely to indicate that they didn't make up their minds until the day of the election or a couple of days previously. The research also indicated that women prefer different sources of information to help them in reaching decisions about how to vote. They were less likely than men to rely on newspapers and more likely to nominate TV current affairs and discussion with friends as sources of information during the election campaign' (Lawrence 2000a: 4).

39 In fact Labour has been attempting to do this since the 1980s by conducting extensive research into women's political preferences, modifying policies (such as candidate preselection) and adopting 'women friendly' social and family policies in an effort to court the women's vote (Leithner 1997: 45).

40 Since then a special conference of the Australian Labor Advisory Council (ALAC) (October 2002) aimed at modernizing the party resolved to increase women's representation to 40 per cent. However, significantly, it also resolved that this target did not have to be met until 2012.

41 For example, Renfrow (1994) was pessimistic in the 1990s of any secular cohort change due to the persistence of a conservative gap between young male and female voters. Leithner was equally pessimistic because of doubts that there would be any significant alterations to Australia's sex-segregated workforce (Leithner 1997: 44).

42 Though it is interesting to note that the gender gap on the abortion issue in the US is much narrower than it is for other issues like the use of force and treatment of poor people (Welch and Sigelman 1992: 181).

43 The British Liberal Democrats have traditionally had more support among women than men (Welch and Thomas 1988: 41).

44 As mentioned above, Australian women are more likely to be softly committed voters than men. In Britain women are also more likely to be floating voters. Prior to the 2001 general election 23 per cent of women compared to 18 per cent of men reported that they did not know who they would be voting for at the next election (Stephenson 2001).
45 One commentator has questioned this, however. According to Anna Greenberg, '[t]he future of the gender gap ... is not clear. Younger Americans look different politically from their elders. They are less polarised over race, national security and market capitalism, but more polarised over social issues and social welfare. Some of these differences may disappear as Generation Y ages, experiencing the various events intrinsic to the lifecycle' (Greenberg 2000: 15).
46 See Campbell (Chapter 3, this volume) for further exploration of this topic.

References

AM Radio transcript (2002) 'Labor women criticise Hawke/Wran report', Thursday 8 August.

Aitken, D. (1977) *Stability and Change in Australian Politics*, 2nd edition, Canberra: Australian National University Press.

Bean, C. and McAllister, I. (2002) 'From impossibility to certainty: explaining the coalition's victory in 2001', in J. Warhurst and M. Simms (eds) *The Centenary Election*, St. Lucia: University of Queensland Press.

Butler, D. and Kavanagh, D. (2002) *The British General Election of 2001*, Palgrave: New York.

Carroll, S.J. (1988) 'Women's autonomy and the gender gap: 1980 and 1982', in C. Mueller (ed.) *The Politics of the Gender Gap: The Social Construction of Political Influence*, Newbury Park: Sage.

Center for Policy Alternatives (2000a) 'Does "W" really stand for women? Gore vs. Bush – who captured the women's vote?', Press release 10 November. Online. Available at: www.cfpa/pressroom/archives/prcomplete.cfm?ID=135 (accessed 30 August 2002).

—— (2000b) 'The gender gap', *Alternatives*, 8(3) May 2000. Online. Available at: www.cfpa.org/alternatives/altbodyID.cfm?ID=254 (accessed 30 August 2002).

Chaney, C., Alvarez, R.M., and Nagler, J. (1998) 'Explaining the gender gap in US presidential elections, 1980–1992', *Political Research Quarterly*, 51(2): 311–39.

Chodorow, N. (1974) 'Family structure and feminine personality', in M.Z. Rosald and L. Lamphere (eds) *Women, Culture, Society*, Stanford: Stanford University Press.

Christy, C. (1994) 'Trends in sex differences in political participation: a comparative perspective', in M. Githens, P. Norris, and J. Lovenduski (eds) *Different Roles, Different Voices*, New York: HarperCollins.

CNN (2004) 'Election Results'. Online. Available at: www.cnn.com/ELECTION/2004/pages/results/states/US/P/00/epolls.0.html (accessed 14 February 2005).

Conover, P. (1994) 'Feminists and the gender gap', in M. Githens, P. Norris, and J. Lovenduski (eds) *Different Roles, Different Voices*, New York: HarperCollins.

Cook, E., and Wilcox, C. (1991) 'Feminism and the gender gap: a second look', *Journal of Politics*, 53: 1111–22.

Curtin, J. (1997) 'The gender gap in Australian elections', *Research Paper No. 3, 1997–98*, Canberra: Department of the Parliamentary Library.

—— (2001) 'Voting patterns and the gender gap: rural and regional dimensions', *Research Note 19*, Canberra: Department of the Parliamentary Library.

De Vaus, D., and McAllister, I. (1989) 'The changing politics of women: gender and political alignment in 11 nations', *European Journal of Political Research*, 17: 241–62.

Deitch, C. (1988) 'Sex differences in support for government spending', in C. Mueller (ed.) *The Politics of the Gender Gap: The Social Construction of Political Influence*, Newbury Park: Sage.

Di Vall, L. (1996) '1996 election overview', *American Viewpoint*, 2 December. Online. Available at: www.amview.com/essays/linda/redbob.html (accessed 30 August 2002).

EMILY's List (1997) *Women's Monitor*, November 1996 Report. Online. Available at: www.emily'slist.org/monitor/novmber96/1196_3.html (accessed 30 August 2002).

Erie, S.P. and Rein, M. (1988) 'Women and the welfare state', in C. Mueller (ed.) *The Politics of the Gender Gap: The Social Construction of Political Influence*, Newbury Park: Sage.

Frankovic, K. (1982) 'Sex and politics: new alignments, old issues', *PS: Political Science and Politics*, 15: 439–48.

Freeman, J. (1994) 'Feminism vs family values: women at the 1992 democratic and republican conventions', in M. Githens, P. Norris, and J. Lovenduski (eds) *Different Roles, Different Voices*, New York: HarperCollins.

Gilligan, C. (1982) *In a Different Voice*, Cambridge, Massachusetts: Harvard University Press.

Goldberg, G. and Kremen, E. (1994) 'The feminization of poverty: not only in America', in M. Githens, P. Norris, and J. Lovenduski (eds) *Different Roles, Different Voices*, New York: HarperCollins.

Goot, M. (1996) 'Class voting, issues voting and electoral volatility', in J. Brett, J. Gillespie, and M. Goot (eds) *Developments in Australian Politics*, Melbourne: Macmillan.

Gow, D. and Renfrow, P. (1996) 'Gender and the vote at the 1996 federal election', *Proceedings of the Australasian Political Studies Association Annual Conference*, Political Science Department, University of Western Australia.

Greenberg, A. (1998) 'Deconstructing the gender gap', The John F. Kennedy School of Government, Harvard University Working Paper Series. Online. Available at: www.ksg.harvard.edu/prg/greenb/gengap.htm, pp. 1–20 (accessed 20 August 2002).

—— (2000) 'Why men leave: gender and partisanship in the 1990s'. Online. Available at: www.ksg.harvard.edu/prg/greenb/whymenleave.pdf (accessed 17 February 2005).

Hayes, B.C. (1997) 'Gender, feminism and electoral behaviour in Britain', *Electoral Studies*, 16(2): 203–16.

Hayes, B.C. and Bean, C.S. (1994) 'Political attitudes and partnership among Australian couples: do wives matter?', *Women and Politics*, 14(1): 53–81.

Hayes, B.C. and McAllister, I. (1997) 'Gender, party leaders, and election outcomes in Australia, Britain and the United States', *Comparative Political Studies*, 30(1): 3–26.

Herek, G.M. (2002) 'Gender gaps in public opinion about lesbians and gay men', *Public Opinion Quarterly*, 66(Spring): 40–67.

Inglehart, R. and Norris, P. (2000) 'The developmental theory of the gender gap: women's and men's voting behaviour in global perspective', *International Political Science Review*, 21(4): 441–63.

Iverson, T. and Rosenbluth F. (2003) 'The political economy of gender: explaining cross-national variation in the gender division of labour and the gender voting gap', *Proceedings of the Annual Meeting of the American Political Science Association*, 28–31 August, Philadelphia.

Jelen, T., Thomas, S., and Wilcox, C. (1994) 'The gender gap in comparative perspective', *European Journal of Political Research*, 25: 171–86.

Kathlene, L. (1989) 'Uncovering the political impacts of gender: an exploratory study', *The Western Political Quarterly*, 42(2): 397–421.

Kaufman, K. and Petrocik, J.R. (1999) 'The changing politics of American men: understanding the sources of the gender gap', *American Journal of Political Science*, 43(3): 864–99.

Kenski, H.C. (1988) 'The gender factor in a changing electorate', in C. Mueller (ed.) *The Politics of the Gender Gap: The Social Construction of Political Influence*, Newbury Park: Sage.

Killick, S. (2002) 'National Chairperson's Report', *Inkwel*, Women's Electoral Lobby, January. Online. Available at: www.wel.org.au/inkwel/ink0201/chair.htm#election (accessed 30 August 2002).

Koretz, G. (2002) 'Divorce and women voters', *Business Week*, Issue 3773, 3 November: 22.

Ladd, E.C. (1997) 'Media framing of the gender gap', in P. Norris (ed.) *Women, Media and Politics*, Oxford: Oxford University Press.

Lawrence, C. (2000a) 'The gender gap in political behaviour'. Online. Available at: www.carmenlawrence.com/says/papers/gendergap.htm (accessed 16 September 2002).

—— (2000b) 'The gender gap in political behaviour'. Online. Available at: www.plutopress.com/news/c_lawrence.html (accessed 16 September 2002).

Leithner, C. (1997) 'A gender gap in Australia? Commonwealth elections 1910–96', *Australian Journal of Political Science*, 32(1): 29–47.

Lien, P. (1998) 'Does the gender gap in political attitudes and behaviour vary across racial groups?', *Political Research Quarterly*, 51(4): 869–94.

Lipset, S. (1960) *Political Man*, Garden City: Doubleday.

Lovenduski, J. (1996) 'Sex, gender and British politics', *Parliamentary Affairs*, 49(10): 1–16.

Lovenduski, J. and Randall, V. (1993) *Contemporary Feminist Politics*, Oxford: Oxford University Press.

McAllister, I. (1992) *Political Behaviour: Citizens, Parties and Elites in Australia*, Melbourne: Longman Cheshire.

Mattei, L.R. and Mattei, F. (1998) 'If men stayed home ... The gender gap in recent Congressional elections', *Political Research Quarterly*, 51(2): 411–36.

Miller, A.H. and Malanchuk, O. (1983) 'The gender gap in the 1982 election', *Proceedings of the Annual Meeting of the American Political Science Association*, 28–31 August, Denver.

Mueller, C.M. (1988) 'The empowerment of women: polling and the women's voting bloc', in C. Mueller (ed.) *The Politics of the Gender Gap: The Social Construction of Political Influence*, Newbury Park: Sage.

NewsPoll (2002) 'Federal politics: Geographical and demographic analysis-voting intentions'. Online. Available at: www.newspoll.com.au/cgi-bin/display_poll_data.pl (accessed 29 August 2002).

Norrander, B. (1997) 'The independence gap and the gender gap', *Public Opinion Quarterly*, 61(3): 464–70.

—— (1999) 'The evolution of the gender gap', *Public Opinion Quarterly*, 63(4): 566–73.

Norris, P. (1988) 'The gender gap: a cross-national trend?', in C. Mueller (ed.) *The Politics of the Gender Gap: The Social Construction of Political Influence*, Newbury Park: Sage.

—— (1994) 'Elections and political attitudes', in M. Githens, P. Norris, and J. Lovenduski (eds) *Different Roles, Different Voices*, New York: HarperCollins.

—— (1996a) 'Gender realignment in comparative perspective', in M. Simms (ed.) *The Paradox of Parties in the 1990s*, St Leonards: Allen and Unwin.

—— (1996b) 'Mobilizing the "women's vote": the gender-generation gap in voting behaviour', *Parliamentary Affairs*, 49(2): 333–443.

—— (1999) 'Gender: a gender-generation gap', in G. Evans and P. Norris (eds) *Critical Elections*, London: Sage.

—— (2000) 'Gender and contemporary British politics', in C. Hay (ed.) *British Politics Today*, Cambridge: Polity Press.

—— (2004) 'The gender gap: old challenges, new approaches', in Susan Carroll (ed.) *Women and American Politics: Agenda Setting for the 21st Century*, Oxford: Oxford University Press.

Norris, P., Lovenduski, J., and Campbell, R. (2004) *Gender and Political Participation*, commissioned by the Electoral Commission of the UK. Online. Available at: www.electoralcommission.org.uk (accessed 14 February 2005).

Papadakis, E. (1993) *Politics and the Environment*, Sydney: Allen and Unwin.

Parliamentary Library (2005) *Commonwealth Election 2004*, Research Brief No. 13, 14 March. Online. Available at: www.aph.gov.au/library/pubs/RB/2004–05/05rb13.pdf (accessed 19 March 2005).

Phillips, A. (1995) *The Politics of Presence*, Oxford: Clarendon Press.

Plissner, M. (1983) 'The marriage gap', *Public Opinion*, 6(February/March): 53.

Prestage, J. (1994) 'The case of African American women and politics', *PS-Political Science and Politics*, 27(4): 720–1.

Renfrow, P. (1994) 'The gender gap in the 1993 election', *Australian Journal of Political Science*, 29(Special Issue): 118–33.

Robb, A. (1996) 'Is there a gender gap in Australia?', in M. Simms (ed.) *The Paradox of Parties: Australian Political Parties in the 1990s*, St Leonards: Allen and Unwin.

Rose, R. and McAllister, I. (1990) *The Loyalties of Voters*, London: Sage.

Sawer, M. (2002a) 'In safe hands? Women in the 2001 election', *Inkwel*, January. Online. Available at: www.wel.org.au/inkwel/ink0201/msawer.htm (accessed 16 September 2002).

—— (2002b) 'The representation of women in Australia: meaning and make-believe', *Parliamentary Affairs*, 55(1): 5–18.

Sawer, M. and Simms, M. (1993) *A Woman's Place: Women and Politics In Australia*, 2nd edition, Sydney: Allen and Unwin.

Seltzer, R., Newman, J., and Leighton, M. (1997) *Sex as a Political Variable*, Boulder: Lynne Rienner Publishers.

Short, C. (1996) 'Women and the labour party', *Parliamentary Affairs*, 49(1): 17–25.

Squires, J. and Wickham-Jones, M. (2002) 'Mainstreaming in Westminster and Whitehall: from Labour Ministry for Women to the Women and Equality Unit', *Parliamentary Affairs*, 55(1): 57–70.

Stephenson, M. (2001) 'Women voters dissatisfied with political parties claims Fawcett'. Online. Available at: www.mori.com/pubinfo/fawcett.shtml (accessed 2 July 2002).

Studlar, D., McAllister, I., and Hayes, B. (1998) 'Explaining the gender gap in voting: a cross-national analysis', *Social Science Quarterly*, 79(4): 779–98.

Trevor, M.C. (1999) 'Political socialization, party identification and the gender gap', *Public Opinion Quarterly*, 63(1): 62–89.

Walker, N. (1994) 'What we know about women voters in Britain, France and West Germany', in M. Githens, P. Norris, and J. Lovenduski (eds) *Different Roles, Different Voices*, New York: HarperCollins.

Welch, S. (1977) 'Women as political animals? A test of some explanations for male–female political participation difference', *American Journal of Political Science*, 21: 711–30.

Welch, S. and Sigelman, L. (1992) 'A gender gap among Hispanics? A comparison with blacks and anglos', *The Western Political Quarterly*, 45(1): 181–99.

Welch, S. and Thomas, S. (1988) 'Explaining the gender gap in British public opinion', *Women and Politics*, 8(3/4): 25–44.

Wilcox, C. (1991) 'Support for gender equality in West Europe: A longitudinal analysis', *European Journal of Political Research*, 20: 127–47.

Wirls, D. (1986) 'Reinterpreting the gender gap', *Public Opinion Quarterly*, 50(3): 316–30.

5 Advancing women's interests in formal politics

The politics of presence and proportional representation in the Antipodes[1]

Jennifer Curtin

The objective of making existing representative democracies more inclusive of women has not always been a strategy acceptable to all feminists. Claims by women for the extension of citizenship rights, including the right to vote and stand for parliament, while appearing universal, were often very partial. For example, Social Democrat women in Austria abandoned their call for universal women's suffrage in 1906 to concentrate on the fight for universal manhood suffrage. However, achievement of the latter meant propertied women, who had the vote, lost it in favour of working class men. In Australia and the United States, the political rights of indigenous and black women were often neglected by suffragists in their campaign for the vote. In the 1960s and 1970s, many in the western women's liberation movement countered the feminist reformist agenda with a strategy of redefining the 'political'. While the aim was a positive one – namely, to 'reveal and valorise women's participation' outside formal politics (Squires 1999: 195) – an additional (negative) consequence was that feminist engagement with formal politics became 'delegitimized' (Vickers, Chapter 2, this volume). Institutions of government were labelled as inherently male, impenetrable and where the interests of men would ultimately dominate. If women participated at all, it was seen as either tokenism or co-option.

However, as Vickers argues in her chapter in this book, the dissolution of the meaning of 'politics', to the point where formal politics is not recognized as a site of institutional power requiring feminist critique, is not in the interests of women. So although it is now accepted amongst feminist activists and feminist political scientists that an objective set of interests common to all women is neither real nor desirable, the argument can still be made that one 'objective' women's interest is having a political presence (Phillips 1991: 72). Increasing the presence of women in legislatures is important, not only because political participation in a democracy should be equally open to all citizens, women and men, but because women may bring new perspectives to bear on existing ways of interpreting politics and operating in the legislative environment. More-over, given that women's experiences and claims are recognized as mul-tiple and diverse, the more women there are elected, the more likely that the diversity between women will be reflected in formal politics and, as a consequence, in the definition and construction of policies concerning the lives of women (Phillips 1995).

The subject of women's under-representation in legislatures regained momentum in the 1990s, with many national and international women's organizations identifying the issue as warranting immediate attention by governments and political parties. With this has come an increase in acad-emic research focusing on the factors that either inhibit or enhance women's participation in electoral politics. The selection and election of women (descriptive representation), and what women do in the interests of women once elected (substantive representation) are themes which res-onate in the recent works of feminist political scientists.

Over time, considerable attention has been given to the extent to which proportional representation voting systems are more conducive to women's entry into formal politics. Aggregate level cross-national compar-isons indicate that women's political representation tends to reach over 30 per cent in countries with proportional or mixed systems (Castles 1981; Norris 1985; Rule 1994). Norris has gone as far as to argue that cross-national differences in the political position of women are unlikely to diminish without electoral reform, that is, the adoption of proportional systems (Norris 1985: 100). However, electoral reform is not an easy quest, and nor can proportional representation be seen as a global panacea for women's under-representation. As Butler argues, 'an electoral system cannot be understood in isolation from the political system of which it is a part' (Butler 1981: 8). So, while a proportional system may determine the coherence, structure, and number of parties that compete, the character-istics, behaviour, and strategic choices of these political parties may in turn determine the extent to which women's representation is institution-alized within legislatures. Two brief examples highlight the importance of closer investigation of proportional systems and the context within which they operate. The Netherlands and Israel both have party list proportional representation systems, where the whole country constitutes one elec-torate. In the Netherlands, women's representation has been compara-tively high (31.3 per cent), while in Israel the representation of women has remained comparatively low (7.5 per cent). Labour Party women in Israel began lobbying for a candidate gender quota in the mid 1970s, but, to date, the reality remains that the political culture, both explicitly and implicitly, has constrained women's political representation (cf. Hertzog 1996; Curtin 1999).

This chapter examines the recent impact of proportional representa-tion on women's legislative presence in four Australasian political systems: New Zealand and the Australian Capital Territory's (ACT) Legislative

Assembly (where the advent of proportional representation is relatively recent), the Australian Senate and the lower house in the state of Tasmania (where proportional systems have been in place for more than 50 years). It is not uncommon to compare sub-national systems for insight into the significance of proportional systems to women's electoral success (Darcy *et al.* 1993; Welch and Studlar 1990), and a number of common features make comparisons between New Zealand and Australia possible. Both were pioneers in providing women with the franchise: New Zealand women gained the vote in 1893 and Australian women won the right both to vote and to stand for parliament in 1902. These two countries are both parliamentary democracies derived from the British Westminster system of government, although in each the Westminster model has been modified for a variety of reasons. The adoption of proportional representation has been one such modification, albeit at different times over the past 100 years. In addition, both have had vibrant feminist movements that have taken a largely reformist position on the political rights of women.

Given the broad similarity of political institutions and political culture, what can these cases tell us about the extent to which contextual factors might mediate the impact of proportional representation? The evidence presented here indicates that, while there is now a critical mass of women standing as candidates in all four systems, they are yet to reach 40 per cent of those elected. Why, then, has proportional representation failed to achieve equal representation for women, and what does this mean for those interested in pursuing strategies aimed at advancing women's presence in formal politics?

Women and proportional representation

Assessing the effect of an electoral system on the representation of women is not a recent phenomenon (Duverger 1955). In 1976, Enid Lakeman surveyed the phenomenon from a broad cross-national perspective and argued that proportional representation was more conducive to the representation of women than were single-member systems. Since then, other quantitative studies have analysed the impact of socio-economic and cultural factors as well as institutional factors in determining women's political representation (Rule 1987, 1994; Norris 1985, 1987). These works confirmed that the presence of proportional representation significantly increased the chances of women being elected to parliament.

However, these findings need qualification. Not only are there differences between majority systems and proportional systems, but significant differences exist among proportional systems. Countries such as Israel and Ireland feature low levels of female representation, while Nordic countries have continued to lead the field in women's legislative presence. In explaining these differences, district magnitude (denoting numbers of candidates elected within a given district) is the variable that matters most.

For example, Rule (1994) argues that to ensure female representation, districts with a minimum of five members is a necessary condition, while ten to 15 member districts will substantially increase women's chances of election. This is partly because the threshold quota decreases as the number of members per district increases. But it is also because in multi-member districts there is less intra-party competition for selection and as a result parties are more likely to recruit women. Historically, political parties were averse to selecting women in single-member or small districts, because party officials perceived (incorrectly) that women were vote-losers (Mackerras 1977, 1980; Norris 1985: 95).

Several country case studies highlight the importance of district magnitude in more detail. Engstrom's (1987) work on Ireland's single transferable vote (STV) system indicates that the electoral opportunities open to women expand or contract as district magnitudes increase or decrease. There, women fare much worse in three seat districts (in terms of both selection as candidates and election) than in the five seat districts. In a comparison of France and Italy (both party-list systems) Beckwith (1992) identifies the importance of district magnitude to the election of women. In the 1986 election in France, under proportional representation, there were few districts of large magnitude. Amongst the metropolitan districts, 14 had ten or more representatives, while 34 had three or less. Women constituted only 5.7 per cent of those elected, 0.4 per cent more than in the 1981 election. The same result occurred again under a non-proportional system in 1988. However, in Italy, where the district magnitude is on average much larger than that in France, the percentage of women in the Italian Chamber of Deputies stood at 12.8 per cent in 1987.

In an attempt to temper the idea that proportional representation is a panacea to women's under-representation, some scholars have looked more closely at other political and cultural factors. So, while Beckwith (1992) acknowledges the importance of district size, she also argues that the behaviour and strategic choices of political parties within proportional systems warrant scrutiny. In a similar vein, Lane (1995) argues that in Malta, a country with a single transferable vote system, the under-representation of women is not solely a result of small districts but is exacerbated by the lack of recruitment of women by both the Labour and Nationalist parties. Lane notes that while traditional social values play a part in reducing women's opportunity to participate politically, organizational barriers within the party systems hinder women's advancement, a dynamic not reserved for 'conservative' cultures. These factors could be considered too subtle for operationalization and use in quantitative cross-national analysis.

There are a number of other factors that might account for the variation in women's representation in proportional systems. First, party list systems are often more proportional in the sense that a minimum threshold quota is set and once a party reaches this quota it receives a proportion of the seats according to the proportion of the vote received. The threshold quota in such systems is often as low as 5 per cent, but is even lower in some (for example it is 2 per cent in Israel). In single transferable vote systems, the threshold quota depends on the size of the district, but it is generally higher than those in list systems.

The implications of a low threshold quota for women's representation are twofold and somewhat contradictory. On the one hand, minor party candidates and independents find it more difficult to obtain the required quota in electorates with fewer members. This can have an impact on women's representation given minor parties are often more open to standing women as candidates (cf. Curtin and Sexton 2004; Lakeman 1976; Lane 1995; Matland and Studlar 1996; McLeay 1993). On the other hand, the higher the threshold quota, the more likely the bigger parties are to win more seats, allowing candidates further down the party list (often women) to be elected. Lower threshold quotas may result in more parties gaining representation, but with only one or two candidates elected from each. Given that women are more likely to be further down on a party list, low threshold quotas could prevent women being elected.

Second, some list systems allow voters either to choose the order of the list candidates (open lists) or to record a vote for the party list as ordered by the party organisation (closed list). By contrast, STV systems usually require voters to list the candidates according to their preference, with or without regard to party direction. In theory, a preference for women candidates could emerge, whereby voters choose women candidates across parties. Individual preferences are feasible in STV systems where electorate magnitude is not excessive. However, the larger the list, the more incentive there is for voters to accept the party's rankings, especially in systems where voters must exhaust all possible preferences for the vote to count (for example, the Australian Senate).

Lakeman (1976) argues it is worth distinguishing between the inclinations of a party organisation and those of the voters. She notes that one may be more advanced than the other and so results would be affected by the degree to which an individual's chance of election depends on the choice of a party organization or on that of the voters. It is (now) assumed that most political parties will devise lists of candidates that are representative of the main groups in society, including both sexes, thereby maximizing their appeal. Matland and Studlar (1996) have suggested that the increased (s)election of women is a result of a gender-specific contagion effect, which is most successful in multi-member proportional systems. The argument is that as a small but competitive (and usually left-leaning) party starts to nominate more women candidates, larger parties will imitate them, for two reasons. First, because the smaller parties demonstrate there is no electoral penalty in selecting women and second, the larger parties are afraid of losing votes to the smaller party if they are not seen to be selecting women, especially if the parties concerned are ideologically close.

However, even with the pressure of competing for votes, evidence suggests political parties have been slow to recruit women as candidates without additional pressure being placed on them by women's organizations, either within or outside the party system. For example, Sweden has had proportional representation since 1907, but in the mid 1980s women became concerned that their political representation was inadequate. A 1987 commission of inquiry into women's representation in public life recommended that parties give each alternate position on their respective lists to a woman. However, with the defeat of the Social Democratic Government in 1991, women's representation in Parliament dropped from 38 per cent to 33.5 per cent. The advent of this decline, so soon after the 1987 public inquiry, led a number of high-profile women to threaten to create a women's party should the major parties not take the issue of women's representation more seriously. This threat had force, with opinion polls indicating that around 40 per cent of voters of both sexes would consider voting for a women's party. As a result, the 'layering' of party lists was implemented by four of the five major parties and in 1994 women's representation rose to 42 per cent, with 50 per cent women in the government (Curtin and Higgins 1998: 81).

In France, where proportional list systems exist for regional, Senate and municipal elections, feminist activists were influential in the adoption in 2000 of a constitutional amendment known as the 'Parity Law'.[2] The law requires political parties to ensure 50 per cent of their list candidates are women or else risk financial penalty. At the 2001 Senate elections, where one-third of Senate seats were up for election, women won 21.5 per cent of the seats. The result may not appear spectacular compared to that of Sweden, but it did represent an 84.7 per cent gain in women's total Senate representation (an increase of 5.9 per cent to 10.9 per cent).

In summary, while proportional representation has the capacity to enhance the representation of women in formal politics, the propensity for it to do so is dependent on a number of factors: the variant of proportional representation used, the political culture which underpins it and the extent to which feminist strategies challenge political parties' structures and ideas about who gets (s)elected to legislatures.

Proportional representation in Australia and New Zealand

Both Tasmania and the Australian Capital Territory (ACT) use a variant of the STV known as Hare-Clark.[3] In Tasmania, Hare-Clark has been in place since 1909. Until 1998, there were five districts, each with seven members (35 in total). In July 1998, the two major parties supported a legislative change that reduced the district magnitude to five members per district (25 members in total). The aim of the change was to limit the opportunity of the election of non-major party candidates by significantly increasing the quota. However, the proportional system has not resulted in a significant women's presence over time. While the representation of women in Tasmania's House of Assembly (lower house) stood at a record 31.4 per cent prior to the 1998 election, this is a recent phenomenon. It was not until 1955 that the first two women were elected and there remained only two women in the Assembly until 1964. No women were elected again until 1976. In 1986 four women were elected and by 1992 this had increased to seven (20 per cent).

The ACT is a small territory, encompassing Australia's capital city, Canberra, and its surrounds and has a population of approximately 300,000. It has had self-government only since 1989, and Hare-Clark since 1995. There are three districts, two with five members and one with seven members. In 1989 women constituted 23.5 per cent of the Assembly, increasing in 1992 to 35.3 per cent. Two women held the highest elected position of Chief Minister for a total of eight years between 1989 and 2001.

In both the ACT and Tasmania, the Hare-Clark system has been combined with Robson Rotation, which allows for the randomization of candidates' names so that no candidate has the advantage of appearing in the same position on every ballot paper. To some extent Robson Rotation can undermine the recurrent problem of women being placed in non-winnable positions on party lists. While parties have been able to provide how-to-vote tickets prior to the election to guide voter preferences (a commonplace in Australian elections), distribution is prohibited at polling booths.

The Australian Senate also uses a form of STV whereby each state constitutes one electorate with 12 elected members, a sizeable district magnitude. However, half Senate elections are the norm, reducing the district magnitude to six, with six senators elected for a six-year term at each federal election (held every three years).[4] With the introduction of above the line voting in 1983, the likelihood of voters listing the candidates individually has diminished substantially.[5] Now, around 94 per cent of voters choose to vote above the line, converting what is technically an STV system into a quasi-party-list system.

The first Senate election using proportional representation occurred in 1949. Prior to this date, two women had been elected to the Senate. The first, Dorothy Tangney, was elected in 1943, and remained in parliament for 25 years. The second, Annabelle Rankin, was elected in 1947 and also served as a senator for over 20 years. With the advent of proportional representation, an unprecedented number of women stood as candidates for election in 1949, although only two additional women were elected. A significant increase finally occurred in the 1980s, with the percentage of women senators reaching 22 per cent in 1987.

For most of its democratic history, New Zealand had a first-past-the-post electoral system. The first woman elected under this system was Elizabeth McCombs in 1933. Between 1935 and 1975 only 14 other women became parliamentarians. Since 1984 there has been a more rapid growth in women's representation, reaching 21 per cent in 1993. In the last ten years, there have been two women Prime Ministers: Jenny Shipley (National Party, 1997–1999) and Helen Clark (Labour Party, 1999–2006+).[6] In 1996, as a result of a Royal Commission, two referendums and many years of voter discontent, the mixed member proportional representation system (MMP) was introduced, providing electors with two votes. One is used to elect an electorate representative by means of a majority system and the second to elect representatives from a party list using the 'Sainte-Lague' variant of proportional representation. However, voters cannot choose the candidates they prefer from party lists: voters can only select their preferred party. The threshold quota for seat allocation is set at 5 per cent, or the party must win at least one electorate to achieve representation. After the first election under MMP the representation of women in parliament increased to 29 per cent.

   This brief overview indicates that the relatively early emergence of proportional representation in Tasmania and the Australian Senate has not in itself guaranteed the presence of women in parliament. By contrast, in the ACT and New Zealand, where proportional representation has been introduced only recently, women have constituted a significant percentage of those elected (23 per cent and 29 per cent respectively). As such, there appears to be a relationship between the politicization of the issue of women's under-representation in formal politics by second wave feminists, and the increase in the numbers of women parliamentarians (cf. Curtin and Sawer 1996; McLeay 1993; Sawer and Simms 1993).

Selecting and electing women in the Antipodes

While women's election to parliament is clearly related to the presence/absence of a proportional representation system, it is also dependent on the parties' propensity to attract women members and recruit women candidates. There are a number of constraints – organizational and cultural – that undermine the political recruitment of women (Lovenduski and Norris 1993). Yet if we assume that 1) proportional systems allow for multi-member districts, thereby encouraging the selection of women, and 2) the representation of women in parliament is sufficiently politicized to warrant attention by political parties, then we should perhaps expect to see a high percentage of women as candidates in the four cases explored here.

   The data in Table 5.1 indicate that there is now a critical mass of women standing as candidates in all three Australian constituencies, if we take critical mass to be over 30 per cent. In New Zealand, women have constituted over 30 per cent of candidates only once since 1996. Although a focus on only three elections does not allow for the prediction of any emerging trends, the percentage of women candidates has tended to

Table 5.1 Women candidates and politicians 1995–2002 (per cent)

	1995–1996		1998–1999		2001–2002	
	Women candidates	*Women elected*	*Women candidates*	*Women elected*	*Women candidates*	*Women elected*
ACT	40.5	35.3	37.0	11.8	42.5	35.3
Tasmania	31.0	31.4	32.6	28.0	37.5	28.0
Australian Senate	33.7	36.8* (30.3)	30.3	26.3* (28.9)	32.6	42.1* (30.3)
NZ	26.8	29.0	33.0	31.0	28.7	28.3

Sources: ACT Electoral Commission; Tasmanian Electoral Office; Australian Electoral Commission; New Zealand Electoral Commission.

Note
* These are the results of half Senate elections only. Total female representation in the Senate (noted in brackets) is dependent on results of previous half Senate elections.

increase over this time. However, there have been no instances where the proportion of women candidates has reached 50 per cent. The ACT has the highest rates of candidacy for women, and this may be related to district magnitude. In 2001, for example, over half of the women candidates that stood for election in the ACT did so in the seven-member district. In the five-member districts women made up approximately one quarter of total candidates. In the 2004 ACT election, women represented 40 per cent of candidates and 35 per cent of those elected, with the positioning of women candidates spread more evenly across all three districts.

In only four of the 12 elections listed in Table 5.1 has the proportion of women elected reflected the proportion of women candidates. These are the 1996 elections in Tasmania and the Senate, and the New Zealand elections in 1999 and 2002. Overall, there is a closer match between the proportion of candidates and the proportion of women elected in the New Zealand parliament and the Australian Senate, where closed lists are the norm.

Women first achieved a critical mass in the Senate in 1996. Since that time, however, women's representation has fluctuated. While women constituted 42 per cent of those elected at the 2001 half Senate election, the total representation of women in the Senate stands at just over 30 per cent. The 2001 result saw women win four of the six seats available in two states (New South Wales and South Australia) and women won at least one seat in the other states and territories. Only three of the 16 women elected were from minor parties (with a total of four women from minor parties in the full Senate) suggesting that the major parties have become more conscientious about gender equality within their ranks (five Liberal and seven Labor women senators were elected). In the case of the Labor Party (ALP), this result has been prompted by the adoption in 1994 of a candidate gender quota aimed at achieving 35 per cent representation of women in all its parliamentary parties (state and federal) by 2002. This quota was extended to 40 per cent in 2002, with a target date of 2012. In the most recent federal election, held in October 2004, women constituted 41 per cent of Senate candidates and 35 per cent of those elected. The result means that from July 2005 the proportion of women senators will be 35.5 per cent, the highest in the history of the Senate. Of the 27 women senators, five are from minor parties, nine are from the Liberal-National (conservative) parties and 13 are from the ALP.

In the case of New Zealand, despite the presence of proportional representation, the percentage of women candidates has only once reached 30 per cent, although the figure in Table 5.1 is a combination of both list and electorate candidate numbers. Looking at the list and electorate candidate percentages separately, there are several points of interest (Table 5.2). Party lists still attract a higher percentage of women candidates than do electorate seats, where a majority voting system operates. However, while in 1996 the majority of women politicians were elected from party lists, since then the percentage of women winning electorate seats has increased significantly. The 2002 result indicates that the proportion of electorate seats won by women was almost the same as the proportion of list seats won by women. Women's improved success rate in electorate seats may be related to swing, in that there was a considerable increase in electorate seats won by the Labour Party in both these elections, and Labour has a better history than the National (conservative) Party at selecting (and electing) women candidates. Nevertheless, the result may also indicate that major parties now view women's candidacy in single member electorates as both viable and necessary.

It is worth briefly comparing New Zealand with Germany, since the mixed member proportional (MMP) system adopted by New Zealand in 1996 was derived from the German model. In the Bundestag, the multi-member system contributes considerably more women than does the single member component. For example in 1994 women won 19 per cent of seats by plurality election and 26 per cent by proportional election. This is despite the presence of (non-mandatory) quotas for women in most of the parties contesting elections (Caul 2001; Kolinsky 1991). By contrast, candidate quotas are not a feature of New Zealand's political parties. Indeed, NZ Labour women debated the issue of quotas, but decided instead to work within party ranks to advance the cause of women's selection and election, with considerable success (Curtin 1997; Curtin and Sawer 1996; Levine and Roberts 2001).

Two election results in particular are worth exploring further in order to elucidate the difficulties associated with assuming that proportional representation can ensure women equality in political presence. The first is the ACT 1998 election where women won only 11 per cent of the seats; and the second the Tasmanian 1998 election, where the district magnitude had been reduced just prior to the election.

At the 1998 ACT election, despite the presence of a critical mass of women candidates and a Labor Party quota in force, only two women were elected to the 17 member parliament. One was from the Greens and the other was the Liberal Chief Minister. Both were elected from the seven-member district. No ALP women were successful. These results run counter to expectations. It is often assumed that left wing parties will nom-

Table 5.2 New Zealand women list and electorate candidates and politicians (per cent)

Election	Women list candidates	Women list politicians	Women electorate candidates	Women electorate seats
1996	32.5	41.8	21.1	13.8
1999	41.6	34.0	27.4	23.8
2002	32.2	29.4	21.3	27.5

Source: New Zealand Electoral Commission.

inate and elect more women to office than right wing parties because of their more egalitarian tendencies, their association with the women's movements, and their recognition of women as a political constituency (Jenson 1982; Lovenduski and Norris 1993; Matland and Studlar 1996). In the ACT, prior to the 2001 election, Labor had consistently selected more women candidates than the Liberals. In addition to the federally adopted candidate gender quota, the ACT branch of the Labor Party had a requirement that 50 per cent of its candidates be women. In the 1998 election, this quota was not filled.

Moreover, prior to the introduction of Robson Rotation in 1995, the ACT ALP had put a number of women in winnable positions on their party lists, leading to more than 40 per cent women in the parliamentary party. In the 1998 election, the advent of Robson Rotation and the removal of how-to-vote cards, while maximizing voter control over the choice of candidate elected, made it impossible for political parties to place women candidates in guaranteed winnable positions. ALP women candidates were not helped in their cause by the decision of the ACT branch of the party to disallow individual candidates from receiving separate funding. As a result, four women candidates missed out on receiving $1,500 each towards their campaign from EMILY's List – an organization developed to support female candidates.

In theory, Hare-Clark as an open list system could give women a better chance because voters can select women across the parties. Analysis of voter preference can provide an indication of a women's vote, or whether there was voter prejudice against women candidates. Results from the 1998 ACT election indicate that there was an element of a pure female vote, but this was not high – approximated at 4 per cent (Hull 1998). At the same time, there was no obvious prejudice against women candidates, with 40 per cent of the formal first preference votes cast for women (ACTEC 1998) (although it is likely that Chief Minister Kate Carnell's personal vote, which was three times higher than the next best candidate, contributed significantly to this figure). Indeed, for five of the nine years leading up to the 1998 election, the ACT had a female Chief Minister, so arguably voters had adequate exposure to women in Parliament. That only two women were elected brings into question the notion that the institutionalization and visibility of women can, in itself, ensure a continued female parliamentary presence.

In the 1998 ACT election, women's candidacy rates were comparable with previous years but did not translate into seats for women. This result suggests that party-chosen lists rather than random lists (that is, voter choice) are of more benefit to the election of women, despite the Australian women's movement's distrust of political parties and their commitment to gender equity (Sawer 2000). Furthermore, because the Hare-Clark system favours candidate recognition over party recognition, several paradoxes emerge for an analysis of women's electoral success.

First, the priority of candidate recognition encourages intra-party competition at the level of election; the same factor which multi-member districts are supposed to dilute at the level of selection. In other words, women may be more likely to get selected in a multi-member system, but in an open list system, their chances of election are undermined by the need to then compete with their party colleagues for votes. Second, research indicates incumbency clearly matters to the re-election prospects of candidates. However, turnover is higher in proportional systems than in majoritarian systems, and when combined with the open list system, makes the incumbency effect less predictable and the issue of voter volatility more salient (Matland and Studlar 2004).

While less exceptional than the ACT 1998 election, the Tasmanian election of the same year provides an interesting comparison of what happens to women's selection and election when district magnitude is reduced in a proportional representation system. Prior to the 1998 election, the Tasmanian Parliament passed a bill to reduce the size of the House of Assembly by ten, from 35 to 25. The existing five divisions, which had seven members each following the 1959 election, were reduced to five members each, thereby increasing the threshold quota from 12.5 per cent to 16.7 per cent. The major parties were united in their support for the change.

It was thought, not surprisingly, that this reform would deny the Greens a presence in the lower house (Bennett 1998). Strong fears were expressed by the Women's Electoral Lobby that it would lead to a reduction in the numbers of women elected (WEL 1998). These two possible outcomes were not unrelated in the Tasmanian context. While there had been an increase in the percentage of women candidates standing for the House of Assembly in Tasmania, from 10 per cent in 1980 to 37 per cent in 2002, most of this increase occurred in 1989 when a large number of women stood as Democrat and Independent candidates. Then, in 1992, the Greens entered the election contest with 15 women candidates, two of whom were elected. Women's representation peaked at 31.4 per cent in 1996, and three out of the seven women elected were from the Greens.

While the percentage of women candidates in the Tasmanian election of 1998 was comparable to 1995, women's representation did drop from 31 per cent to 28 per cent in 1998 and it has remained at 28 per cent. The Greens retained only one elected representative in 1998 (a woman) and their total representation was reduced by three. The Greens won four seats again in 2002, although only one was a woman (the Greens' Leader). The Labor Party substantially increased from five to 14 its number of female candidates in 1996, with women gaining only three of the 16 Labor seats. It is difficult to determine if the increase in Labor women candidates is a result of a contagion effect or because of the quota rule established by the party in 1994. Either way, seven women were elected in both 1998 and 2002, the same number as in 1992, despite the reduction from 35 to 25 elected members.

What is evident from this brief analysis of the Tasmanian election is that, while the size of districts does matter, it is not the only factor in increasing women's representation. Decreasing the size of the Tasmania divisions from seven to five did not lead to a drastic reduction in the representation of women, despite the decrease in the number of Green candidates elected and despite the fact that nine sitting members lost their seats (four of whom were women). While the Greens' election to both the Tasmanian and ACT Parliaments has enhanced the political presence of women in the past, even in a proportional system minor parties cannot be solely relied upon to provide gender balance in parliamentary representation.

Conclusion

There is no doubt that proportional representation provides more opportunities for increasing women's presence in formal politics. But this effect should not be taken as a given. In New Zealand (prior to electoral reform in 1996) women's parliamentary representation had reached 21 per cent, exceptionally high for a country with a first-past-the-post electoral system. One explanation put forward as to why women managed to attain this presence is that Labour and to a lesser extent National (conservative) women have created and utilized institutional structures within their parties to facilitate their entry into Parliament, and ultimately parliamentary leadership. In the United Kingdom, another country with a first-past-the-post system, the Labour Party introduced in 1993 women-only shortlists in 50 per cent of winnable and 'inheritor' seats in which a Labour MP retired. This policy was ruled unlawful in 1995, but by this time 35 women had been selected using the system, and the result of the 1997 election saw the percentage of Labour women elected double – from 9.2 per cent to 18 per cent. These examples indicate that alternative strategies exist to facilitate women's entry into parliament in single-member systems. Similarly, the examples presented here suggest that proportional representation alone may not prove sufficient to maintain a strong female presence or to increase the proportion of women elected beyond 40 per cent. For example, while district magnitude matters, it does not explain why women's representation in New Zealand, where the number of list seats averages around 53, remains the same as or lower than in Australia's proportional systems.

Second, while gender quota rules may be useful in ensuring parties select women as candidates, they cannot guarantee the representation of women in systems where voter choice dominates the electoral process. Third, more research is needed to gauge whether the arrival of new (left-leaning) parties in Australia has had a direct impact on the numbers of women elected to parliament. It certainly seems that in the case of Tasmania, the election of Green candidates has coincided with the increase of women's representation. This may represent an example of a contagion effect, whereby the selection and election of Green women candidates has stimulated the major parties to select women (cf. Curtin and Sexton 2004). Finally, the contagion effect may also have another dimension. In the case of New Zealand, the introduction of a proportional element to the system has led to an extraordinarily high number of women winning seats elected by majority election.

Lovenduski (1993) has reminded us that when first wave feminists fought for the enfranchisement of women, they also wanted to win the right for women to stand for parliament, because they recognized that the representation of women's interests required their presence in parliament. While the feminist movements in the 1960s and 1970s ensured women's concerns were voiced effectively outside the parliamentary arena, the focus of feminists from the 1990s and into the current period returned to the importance of political institutions and electoral processes. In particular, women's representation in formal politics has gained and maintained both national and international attention, as a strategy for ensuring women's issues remain on the policy agenda. However, commitment by only one party (such as the ALP) to increasing women's presence is unlikely to lead to a drastic rise, especially when that party is in opposition. Consideration also needs to be given to the vagaries of the particular proportional representation system adopted, thereby requiring parties not only to recruit more women candidates, but also to ensure that these candidates are given a high profile and/or are positioned in winnable positions on party lists. In other words, while political parties are often portrayed as in decline, it is in these institutions that women must place their efforts if they are to go beyond 40 per cent representation.

Notes

1 A different version of this argument first appeared in *Policy, Organization and Society*, as 'Women and proportional representation in Australia and New Zealand', 22(1): 2003. The author gratefully acknowledges thair permission to reproduce substantial portions of that article here.
2 An article written by ten former women ministers published in the magazine *L'Express* in 1996 was particularly important to the successful adoption of the amendment (Sineau 2003).
3 The Hare-Clark electoral system is a single transferable vote (STV) method of proportional representation used in multi-member electorates. However, it differs from other STV methods in several ways: there is a technical difference in the way votes are transferred from candidates elected on the first count and candidates eliminated; Hare-Clark is usually used in conjunction with Robson Rotation; and, casual vacancies are filled by a recount rather than a casual vacancy (see Newman, 1989 for more detail on technicalities).
4 Under the deadlock provision as per Section 57 of the Australian Constitution, a 'double dissolution' of both houses is permitted, at which all senators face election. This reduces by half the threshold quota required for re-election.

There have been five double dissolution elections since federation in 1901. Stand alone Senate elections can occur but are unusual – the last one occurred in 1970.
5 Voters may choose to vote above the line for a particular party, thereby accepting the party's ordering of candidates, or they may vote below the line. Voting below the line requires the voter to number all the candidates standing, in order of preference. Failure to do so renders the vote invalid.
6 NZ Labour was re-elected as a minority government in 2005, with Helen Clark as Prime Minister.

References

ACTEC (1998) *ACT Election Statistics*, Canberra: Australian Capital Territory Electoral Commission. Online. Available at: www.elections.act.gov.au (accessed 10 February 2005).

Amy, D.J. (2000) *Behind the Ballot Box: A Citizen's Guide to Voting Systems*, Westport: Praeger Publishing.

Australian Electoral Commission. Online. Available at: www.aec.gov.au (accessed 10 February 2005).

Beckwith, K. (1992) 'Comparative research and electoral systems: Lessons from France and Italy', *Women and Politics*, 12(1): 1–34.

Bennett, S. (1998) *The Reduction in the Size of the Tasmanian Parliament*, Research Note 2, Canberra: Department of the Parliamentary Library.

Butler, D. (1981) 'Electoral systems', in D. Butler, H.R. Penniman, and A. Renny (eds) *Democracy at the Polls: A Comparative Study of Competitive National Elections*, Washington: American Enterprise Institute for Public Policy Research.

Castles, F.G. (1981) 'Female legislative representation and the electoral system', *Politics*, 1(1): 21–6.

Caul, M. (2001) 'Political parties and the adoption of candidate gender quotas: a cross-national analysis', *The Journal of Politics*, 63(4): 1214–29.

Curtin, J. (1997) *Gender and Political Leadership in New Zealand*, Research Note 14, Canberra: Department of the Parliamentary Library.

—— (1999) *Women and Trade Unions: A Comparative Perspective*, Aldershot: Ashgate.

Curtin, J. and Higgins, W. (1998) 'Feminism and unionism in Sweden', *Politics and Society*, 26(1): 69–94.

Curtin, J. and Sawer, M. (1996) 'Gender equity and the shrinking state', in F.G. Castles, R. Gerritsen, and J. Vowles (eds) *The Great Experiment: Labour Parties and Public Policy Transformation in Australia and New Zealand*, Sydney: Allen and Unwin.

Curtin, J. and Sexton, K. (2004) 'Are quotas contagious? Promoting women's parliamentary presence in Australia', paper presented at Canadian Political Science Association Meeting, Winnipeg, June.

Darcy, R., Hadley, C., and Kirksey, J. (1993) 'Election systems and the representation of black women in American state legislatures', *Women and Politics*, 13(2): 73–89.

Duverger, M. (1955) *The Political Role of Women*, Paris: UNESCO.

Engstrom, R. (1987) 'District magnitudes and the election of women to the Irish Dail', *Electoral Studies*, 6(2): 123–32.

Hertzog, H. (1996) 'Why so few? The political culture of gender in Israel', *International Review of Women and Leadership*, 2(1): 1–18.

Hull, C. (1998) 'The count: how it happened', *The Canberra Times*, 17 March.

Jenson, J. (1982) 'The modern women's movement in Italy, France and Great Britain: differences in life cycles', *Comparative Social Research*, 5: 341–75.

Kolinsky, E. (1991) 'Political participation and parliamentary careers: women's quotas in West Germany', *West European Politics*, 14(1): 56–72.

Lakeman, E. (1976) 'Electoral systems and women in parliament', *The Parliamentarian*, 57: 159–62.

Lane, J. (1995) 'The election of women under proportional representation: the case of Malta', *Democratization*, 2(2): 140–57.

Levine, S. and Roberts, N. (2001) 'The 1999 election results', in R. Miller (ed.) *New Zealand Government and Politics*, Auckland: Oxford University Press.

Lovenduski, J. (1993) 'Introduction: the dynamics of gender and party', in J. Lovenduski and P. Norris (eds) *Gender and Party Politics*, London: Sage.

Lovenduski, J. and Norris, P. (1993) *Gender and Party Politics*, London: Sage.

Mackerras, M. (1977) 'Do women candidates lose votes?', *Australian Quarterly*, 49(3): 6–10.

—— (1980) 'Do women candidates lose votes? Further evidence', *Australian Quarterly*, 52(4): 450–5.

McLeay, E. (1993) 'Women and the problem of parliamentary representation: a comparative perspective', H. Catt and E. McLeay (eds) *Women and Politics in New Zealand*, Wellington: Victoria University Press.

Matland, R. and Studlar, D. (1996) 'The contagion of women candidates in single-member district and proportional representation electoral systems: Canada and Norway', *Journal of Politics*, 55(3): 707–33.

—— (2004) 'Determinants of legislative turnover: a cross-national analysis', *Journal of Political Science*, 34(1): 87–99.

Newman, G. (1989) *Electoral Systems*, Research Paper, September, Canberra: Department of the Parliamentary Library.

—— (1996) *New Zealand's New Electoral System: From FPP to MMP*, Research Note 6, Canberra: Department of the Parliamentary Library.

New Zealand Electoral Commission. Online. Available at: www.elections.org.nz (accessed 10 September 2003).

Norris, P. (1985) 'Women's legislative participation in Western Europe', *West European Politics*, 8(4): 90–101.

—— (1987) *Politics and Sexual Equality*, Boulder: Reinner.

Phillips, A. (1991) *Engendering Democracy*, Cambridge: Polity Press.

—— (1995) *The Politics of Presence*, Oxford: Clarendon Press.

Rule, W. (1987) 'Electoral systems, contextual factors and women's opportunities for election to parliament in twenty-three democracies', *Western Political Quarterly*, 40(3): 447–98.

—— (1994) 'Parliaments of, by, and for the people: except for women?', in W. Rule and J.F. Zimmerman (eds) *Electoral Systems in Comparative Perspective*, Westport: Greenwood Press.

Rydon, J. (1994) 'Representation of women and ethnic minorities in the parliaments of Australia and New Zealand', in W. Rule and J.F. Zimmerman (eds) *Electoral Systems in Comparative Perspective*, Westport: Greenwood Press.

Sawer, M. (2000) 'Parliamentary representation of women: from discourses of justice to strategies of accountability', *International Political Science Review*, 21(4): 361–80.

Sawer, M. and Simms, M. (1993) *Woman's Place: Women and Politics in Australia,* Sydney: Allen and Unwin.

Sineau, M. (2003) 'La Parité in politics: from a radical idea to a consensual reform', in R. Célestin, E. DalMolin and I. de Courtivron (eds) *Beyond French Feminisms: Debates on Women, Politics, and Culture in France, 1980–2001,* New York: Palgrave Macmillan.

Squires, J. (1999) *Gender in Political Theory,* Malden: Polity Press.

Tasmanian Electoral Office (2005). Online. Available at: www.electoral.tas.gov.au (accessed 2 February 2005).

Uhr, J. (1999) 'Why we chose proportional representation', in M. Sawer and S. Miskin (eds) *Representation and Institutional Change: 50 Years of Proportional Representation in the Senate,* Canberra: ANU/Senate.

WEL (1998) 'Speech to the "Save our Democracy" Rally', August, Hobart: Women's Electoral Lobby.

Welch, S. and Studlar, D.T. (1990) 'Multi-member districts and the representation of women: evidence from Britain and the United States', *Journal of Politics,* 52(2): 391–412.

6 From women's interests to special interests

Reframing equality claims

Marian Sawer[1]

The year 1975 was International Women's Year (IWY), designated as such by the United Nations three years before. IWY was an international consciousness-raising exercise, extending to the international sphere the kind of gender mobilisation that had been taking place in many western countries from the late 1960s. A World Conference on Women held in Mexico City was its focal point and out of it came both a UN Decade for Women and a World Plan of Action agreed to by UN member states. The Plan of Action aimed to eliminate discrimination and promote the status of women, to integrate women in development and to increase the involvement of women in political life and international peace-making. For these things to happen, it was agreed, there needed to be national machinery to advance the equality of women. As we shall see, by the end of the UN Decade for Women more than two-thirds of UN member states had adopted such machinery. The early initiatives by countries such as Australia and Canada were being emulated in most parts of the world.

This chapter will examine the current fortunes of the idea that women need mandated machinery of government to advance their interests. As Jill Vickers points out in Chapter 2, the idea that women have shared interests is not a currently fashionable one within feminist scholarship. In 1975, however, the disputes tended to be less about whether the subordination of women was a shared problem and more about whether the solution lay in reform or revolution. This chapter is about the reform side of this story, and the attempts to make the state more responsive to its female citizens. It will begin by outlining some of the current applied discourse about government machinery for women. It will then argue that shifting discourses in the English-speaking democracies, in particular, have reshaped attitudes to using the state to promote equal opportunity and the status of women. The state itself has been undergoing changes that make such mandates more problematic. In addition, the retreat of many parts of the women's movement from policy engagement and the rise of vocal men's rights movements have meant increased contestation over even statistical indicators of inequality.

Resources provided by the state to enable women from diverse backgrounds to have a voice in the policy process are now depicted as part of the cosy conspiracy between bureaucrats (or femocrats) and rent-seeking 'special interests' who seek a better return through the state than they can obtain through the market or through marriage. Thirty years ago the idea of equal opportunity meant making claims on the state to ensure that all women, as well as men, had the opportunity to develop their full potential and to participate equally in the life of the community. Today such claims are decried as an elite agenda pursued at the expense of ordinary citizens and taxpayers. How did we get from there to here?

Machinery of government for women

IWY was a milestone in disseminating new kinds of thinking about how government could be made to operate for the benefit of women as well as men. The Australian Elizabeth Reid, who chaired the drafting group working on the World Plan of Action at the preparatory meeting in New York, had firm ideas on the need for presence in the heart of government, to ensure all policy proposals were analysed for impact on women. It could not be assumed that any proposals, whether to do with tax, tariffs or transport, would be gender-neutral, given the different location of women and men in the social division of labour or the false supposition of income-pooling within families. Previously, public servants had assumed that policies that would benefit men would also benefit women – a presumption most blatantly displayed in overseas aid policies where development policies targeted at men notoriously increased the workloads of women left behind in the subsistence farming sector.

The sharing of these ideas at IWY meetings and at three subsequent UN World Conferences on Women resulted in a global diffusion of policy innovation that was unprecedented in its rapidity (True and Mintrom 2001). Government machinery to advance the status of women had been adopted by 127 countries by 1985, and by 165 countries by 2004. The institutionalising of feminist ideas in international discourses and bureaucratic innovation was barely reflected in theorising at the time on the subject of feminism and the state. Much of this theorising was produced in the United Kingdom and the United States of America, the two countries where feminist impact on state structures had been least (see also Vickers, this volume). There was a corresponding tendency to theorise the state as driven by some unitary logic, whether serving the interests of capitalism or of patriarchy (Wilson 1977; Ferguson 1984; MacKinnon 1989). Even in countries like Australia, Canada, and New Zealand, feminist writing about the state was often refracted through imported theoretical lenses that were of little assistance in resolving issues confronting feminists working through the state. So the applied discussion concerning machinery of government tended to be conducted in a parallel universe to that of feminist theory, a universe peopled by feminist bureaucrats (femocrats), women's advocacy organisations and feminists working through multilateral organisations such as the UN.[2]

In this applied discourse about how gender equality may best be advanced within government there has been much emphasis on the *location* of gender units. Because it is economic policy that tends to have the most direct impact on women's lives, it is argued that mechanisms to promote gender equality should be centrally located in government, where they will be able to monitor all policy for gender impact, including economic policy. Such a key location might be in a co-ordinating agency such as a prime minister's office or department, a cabinet office, or a planning commission.

The *authority* behind gender units is also crucial. Only the imprimatur of the head of government is likely to be sufficient to overturn entrenched norms and enable new cross-government approaches. The backing of the head of government and location in their office or portfolio is often the only way to ensure access to top-level decision-making. However, because of the role of the head of government in chairing cabinet, it has been found useful to have another cabinet minister assisting the prime minister on the status of women, who can be less constrained in their advocacy. Such considerations of the importance of location and authority lie behind the relevant part of the Beijing Platform for Action (para. 201) recommending location of national machineries at the highest possible level in government.

In federal systems the central location of gender units is also important for the purpose of having access to and input into the process of intergovernmental decision-making. The devolution of areas of responsibility to another level of government, without stipulations of gender outcomes, may result in hard-fought gains being lost in areas such as women's services. Access to forums where the federal division of powers is being renegotiated is therefore important, as is a co-ordinating role in relation to intergovernmental meetings of ministers and officials responsible for the status of women.

A self-standing ministry within government may have advantages in terms of greater visibility and 'ownership' by women in the community to whom it delivers programmes. Its policy clout will, however, be very dependent on the status of its minister. Another alternative, often preferred by governments, is to hive off gender units to social welfare or similar areas of government. Location in a programme delivery department might mean access to budgetary resources for services. But it is difficult to undertake from such a location the role of supporting and acting as a catalyst in gender mainstreaming across government. This is the role for national machinery envisaged by the Beijing Platform for Action and other international documents:

> Mainstreaming a gender perspective is the process of assessing the implications for women and men of any planned action, including

legislation, policy or programs, in all areas and at all levels. It is a strategy of making women's as well as men's concerns and experiences an integral dimension of the design, implementation, monitoring and evaluation of policies and programs in all political, economic and societal spheres, so that women and men benefit equally and inequality is not perpetuated. The ultimate goal is to achieve gender equality.

(UN 1997: 1)

There is no one answer to the optimal design of gender mechanisms within government. While central location can ensure access to cabinet submissions from across government, there can also be disadvantages in terms of links to women in the community. Central location means placing a heavy premium on policy expertise and confidentiality, rather than the kind of outreach and budgetary resources associated with programme delivery. Often women in the community will not feel any 'ownership' of processes of gender monitoring and gender audit conducted by gender specialists in the recesses of government.

In Australia there was more 'ownership' of the insider model of women's policy machinery than in many countries. It was an influential women's non-government organisation, Women's Electoral Lobby, that promoted the advantages of central location in the early 1970s and drew up the wheel model subsequently adopted at national and sub-national levels of government. The wheel was constituted by a hub at the centre of government and spokes in line departments. Gough Whitlam, the prime minister of the day, spoke in 1975 of how his women's adviser had always had the right to see any Cabinet documents to advise on gender implications and of how it was 'proper that there should be in the Department of Prime Minister and Cabinet appropriate machinery for doing these things on a continuing and official basis' (Whitlam 1975: 1926).

At the height of influence of feminist thinking on government, in the 1980s and early 1990s, such policy wheels existed in all of Australia's governments, at Commonwealth, State and Territory levels. However, the central location of women's policy machinery depended heavily on political will and the perception that political pain would be inflicted if it were downgraded. Even at this time, analysis of the detrimental impact of policy proposals did not necessarily change the outcome. One example is the fate of universal family allowances paid to mothers of dependent children. The Commonwealth Office of the Status of Women commissioned survey research on such mothers in 1985 and found that for 90 per cent of them family allowances were very important and for 40 per cent they were their only independent source of income (OSW 1985). Despite these findings, as well as data querying assumptions about 'pooling' of family income, family allowances fell victim to the Labor government's determination to cut 'middle-class' welfare. Means-testing of family allowances on 'family income' was introduced in 1987.

With the discursive changes of the 1990s (discussed below), the political will to allow disaggregated gender analysis of major government policy directions, particularly economic directions, tended to disappear. Gender units were moved out of their central locations into programme delivery departments while whole-of-government co-ordinating functions, such as the preparation of women's budget statements, were lost. This process was completed at the national level in Australia in 2004 with the relegation of the Office of the Status of Women from the Department of Prime Minister and Cabinet to the Department of Family and Community Services. The renamed Office for Women has now been placed where it can have no routine access to Cabinet submissions from across government and women are once again submerged in the family.

The usual excuse for the relegation and/or dismantling of gender analysis units is that the responsibility for gender analysis is being mainstreamed (discussed further below). Although responsibility allegedly inheres in all policy officers, in fact it is nobody's job and no capacity building or training has been provided for the purpose of fostering gender expertise (Donaghy forthcoming). The femocrat who headed the Australian Office of the Status of Women at the height of its power and influence has recently published a book with an eloquent title. *The End of Equality* charts the dismantling of feminist initiatives within government (Summers 2003).

Arm's-length statutory bodies and commissions

The advantages of statutory bodies such as human rights agencies is their relative independence from government and their public voice, creating the potential to bring pressure on government from outside. A recent example of this in Australia has been the high-profile campaign for paid maternity leave by the Commonwealth Sex Discrimination Commissioner in the context of an extremely conservative Commonwealth government. While mechanisms within government were unable to promote this issue, the statutory independence of the sex discrimination commissioner (and her media skills) and the creation of alliances with bodies such as the Australian Council of Trade Unions helped build momentum. The outcome was not paid maternity leave in a form meeting International Labour Organization (ILO) Convention 183 standards but a compromise in the form of a universal maternity payment. Thanks to the rise of populist discourse, paid maternity leave for women in the workforce was framed by government as discriminating against women who were full-time homemakers.

National human rights institutions are one step removed from majoritarian or populist influences on government, but they also have outreach in the community arising from their community education and complaint-handling functions. The downside also derives from their status as bodies outside government – their lack of access to confidential government processes and inability to provide advice before governments have invested political capital in new proposals.

One source of leverage for human rights and equal opportunity commissions is their linkages to international bodies and responsibilities under international human rights instruments to which governments have acceded. In terms of promoting gender equality the leverage of human rights agencies would be significantly enhanced if they had de facto independent status at meetings of the UN Commission on the Status of Women (CSW) rather than having to function as part of government delegations. This would reflect both their significant role in advancing gender equality and their arm's-length relationship with government.

Advisory and consultative bodies

A third type of national mechanisms is advisory and consultative bodies, which frequently prepare the way for the establishment of agencies inside and outside government to advance gender equality. These bodies are often able to commission and promote research on issues of concern to women in the community, which might be too politically sensitive to be commissioned directly from within government.

Advisory and consultative bodies can also act as a 'parachute' for women's policy machinery inside government by including representatives from a broad political spectrum that will leap to its defence when government changes. They can promote broader understanding of the functions of women's policy units among women's organisations, although they can also become too much the captive of government agendas.

An *alternative* to advisory or consultative bodies, given their resource-intensive nature, is the provision of operational funding to support community-based peak bodies and the networking of non-governmental organisations (NGOs) in the women's sector. Such resourcing enables the participation of NGOs in national policy processes in addition to their activities at the local level. It requires government commitment to the idea of 'critical partnership', whereby the provision of government resources is not contingent on NGOs refraining from criticism of government policies. There needs to be acceptance of the functions of NGOs in representing to government the perspectives and experiences of groups whose lives are significantly affected by government policy, including sole parents, refugee women, lesbians, and women with disabilities. In countries such as Australia and Canada it is the provision of operational funding that has enabled advocacy bodies representing disadvantaged and often unpopular groups of women to achieve voice and presence in policy processes (Sawer 2002).

One topical issue is the more effective use of information technology to facilitate the interface between gender units and women in the community. While NGO websites include links to government gender units, this is rarely reciprocated by government websites. The latter are also notable for the absence of interactive components whereby women in the community can convey their views to government – apart from 'customer' surveys on the actual design of the website.

Unfortunately over the past decade in Australia there has been increased government distrust of the representational functions of NGOs and the defunding of those seen to be representing constituencies outside the mainstream and/or those critical of government (Maddison *et al.* 2004). At the international level the Australian government has reacted sharply to criticisms by UN human rights committees based on NGO reports. In September 2000 the Australian foreign minister told the UN General Assembly that treaty committees were losing credibility because they were too accepting of NGO submissions and did not pay sufficient attention to the views of democratically elected governments. This statement confirmed the views expressed in a joint ministerial media release announcing a review of Australia's participation in the UN human rights system and stating the need to ensure the primary role of governments and the subordinate role of NGOs (Joint Media Release FA 97 2000). These views gave little recognition to the vital role played by NGOs in the UN human rights monitoring system or to the lack of interest on the part of democratically elected governments in exposing their own human rights breaches.

Parliamentary bodies

Sometimes overlooked in the past has been the role of parliamentary bodies in the promotion of gender equality and the empowerment of women. Standing committees on women's rights or equal opportunities, such as found in European and many other parliaments, have played a significant part in agenda setting on equality issues or in 'equality proofing' of legislative proposals (Sawer 2000). Australia has lacked such standing committees on equal opportunity but has had enquiry references given to other standing committees. For example, at the federal level, a 1992 report by a Legal and Constitutional Affairs Committee, *Half Way to Equal*, was a milestone in the strengthening of sex discrimination and equal opportunity legislation. In Sweden all parliamentary enquiries have a mandate to examine gender implications of proposals.

Women's caucuses within parliament or within parliamentary parties may also have a significant role in gender mainstreaming and in identifying the gender implications of policy. While in some parts of the world such caucuses bring together women from different parties, in Australia, New Zealand, and Canada they occur within particular parliamentary parties. For example, in Australia, the Labor Party's Status of Women Committee (which can be attended both by parliamentarians and staffers) has been meeting weekly during parliamentary sitting weeks since 1981. By contrast, the conservative parties lack such a body and their women MPs are less likely to act collectively to raise gender issues.

Standing committees on equal opportunity and women's caucuses provide a mandate for gender-focused work and legitimate the introduction of feminist discourses. They have an important role to play in raising awareness of gender issues at the parliamentary level and in ensuring gender perspectives are represented in public debate. These bodies can provide significant forums for NGOs and academic experts to give evidence on the gender impact of policy and may enhance the work of gender equality mechanisms within government. Women's caucuses may perform a capacity-building role for women parliamentarians as well providing them with a collective voice.

International parliamentary bodies like the Inter-Parliamentary Union (IPU) and the Commonwealth Parliamentary Association have also played a supportive role in gender mainstreaming, as has the International Institute for Democracy and Electoral Assistance (IDEA) in Stockholm. Beyond promoting and monitoring strategies to increase the presence of women in parliament, such bodies look at how women parliamentarians may become more effective in representing the views of women in the community. They also promote partnerships over CEDAW implementation and reporting. The handbook on CEDAW for parliamentarians, prepared by the UN and the IPU, highlights good practices in relation to parliamentary involvement. In the Netherlands, for example, the government is legally obliged to report to parliament every four years on CEDAW implementation before the periodic report is submitted. The government is also required to present the concluding comments of the CEDAW Committee to parliament (UN 2003: 66).

The different roles played in gender mainstreaming by national mechanisms within government, national human rights institutions, advisory and consultative bodies, NGOs, parliamentary and regional bodies relate in part to the changing nature of governance and the changing role of the state. Where once the state may have played a central role in provision of social infrastructure, its role in direct service provision may now be reduced, raising new issues of gender accountability. Bodies outside executive government may become more important and so may partnerships and synergies between bodies inside and outside government. These partnerships must not be at the expense of qualities such as independence and separation of powers, which make such partnerships fruitful in the first place.

New constraints on state action on women's interests

Constraints over the decade since the Beijing Conference may be summarised as: importation of private sector models of governance into the public sector; decreased visibility of the women's movement; 'backlash' against perceived gains by women; and discursive shifts resulting in the displacement of gender equality issues. Because of the overarching importance of the shifts in discourse, which have made issues of gender inequality harder to see, this will be the constraint given most attention but the changing configuration of the state is also relevant.

The new public management

A significant structural constraint for mechanisms to advance gender equality arises in many countries from the nature of the new public management (NPM) – the introduction into the public sector of techniques of private sector corporate governance. NPM has been disseminated through the Organization for Economic Cooperation and Development (OECD) and has affected even the relatively women-friendly Nordic welfare states (Kantola and Dahl 2005). The new philosophy that services should be delivered through markets or market-like arrangements has had a significant impact on the 'public caring' required if women are to have equal opportunity.

Other consequences of NPM have included the devaluation of 'in-house' policy expertise of all kinds, including gender expertise, in favour of management skills and contracting out government services. Without gender expertise it is difficult to evaluate policy for gender impact or to audit the gender outcomes of government activity, while contracting out famously makes all forms of accountability more difficult. It is sometimes argued that accountability for gender equity can be written into performance agreements between chief executive officers and ministers – but without independent and expert scrutiny this is unlikely to be effective and more likely to be an empty formality.

Along with contracting out has come increased volatility of bureaucratic structures and a continuously changing environment. Within this environment it is difficult to sustain the structures needed for long-term projects like advancing gender equality and there is an ongoing loss of corporate memory. Moreover, within the commercial product format and outcomes focus associated with NPM there is a devaluing of process, including the kind of consultative policy processes and democratic forms of service delivery required for the empowerment of women.

A related problem is the introduction of compulsory competitive tendering processes in all areas of service provision. The tendering process makes little room for policy advocacy and community education functions associated with second-wave women's services, let alone the kind of democratic structures and collective decision-making intended to achieve women's empowerment. NPM is also at odds with the organisational philosophy of services provided from within government, such as the women's information services that exist in all Australian jurisdictions. The women's information services have let women talk until they reach the real question that is of concern to them, rather than trying to reach preset quantitative targets (which is a feature of NPM processes).

Decreased visibility of the women's movement

In many western countries the women's movement is much less visible as an oppositional force than it was 20 years ago. There has been a marked decline in the number of 'collective action events' in support of women's rights (Staggenborg and Taylor 2005: 45). There are many debates over why this is so – including the natural cycles of social movements, shifts in the political opportunity structure, the 'institutionalisation' of the women's movement or its diversification and fragmentation. In both waves, the women's movement successfully mobilized gender identity as a basis for political action. This required a discursive strategy that played down differences between women, and played up common experiences of subordination, in order to activate a constituency for change and create a political base for claims for gender equality. In recent years, as pointed out by Vickers in this book, such essentialism has been much contested by post-modernist theorists who perceive the category 'women' as privileging a white, middle-class and heterosexual identity and imposing a rigid construct on fluid and intersecting identities. An even more important source of the demobilising of gender identity has been the increased dominance of neo-liberal discourse. The latter replaces collective identities with the construct of the individual who is author of their own choices, unconstrained by inequalities of power or expectations. The constraints posed by the dominance of neo-liberal discourse are discussed further below.

Some believe the women's movement is in abeyance – hibernating in 'abeyance structures' that preserve the collective identity and values of the social movement, while giving up on broader policy engagement until the arrival of the next wave (Bagguley 2002). Others suggest that the women's movement has forsaken public protest for less visible forms of contention or 'unobtrusive mobilisation' within the whole spectrum of government, non-government and civil society institutions (Katzenstein 1998). The latter can in turn be interpreted as a sign of social movement 'success' or, on the other hand, of incorporation and co-option (see Roth, Chapter 8, this volume, on this point). Either way, International Women's Day and Reclaim the Night marches no longer attract big crowds of women, although women can still be mobilised to protect the right to abortion. Women's studies programmes and research centres with links to women's NGOs have often been replaced by 'gender studies' that tend to lack a comparable community base. Curriculum has shifted from political economy and concerns with labour market segmentation to cultural critique and concerns with the body. Feminist 'women's pages' in the mainstream press have largely been scrapped and feminist broadcasting has lost its high profile vehicles.[3] The 'narrow-casting' provided by feminist e-lists means that feminist perspectives are still shared on policy developments of the day, and often on a more global basis than in the past, but this is no substitute for more publicly visible forms of oppositional discourse.

For whatever reason, the men's rights movement has been much more successful in mobilising letter-writing campaigns and lobbying on issues like child support than today's women's movement and, in Australia, has been able generate almost two-thirds of submissions to parliamentary enquiries on such issues. In general, governments are less afraid of stirring up feminists than previously and have blithely introduced policy changes that, for example, have increased effective marginal tax rates for second earners.

Backlash politics

The so-called backlash against the women's movement has also been identified in many countries, both East and West. It is associated with the men's rights movement that seeks to roll back changes in gender relations that followed from second-wave feminism. Men's rights groups proliferated in the 1990s with names such as 'Dads Against Discrimination' (Australia, Canada and the USA), the Men's Rights Agency (Australia) or Men's Equalization Inc. (Canada). They believe that feminists have captured state power and are responsible for policies and legislation that victimise men (Kaye and Tolmie 1998). Particular sources of resentment include child support formulae applied to non-custodial parents, equal opportunity legislation and domestic violence programmes that focus on men as perpetrators. Starting in the USA, men's rights groups seized on unreliable statistics to 'prove' that women were just as violent as men and refused to accept the legitimacy of any domestic violence programmes that did not start from this premise. In Australia, the Men's Rights Agency claimed a victory when an expensive government anti-domestic violence advertising campaign aimed at teenagers and young adults, 'No respect, no relationship', was cancelled just before Christmas 2003, when screening was to begin.

In general men's rights groups view policies that have made it easier for women to leave unhappy or violent relationships and/or to compete on a more equal basis in the paid workforce as undermining the authority of men inside and outside the family. Small steps towards greater gender equity in public policy are vastly exaggerated in the eyes of those who believe they are the new victims of feminist elites and gender bias in the state. In some western countries the rise in political influence of fundamentalist Christian churches has reinforced the anti-feminist backlash.

While the men's rights movement depicts equal opportunity policies as a form of discrimination against men, there are also anti-feminist women's groups that depict equal opportunity as discrimination against women who choose to be economically dependent on men. The discourse of anti-feminist women's groups ties in nicely with the market populist discourse discussed in the next section because it frames equal opportunity measures and paid community services as wasteful as well as discriminatory. Paid maternity leave, subsidized childcare or re-entry allowances and training programmes are all framed as wasteful as well as a form of discrimination against women who have chosen to be homemakers. Tax systems based on the individual are also depicted as discriminating against two-parent single-income families: instead, family unit taxation is favoured that would impose high rates of tax on second earners. Anti-discrimination legislation is opposed on the ground that private employers, with the incentive of the profit motive, will make wiser choices than 'equal opportunity bureaucrats whose salaries are paid by taxpayers' (Francis 1994).

Discursive shifts

One of the greatest constraints on government machinery for women in the English-speaking countries over the last decade has been the rise of market populism and the framing of gender equality initiatives as part of an elite agenda and/or 'special interest pleading'. I shall use the term market populism here rather than 'neo-liberalism' in order to focus on the semantic structure of this new public discourse (for more detail see Sawer and Hindess 2004).

The market populism that now constrains the terms and structures of public policy in English-speaking countries has at least two clearly identifiable elements. First, neo-conservative discourse discrediting the welfare state as the domain of 'new class elites'; and second, public choice discourse unmasking all public interest or social justice advocacy as motivated by rent-seeking and self-interest.

The neo-conservative discourse of 'new-class elites' was an adaptation of a Trotskyist idea originally applied to cognitive elites in the Soviet bloc. In the USA neo-conservative writers applied it to university graduates, radicalised by the social movements of the 1960s. They form a 'class' by virtue of their cultural capital, which fits them for employment in public sector agencies and means they have a class interest in maximising redistribution. They speak a language of public interest and equal opportunity that masks a class interest in expanding the public sector and regulating business.

The new class is associated with values such as feminism, environmentalism, multiculturalism and minority rights more generally but these are depicted as 'fashions', or a form of moral vanity, rather than having any authentic ethical content. They serve to distinguish the elite from ordinary people and are given the label of 'political correctness'. This construction was reinforced by the familiar populist strategy of depicting new class elites as having contempt for the values of ordinary people.

The new class is said to sneer at, despise, have contempt for, look down on, or wince at the values of ordinary people – although no empirical evidence is ever provided of such behaviour. Feminists, particularly those in government, are depicted as having contempt for ordinary women. The idea of contempt is necessary to discredit the values being upheld by the new class – who would want someone contemptuous of them spending their taxes? It should be observed that, unlike the business and financial elites of yesteryear, the new class elite is characteristically made up of teachers, social workers, librarians, and public servants. In other words, they don't have to be well-paid to be labelled as members of the elite – just well-educated and with a set of environmental and human rights values perceived to be at odds with business interests. It may seem odd that groups such as social workers or teachers, also derided as 'bleeding hearts', should despise ordinary people but such contempt is required by the semantic grammar of populism.

Another major source of the language of contemporary market populism is public choice theory, developed in the United States from the 1960s. Public choice theory did not appropriate, as had the neo-conservatives, the quasi-Marxist idea of a class defined by ownership of cultural capital. The public choice school is neo-liberal rather than neo-conservative. It takes over the idea of the utility maximising individual from neoclassical economics and applies it systematically to all collective and institutional behaviour.

Public choice analyses set out to demonstrate that all those purporting to pursue the public interest, such as women's advocacy groups and other NGOs, are really 'special interests' seeking to maximise their returns. The term 'welfare state' is replaced by the concept of the 'over-loaded state', the outcome of a cosy conspiracy between special interests and budget-maximising bureaucrats. This frame was popularised worldwide by a disciple of Milton Friedman in the brilliant television series 'Yes, Minister'. It has also been heavily promoted by free-market think tanks in the English-speaking democracies, with their ready access to the mass media owned by Rupert Murdoch in particular.[4]

One of the most dramatic impacts of public choice discourse in countries such as Australia and Canada has been to delegitimise the advocacy work of NGOs. Public choice has justified changed citizenship regimes and the bypassing of bodies 'representing' the interests of particularly needy sections of the community, whether stigmatised groups such as sex workers or poverty-stricken groups such as sole parents or public housing tenants. Whereas operational funding was previously made available to strengthen 'weak voices' in policy debate and to balance the influence of powerful business and professional interests, this is now framed as privileging various 'industries' that have a vested interest in expanding the welfare state – whether the poverty industry, the multicultural industry, the Aboriginal industry or the feminist industry. Operational funding for NGOs representing disadvantaged sections of the community is replaced by project-funding, tied to competitive tendering for service provision with no scope for representational or advocacy work.

Market populist discourse with its simple 'us and them' frame has been a powerful means of displacing attention from increasing economic inequalities and the injuries of class, gender, and race. To draw attention to such injuries is seen as special pleading that will perpetuate privileged welfare state jobs on the one hand and dependency on the other, all at the expense of ordinary taxpayers. Sole parents, for example, are seeking better rents through the state than they can achieve either through marriage or the market. Feminists in general are guilty of expanding the public provision of community services in order to provide equal opportunity for women, services that could be provided more efficiently by 'families' on an unpaid basis.

Public choice theory also places its own twist on the concept of 'gender mainstreaming', as has been analysed in the New Zealand and British Columbia contexts by Kathy Teghtsoonian. While gender mainstreaming generally involves improved consultation with women over policy and programmes, the New Zealand State Service Commission was warning policy managers against 'capture' of policy by the community: 'Ministers ... will not thank policy analysts for advocating sectoral interests' (quoted in Teghtsoonian 2004: 274, and Teghtsoonian, Chapter 7, this volume).

The 'undemocratic' nature of gender equality norms

One of the characteristic features of the market populist discourse is its distrust of 'non-elected' courts and tribunals and the way they frustrate the will of the people expressed through elected governments. This distrust of the liberal elites said to infest judicial benches is associated with an even greater distrust of international courts and tribunals and the international human rights norms established through UN conventions.

In many western democracies populists have hotly contested the development of international normative regimes upholding women's human rights as well as those of children and minorities. Even in Norway some of these tensions were exposed in a recent report to parliament entitled the *Study of Power and Democracy*. The majority report described the new international framework of human rights law as partially responsible for a diminishing of democracy. A dissenting report by Hege Skjeie contested the notion that improving the rights of minorities and of women through applying international human rights norms could be regarded as a loss of democracy. While signing up to international human rights instruments did bind the hands of legislators and transferred some power to international tribunals, it also increased the power of citizens. Strengthening the rights of individual citizens could not, in her review, be regarded as lessening democracy (Ringen 2004).

Domestic and international courts and tribunals do still recognise the concepts of indirect and systemic discrimination and the injustice of policies or requirements that have disparate impact on particular groups, where this impact is disproportional to demonstrated benefit from the policies. But the market populist framing of such recourse to the courts or international tribunals is that new class elites are unable to accept the verdict of democratic majorities. This reframing of rights protection as undemocratic has reverberations across the policy board and is reflected in attitudes towards asylum seekers, towards the rights of Indigenous minorities, and towards policies and programmes promoting equal opportunity for other groups.

Market populism meets gender mainstreaming

Since 1995 Australians have heard much about the need to 'govern for the mainstream' and to ignore the new class and their associated special interests. In part this language has meant pushing back the jurisprudence developed during the 1970s, which acknowledged the need to accommodate difference in order to promote equality. The concept of *indirect* discrimination introduced in anti-discrimination legislation at this time made it clear that to treat in the same way those who were different in significant ways might simply compound disadvantage. In this new understanding equal treatment meant something more than same treatment. A common example was the old requirement of full-time work and unbroken careers in order to be considered for promotion – in organisations designed for a normative male employee without caring responsibilities.

In the 1990s policies to accommodate difference were relabelled by market populists as 'special treatment of special interests' – equality was once again to mean treating everybody the same, regardless of the impact of such treatment on groups who differed in significant respects from the norm. In Australia even the auditing of policies and programmes for disparate impact became viewed as a form of 'special treatment'. A very similar discursive shift was taking place in Canada, where the Reform Party argued for a return to identical treatment, regardless of difference, rather than the 'sophisticated jurisprudential theories of disparate impact and systemic discrimination that invite judicial revision of legislative decision-making' (Morton and Knopff 2000).

The new international language of gender mainstreaming has been used to legitimate the dismantling of units with expertise in promoting equal opportunity for women and designated groups (see Bacchi and Eveline 2003: 100). This was not the intent of this language. As we have seen, 'gender mainstreaming' was intended to encourage central location of machinery so that economic as well as non-economic areas of policy could be monitored and disaggregated in terms of impact on both men and women. It was a reaction to the propensity of governments to focus only on their 'special initiatives' for women and to locate women's machinery in welfare or community services well away from the central planning or macro-economic policy areas of government, where the decisions of most importance to women's lives were made. 'Gender mainstreaming' was meant to foster a structural approach comparable to the wheel model and gender budgeting exercises pioneered in Australia. Instead it became a pretext for eliminating such structures and processes in the name of 'mainstreaming'.

At the federal level in Australia 'governing for the mainstream' meant abolishing longstanding gender analysis units such as the Women's Bureau in the employment portfolio, dating from 1963 but disappearing in 1997. More recent gender analysis units also disappeared, ranging from the Office of Indigenous Women through the Migrant Women's Advisor, Gender and Curriculum Unit, the Equal Pay Unit, the Work and Family Unit, the Rural and Regional Women's Unit, to say nothing of the women's policy units once found in all portfolios.

Governing for the mainstream has also meant abolishing the Aboriginal and Torres Strait Islander Commission and removing the Office of Multicultural Affairs from the Department of Prime Minister and Cabinet. There is to be no more 'special treatment for special interests'. As already mentioned, the Office of the Status of Women followed suit in 2004. Gender disaggregated data on government performance is much more difficult to obtain and gender expertise is increasingly rare in government. Statistics on issues such as the distribution of unpaid work and the prevalence of family-friendly provisions in industrial agreements is increasingly out of date. Changes have been made to child support formulae without any prior modelling of the effects on sole parent poverty. More and more contradictions emerge in the realm of social policy. 'Dependency', as in the dependency of sole parents, is seen as a major social problem, yet the dependency of married women is actively encouraged through tax and transfer policies and can lead overnight to the wrong kind of dependency. Increased dependency on the whims of employers is encouraged through labour market deregulation and removal of unfair dismissal protections but is never named as such.

A similar trajectory in Canada, accelerating during the 1990s, has been labelled by Janine Brodie as the 'disappearance of the gendered subject'. Brodie writes:

> This process of invisibilization began with the *delegitimization* of women's groups, indeed of virtually all equality-seeking groups as relevant voices in public policy. This phase was followed by the *dismantling* of much of the gender-based policy capacity within the federal government.
>
> (Brodie forthcoming)

Conclusion

What are the implications of this analysis for future strategies? First, it is essential to acknowledge the significance of shifts in public discourse and their implications for gender policy. Here it is crucial to acknowledge the power of language in shaping the world and determining what problems can actually be seen and what is rendered invisible. In 1999 Status of Women Canada did exactly this, funding a round of research grants on shifts in public policy discourse to anticipate their effects on gender issues.

The discourse of market populism creates a world in which gender equality is depicted as an elite project serving special interests. Equality seekers are discredited as part of a rent-seeking elite wanting to live off other people's taxes. The denunciation of 'liberal' elites distracts attention from the actual rise in economic and social inequalities associated with deregulation and globalisation. There is a truncation of 'public caring' in the interests of lower taxes and greater economic competitiveness, despite the effects of this on women's equality.

But while public discourse has shifted in one direction in the English-speaking countries, it did not do so unaided. The shift involved a great deal of concerted effort on the part of think tanks that packaged and sold this new way of looking at the world, and the broadcast and print media that disseminated it on a daily basis.

Alternative ways of looking at the world still thrive on the internet and in multilateral institutions but they need packaging and popularising in the ways that have brought market populism to the fore. We need to ensure that gender equality discourses are not only institutionalised at the international level but that new vectors are found for them at national and sub-national levels. A new way has to be found to contest dominant discourses that sideline equity issues. The strength of regional and international networks is one part of this equation. Finding the right language to contest the seemingly irresistible tug of populism is another. It is a key challenge for the next decade.

Notes

1 My thanks to Megan Kimber for her assistance.
2 This chapter is itself a contribution to such applied discourse and was originally presented at a UN Expert Group Meeting on 'The Role of National Mechanisms in Promoting Gender Equality and Women's Empowerment' (UN 2005).
3 For example, the 'Accent' Page in the Melbourne *Age* and 'Corporate Woman' in the *Australian Financial Review.* The 'Coming Out Show' on Radio National had a devoted following for 25 years before its demise.
4 In the 24 months January 2003 to December 2004, the Murdoch flagship paper *The Australian* carried 126 articles on its Opinion Page sourced from free-market think tanks or authors associated with them and only seven from what might loosely be termed 'progressive' think tanks, including three from a Jesuit social

justice agency. This analysis is exclusive of foreign policy articles, where once again the Murdoch media have a particular bent.

References

Bacchi, C. and Eveline, J. (2003) 'Mainstreaming and neoliberalism: a contested relationship', *Policy & Society*, 22(2): 98–118.

Bagguley, P. (2002) 'Contemporary British feminism: a social movement in abeyance?', *Social Movement Studies*, 1(2): 169–85.

Brodie, J. (forthcoming) 'Putting gender back in: women and social policy reform in Canada', in Y. Abu-Laban (ed.) *Gendering the Nation-State: Canadian and Comparative Perspectives*, Vancouver: University of British Columbia Press.

Donaghy, T. (forthcoming) 'The death of the Australian femocrat', *Australian Journal of Political Science*.

Ferguson, K.E. (1984) *The Feminist Case against Bureaucracy*, Philadelphia: Temple University Press.

Francis, B. (1994) 'Some more equal', Endeavour Forum (previously Women Who Want to be Women). Online. Available at: www.endeavourforum.org.au (accessed 20 October 2004).

Joint Media Release FA 97 (2000) 'Improving the effectiveness of United Nations committees', 29 August. Online. Available at: www.dfat.gov.au/media/releases/foreign/2000/fa097_2000.html (accessed 10 June 2005).

Kantola, J. and Dahl, H.M. (2005) 'From differences between to differences within', *International Feminist Journal of Politics*, 7(1): 49–70.

Katzenstein, M.F. (1998) *Faithful and Fearless: Moving Feminist Protest inside the Church and Miltary*, Katzenstein: Princeton University Press.

Kaye, M. and Tolmie, J. (1998) 'Discoursing dads: the rhetorical devices of fathers' rights groups', *Melbourne University Law Review*, 22: 162–94.

MacKinnon, C. (1989) *Towards a Feminist Theory of the State*, Cambridge, Massachusetts: Harvard University Press.

Maddison, S., Denniss, R., and Hamilton, C. (2004) 'Silencing dissent: non-government organisations and Australian democracy', *Discussion Paper 65*, Canberra: Australia Institute.

Morton, F.L. and Knopff, R. (2000) *The Charter Revolution and the Court Party*, Peterborough: Broadview Press.

OSW (Office of the Status of Women) (1985) *What Women Think: A Survey of Mothers' Attitudes to the Family Allowance, the Dependent Spouse Rebate and Family Finances*, Canberra: CPN Publications.

Ringen, S. (2004) 'Where now democracy?', *Times Literary Supplement*, 13 February.

Sawer, M. (2000) 'Parliamentary representation of women: from discourses of justice to strategies of accountability', *International Political Science Review*, 21(4): 361–80.

—— (2002) 'Governing for the mainstream: implications for community representation', *Australian Journal of Public Administration*, 61(1): 39–49.

—— and Hindess, B. (2004) *Us and Them: Anti-Elitism in Australia*, Perth: Australian Public Intellectual Network.

Staggenborg, S. and Taylor, V. (2005) 'Whatever happened to the women's movement?', *Mobilization: An International Journal*, 10(1): 37–52.

Summers, A. (2003) *The End of Equality: Work, Babies and Women's Choices in 21st Century Australia*, Sydney: Random House.

Teghtsoonian, K. (2004) 'Neoliberalism and gender analysis mainstreaming in Aotearoa/New Zealand', *Australian Journal of Political Science*, 39(2): 267–84.

True, J. and Mintrom, M. (2001) 'Transnational networks and policy diffusion: the case of gender mainstreaming', *International Studies Quarterly*, 45: 27–57.

UN (United Nations) (1997) Economic and Social Council (ECOSOC), Agreed Conclusions 1997/2, doc. A/57/3/Rev.1, Ch. IVA, p. 1.

—— (2003) *The Convention on the Elimination of All Forms of Discrimination against Women and its Optional Protocol: Handbook for Parliamentarians*, Geneva: United Nations and the Inter-Parliamentary Union.

—— (2005) 'The role of national mechanisms in promoting gender equality and the empowerment of women', report of the Expert Group Meeting held in Rome, December 2004. Online. Available at: www.un.org/womenwatch/daw/egm/nationalm2004/ (accessed 10 June 2005).

Whitlam, E.G. (1975) Reply to Parliamentary Question on Women's Affairs, *Commonwealth of Australia Parliamentary Debates, House of Representatives*, 9 October 1975: 1926.

Wilson, E. (1977) *Women and the Welfare State*, London: Tavistock.

7 Disparate fates in challenging times

Women's policy agencies and neoliberalism in Aotearoa/New Zealand and British Columbia[1]

Katherine Teghtsoonian

Introduction[2]

This chapter develops an explanation for the different approaches to existing women's policy agencies adopted by governments of the right elected to office in Aotearoa/New Zealand (in 1990) and in the province of British Columbia (in 2001). In Aotearoa/New Zealand the Ministry of Women's Affairs remained structurally intact, while in British Columbia the Ministry of Women's Equality was eliminated and replaced with a women's policy agency that constitutes a small sub-unit within a much larger ministry. My analysis of these developments focuses on the impact of two institutional features of the women's ministries: (1) the nature of the activities in which they were involved and the different allocations of their budgetary resources that these activities entailed; (2) the relationship between each ministry and community-based women's groups. I also explore the interaction between these institutional variables and the particular way in which a discourse of 'special interests' has been expressed within the party of the right in each case.

One of the first acts of the incoming government formed by the victorious Liberal Party following the May 2001 provincial election in British Columbia was the elimination of the Ministry of Women's Equality. Although the Liberals had seemingly reversed their longstanding opposition to the ministry's existence with a pre-election promise to retain it, once in office they quickly abandoned this commitment. As a result, ten years after its establishment as a free-standing government ministry in 1991, Women's Equality was dismantled and reconfigured as 'Women's Equality and Social Programs', a small sub-unit in the Ministry of Community, Aboriginal and Women's Services (CAWS).[3] CAWS is a sprawling entity established after the 2001 election that incorporated a dizzying array of units and responsibilities transferred from seven different ministries. Initially accounting for a mere 7 per cent of the 1,184 full time employees absorbed by CAWS, Women's Equality and Social Programs had been rendered all but invisible (Teghtsoonian 2003: 33). Disappointing to supporters of the ministry, the restructuring of Women's Equality was consistent with developments elsewhere. In Canadian provinces such as Alberta and Ontario, as well as at the state and federal levels in Australia, governments of the right have undermined the work of women's policy agencies by downsizing or eliminating them, moving them to peripheral locations within the bureaucracy, and reducing the resources available to them (Chappell 2002; Harder 2003; Malloy 1999; Sawer 1999).

Despite having to operate in a similarly inhospitable political context during much of its history, the Ministry of Women's Affairs in Aotearoa/New Zealand has nevertheless experienced a different institutional fate. Established by the Fourth Labour Government elected in 1984, Women's Affairs had been the target of ongoing hostility from socially conservative segments of society and from critics within the right-wing National Party while the latter was in opposition during the 1980s. And yet, after winning the 1990 election, the incoming National government retained Women's Affairs as a free-standing ministry with Cabinet representation. Although calls for the dismantling of the ministry persisted from various quarters while National governed throughout the 1990s, it survived to see the return of the Labour Party to office in the 1999 election.

The disparate fates of the Ministry of Women's Affairs and the Ministry of Women's Equality under governments of the right pose a puzzle that this chapter seeks to unravel. It does so through a comparison of key institutional features of the two ministries that reveals important differences between them. The first is the nature of the activities in which Women's Affairs and Women's Equality were involved and the different allocations of their budgetary resources that these activities entailed. The second, related, feature is the relationship between each ministry and community-based women's groups. Important in their own right, the impact of these institutional differences on the divergent fates of the two ministries has been amplified through their interaction with the particular way in which a discourse of 'special interests' has been expressed within the party of the right in each jurisdiction. I argue that the configuration of these institutional and ideological variables that we see in each case enhanced the vulnerability of the BC ministry, and minimized that of Women's Affairs, to the political agenda of an incoming right-wing government.[4]

In addition to engaging with a number of theoretical issues, the analysis developed below is also important from a practical point of view. Scholars reflecting on experiences in a broad range of countries in the industrialized west have argued that women's policy agencies constitute a key site within government for the substantive representation of women's interests (Chappell 2002; Squires and Wickham-Jones 2002; Stetson and Mazur

1995). For example Laurel Weldon, in summarizing the results of her cross-national study of policies pertaining to violence against women, argues that women's policy agencies and women's community-based activism 'in combination ... give women a stronger voice in the policy-making process than does the presence of women in the legislature' (2002: 1153–4). In light of the significant role that women's policy agencies can play in articulating and promoting the interests of diverse groups of women, it is important to enhance our understanding of the variables that support or detract from their capacity to survive and work effectively on behalf of women.

Before turning to this task, some comment on the understanding of 'women's interests' that informs the analysis in this chapter is warranted. As Jill Vickers notes in Chapter 2 of the present volume, understandings of 'women's interests' and how these ought to be reflected within government or translated into policy decisions remain multiple and contested. This complexity flows, in part, from the diversity of fundamental assumptions and values that underpin competing framings: are women's interests served by outlawing pornography? by policies providing generous financial support for mothers with young children to remain at home full time? through by-laws requiring the registration and licensing of prostitutes? On these and many other issues, there is often disagreement – among feminists, between feminist and non-feminist women's groups, between community-based organizations and government departments, and among different government departments – on the question of how public policy can best serve women's interests. It is also the case that 'women' are a highly diverse group distributed across widely varying social and economic locations. As a result, variously defined groups of women have interests that diverge or conflict: wealthy women who benefit from tax cuts vs. poor women who rely on public services funded by taxes; single mothers needing access to low-cost child care vs. (generally female) child care workers who need higher wages to survive economically; Aboriginal women or women of colour seeking culturally appropriate health and social services delivered by members of their own communities vs. white social service workers seeking to maximize their employment opportunities.

Recognizing these complexities alerts us to the contingent nature of the ways in which women's policy agencies will construct and articulate 'women's interests', and the gulf that may exist between this formulation and the policy goals of various communities of women outside government. While acknowledging these uncertainties and contingencies, the analysis which follows is nevertheless also informed by a belief that women's interests – in all their diversity – are poorly served when government's capacity or willingness to identify and articulate the gendered impact of its policies is reduced. Appropriately structured, and equipped with adequate material and political resources, women's policy agencies

can constitute key institutional spaces within government through which
the gendered dimension of policy choices can be made visible; as such,
they have the potential to play a significant role in supporting women's
diverse interests. It is thus crucial to deepen our understanding of the
factors that operate to shape women's policy agencies' divergent fates.

The Ministry of Women's Affairs and the Ministry of Women's Equality as comparative cases

There are a number of similarities between these two women's policy
agencies and the wider socio-political contexts within which they have
operated that make them useful as cases for comparative analysis. Both
ministries were strongly supported by feminist activists within the governing party that established them, the Labour Party in Aotearoa/New
Zealand and the provincial New Democratic Party in British Columbia,
and initially enjoyed widespread support among community-based
women. Both were entitled to have their minister sit in Cabinet, and each
was initially led by a strong feminist minister who brought additional political resources to bear on her tasks in the women's portfolio.[5] Although
subsequently operating under the direction of less powerful ministers,[6]
both ministries were nevertheless well-institutionalized prior to the election of National in Aotearoa/New Zealand in 1990 and the provincial
Liberal Party in British Columbia in 2001.

As far as the wider context is concerned, we can note that the two ministries were both established within governments based on the general
principles of Westminster-style parliamentary democracy. As a result, they
faced similar constraints in their efforts to secure positive policy developments for women while operating within the conventions of cabinet
government. It is also the case that the populations of Aotearoa/New
Zealand and British Columbia are of similar size and distribution, concentrated in each instance in one major urban centre with residents elsewhere dispersed over geographically diverse rural areas and smaller cities
and towns.[7] In both jurisdictions women's life circumstances vary tremendously, shaped by the experiences of privilege and marginalization that
flow from – among other things – sexual orientation, (dis)ability, class
location, and racialized identities that reflect histories of colonization and
immigration. The two women's ministries have thus pursued their efforts
to develop and maintain a working relationship with community-based
women and women's organizations within broadly similar socio-political
contexts.[8]

One of the most salient contrasts between the two cases lies in the fact
that Women's Affairs was established at the *national* level in Aotearoa/New
Zealand, whereas Women's Equality was established within the *provincial*
government of British Columbia. While there are certainly differences
between national and subnational levels of government that need to be

acknowledged, my analysis is premised on a belief that these are not of sufficient magnitude or relevance to undermine the comparability of the two cases. For example, although provincial governments in Canada do not have as wide-ranging a set of responsibilities as the government of Aotearoa/New Zealand, those that they do have (including health, education, social assistance, and powers of taxation) are both broad and of central importance to women's well-being. And, while is it true that the powers of the Canadian federal government limit the degree of autonomy enjoyed by provincial governments, national governments have themselves been significantly constrained in recent times by the provisions of international agreements and by the perceived imperatives of competitiveness in a global economic environment. I would thus suggest that the differences between the governments of British Columbia and Aoteaora/New Zealand, in terms of the breadth of their responsibilities or the degree of autonomy that they enjoy, are less significant for the purposes of comparative analysis than the many similarities between the two ministries and the wider contexts within which they have operated (for similar case selection see Clark 2002 and Schwartz 1997).

Accounting for disparate fates

Research to date has identified a number of ways in which governments' commitments to neoliberal policy directions and advanced liberal 'technologies of rule', such as balanced budgets, marketized accountability mechanisms and performance indicators (Larner 2000; Rose 1999), have undermined the work of women's policy agencies and have sustained political contexts within which the restructuring or dismantling of these units has been facilitated (Chappell 1995; Eisenstein 1996; Harder 2003; Sawer 1999; Teghtsoonian 2003, 2004). Beyond noting these general tendencies, however, there has been little systematic attention in the literature to a more fine-grained analysis of the features of women's policy agencies or their broader contexts that render them more or less vulnerable to these trends.

A more analytic focus has emerged in research that seeks to identify factors which support, and those which detract from, the effectiveness of existing women's policy agencies. These discussions have generally identified three broad sets of influences: (1) the extent to which the values, goals and ways of working adopted by the women's policy agency are congruent with those of the wider bureaucratic context within which it operates and, more generally, the ideological commitments shaping the government's policy agenda; (2) the political and bureaucratic resources available to the agency; and (3) the nature of the relationship between the community-based women's movement and the women's policy agency (Chappell 2002; Grace 1997; Malloy 1999; Squires and Wickham-Jones 2002; Stephen 2000; Stetson and Mazur 1995; Weldon 2002). Although the discussion below is not intended to assess the effectiveness per se of the two ministries, the general literature exploring this subject is helpful in that it does draw our attention to institutional features of Women's Affairs and Women's Equality on which we can focus for the purposes of a comparative analysis aimed at understanding their different fates under governments of the right. Framing the discussion in these terms will also permit a consideration of the extent to which various features of women's policy agencies which have been identified as contributing to their *effectiveness* may enhance, or undermine, their prospects for *surviving a partisan change in government.*

Conformity to organizational and ideological contexts

Assessments of the effectiveness of women's policy agencies in a number of different jurisdictions have concluded that conformity to the surrounding organizational and ideological contexts contributes positively to these agencies' institutional capacity and their 'survival prospects' (Meyer and Rowan cited in Malloy 1999: 273; see also Squires and Wickham-Jones 2002; Stephen 2000). However, there are a number of ways in which the organizational features of women's policy agencies may depart significantly from those which characterize the wider bureaucratic context within which they operate. For example, agency staff may adopt organizational practices that reflect feminist concerns regarding the hierarchical structures and norms that characterize the wider public service (Iannello 1992). Furthermore, feminist approaches to policy analysis flow from a critique of mainstream 'scientific' methods that fail to address the structural constraints shaping the lives of diverse groups of women as social collectives and that dismiss or diminish the value of qualitative data (Grace 1997; Malloy 1999). Thus the methods of data collection and analysis preferred by feminist staff working within women's policy agencies may be viewed with suspicion by their more conventional counterparts elsewhere in government.

In addition to being set apart from their bureaucratic environment by virtue of a distinctive organizational or methodological profile, women's policy agencies may be characterized by a feminist and equity-seeking orientation that places them at odds ideologically with their political masters. Stetson and Mazur have noted that the ability of women's policy agencies to articulate and promote women's interests will be enhanced in political contexts in which government and society accept the legitimacy of using state mechanisms to address structural inequities (1995: 290). Thus, where progressive governments are in office a congruence between the prevailing ideology and a women's policy agency's equity agenda can enhance the latter's capacity to work on behalf of women. A shift in the partisan complexion of government, however, may well pose a challenge to women's policy agencies and the policy directions they promote.

Commenting on experiences in Australia at both the federal and state level, Louise Chappell has noted 'a pattern of advancement under Labor governments and retreat under conservative governments' on the issues addressed by women's policy agencies, and that the latter 'have tended to be marginalised' under governments of the right (2002: 92; see also Chappell 1995; Sawer 1999).

Although there are broad policy directions and discursive trends that are often identified as flowing from a neoliberal political agenda, neoliberalism in practice is not a monolithic entity, invariant in its manifestations across time and space (Larner 1996, 2000). It is therefore important to retain a sensitivity to local configurations of neoliberalism in attempting to unpack its impact on the interests of diverse groups of women, and the ability of women's policy agencies to articulate and advance these interests. We need also to consider the ways in which neoliberal policy goals and normative commitments have infiltrated the political agenda of governments formed by ostensibly social democratic parties.

For example, although the Fourth Labour Government in Aotearoa/ New Zealand made 'genuine attempts to respond to the demands of women, Maori and the environmental movement' (Larner 1996: 50), it was also an early and vigorous proponent of neoliberal policies and modes of governing. Neoliberal orientations were taken up as well – albeit less comprehensively – by the NDP government in British Columbia during the 1990s. Both women's ministries thus found themselves having to function in a political and ideological environment that was less supportive of feminist policy directions than might have been anticipated given the partisan composition of the governments of which they were a part. These circumstances suggest that it will be useful to begin our analysis with a consideration of the extent to which Women's Affairs and Women's Equality had adjusted to neoliberal imperatives *prior to* the arrival in office of governments of the right, in order to assess the extent to which their relative success in doing so may have influenced their survival prospects when the government changed.

The organizational and ideological shifts implemented in the Ministry of Women's Affairs while the Fourth Labour Government was in office were dramatic and far-reaching. In part, this reflected the fact that the ministry was established – and initially operated – in a radical and unprecedented manner. Under the leadership of its first bureaucratic head, Mary O'Regan, Women's Affairs pioneered a number of departures from civil service practice. These included efforts to minimize hierarchical relationships within the ministry, consulting with Maori women in the community regarding the structure of, and appointments to, Te Ohu Whakatupu (the Maori women's policy analysis unit located within the ministry), allowing Maori applicants for positions in the ministry to have family and community members present during their interviews, making part-time work available, and working to implement biculturalism and anti-racism in the ministry's structure and operation (Curtin 1992; Nathan 1989; O'Regan and Varnham 1992; Washington 1988). Recruited from an activist background, O'Regan was committed to incorporating feminist process into the ministry's work both within government and in its connections with the women of Aotearoa/New Zealand (O'Regan and Varnham 1992).

From the outset, the ministry developed a strong and interactive relationship with a broad range of women's organizations as well as with large numbers of women who were not especially active politically. These linkages were originally fostered through a series of 'women's forums' held around the country prior to the establishment of the ministry, so that the latter project could proceed on the basis of a thorough understanding of the priorities and concerns of a broad spectrum of ordinary women.[9] This initial, powerful connection between Women's Affairs and women in the community was sustained both by ongoing consultations with a range of different women's groups and by ministry staff's understanding of themselves as collectively accountable to women throughout the country, as well as to their minister and the government. As the ministry explained in its post-election briefing to the Labour government returned to office in 1987:

> As public servants, Ministry staff are aware that we must always be loyal to our Minister and to the Government. As the only official agency in the system for women, we are also aware of our accountability to women. For the Maori women in the Ministry there is also the issue of accountability to their iwi. There are obviously times when these lines of accountability are in conflict. We would always hope that we can have frank and open discussion with our Minister in these circumstances.
>
> (MWA 1987: 38)

In terms of both its internal organizational practices as well as its relationship with women outside of government, the ministry thus offered a sharp contrast with established civil service norms.

Remarkable in their own right, the ministry's innovative practices were all the more notable in light of the political direction pursued by the Fourth Labour Government. To the dismay of its erstwhile supporters, the government launched a wide-reaching reform of the economy and the public service that was shaped by neoliberal assumptions and goals (Larner 1996: 50). Through various policy avenues, including the privatization of state enterprises, the deregulation of financial markets and key changes within the civil service, the principles of public choice theory and the privileging of market relationships were brought to life (Kelsey 1995; Larner 1996, 1997). The State Sector Act of 1988 and the Public Finance Act of 1989 entrenched marketized relationships and business models within the public service itself (Boston *et al.* 1996). This new emphasis on efficiency, outputs, and the accountability relationship between bureaucratic and political leaders could hardly be more contrary to the feminist commitment to process, relationship building, and accountability to the community that had characterized the work of Women's Affairs under O'Regan's leadership (O'Regan and Varnham 1992).

A key factor contributing to the survival of the ministry after National's arrival in office in 1990 was the replacement of Mary O'Regan by Judith Aitken in 1988 (Curtin 1992). Committed to the government's neoliberal agenda (Bunkle 1993; Campbell 1988), Aitken moved decisively to undo many of the feminist organizational innovations that had characterized the ministry during its early years, and oversaw the implementation of the new planning, budget and accountability processes required of all government departments under the State Sector Act. In addition to a more hierarchical and managerialist structure, these changes were also reflected in a sometimes awkward business language that came to characterize ministry documents in the late 1980s. For example, in the ministry's 1988 *Statement of Intent* violence against women by abusive partners ('domestic violence') and women's high levels of unemployment are characterized as 'important indicators of inefficiency' in wider economic and social structures and systems of service delivery (MWA 1988b: 4).

Aitken also placed the relationship between ministry staff and the wider community of women on a more conventional footing. In contrast to the emphasis in earlier documents on the ministry*'s accountability* to community-based women, the 1988 *Statement of Intent* reframed the purposes and tone of this relationship in ways that removed its radical edge:

> As a centrally located advisory agency, the Ministry is expected to ensure that its advice to the Minister of Women's Affairs is reliable, comprehensive and timely, which means among other things keeping in direct contact with women in the community, so that the advice proffered to the Government reflects women's own experience, expectations and needs.
>
> (MWA 1988b: 5)

These shifts were deeply disappointing to many of the ministry's supporters in the community. As one feminist commentator regretfully concluded: '[w]hat we have now is a Ministry of Women's Affairs that operates just like any other government department. So be it. We can adjust our expectations accordingly' (Rosier 1989). Nevertheless, the operational style and political discourse adopted by the ministry under Aitken's leadership did serve to demonstrate Women's Affairs' ability to work within the prevailing neoliberal paradigm. Because the Fourth Labour Government was itself so saturated with key neoliberal orientations, Women's Affairs had in many ways adjusted to these prior to the arrival of National in office, undoubtedly enhancing its prospects for survival.

There is a somewhat different story to relate about the Ministry of Women's Equality in British Columbia. Apart from the fact that a free-standing gender-based ministry was a novelty in the Canadian context, there was nothing particularly distinctive about the new ministry's structure, staff or mode of operation. The first Minister, Penny Priddy, did articulate a strong commitment to working in partnership with women's groups throughout the province, but there was no extensive mobilization of the women of British Columbia around the establishment of the ministry analogous to the women's forums that were held in Aotearoa/New Zealand. And, unlike Women's Affairs, there were no moves to depart from established bureau-cratic practice in terms of staff recruitment or internal organizational prac-tices. It is true that, later in the 1990s, Women's Equality forged an innovative trail through the practice of job sharing the position of Deputy Minister, with each of the two part-time occupants of the position working half the week, overlapping on Wednesdays (Pearce 1996). Nevertheless, in general the min-istry undertook no sustained efforts, such as those pursued under O'Regan's leadership at Women's Affairs, aimed at challenging the hierarchical struc-ture of the civil service. Institutionally, then, Women's Equality was broadly in conformity with its wider organizational context from the outset.

Women's Equality was also relatively successful in adjusting to predomi-nant ideological directions and modes of governing, which took on an increasingly neoliberal flavour during the latter part of the 1990s. Plagued by allegations of fiscal mismanagement and intent on demonstrating their credibility as responsible managers of the province's economy, the NDP government under Premiers Clark and Dosanjh implemented a number of neoliberal 'techniques of governance' (Rose 1999). These included a strong rhetorical and practical emphasis on accountability relationships and performance management systems in structuring both the internal operation of government departments and their relationships with service providers in the community. Its efforts to appear fiscally responsible also led the NDP to adopt balanced budget legislation in 2000.

We can see these trends reflected in the emergence of elements of neoliberal discourse in the annual reports and planning documents pro-duced by the Ministry of Women's Equality during the latter half of the 1990s. The ministry's annual 'Strategic Plan' had, by 1995/96, evolved into a 'Business Plan'; during the final year of the NDP's term in office this document had been further transformed into a three-year 'Perform-ance Plan' as prescribed by the government's Budget Transparency and Accountability Act, replete with performance measures and quantitative targets and carefully aligned with the government's wider strategic plan (MWE 1995, 2001a). These planning documents also increasingly emphas-ized working in partnership with the private sector as a ministry goal, and outlined new initiatives to support and encourage women in business and women as entrepreneurs (see, for example, MWE 1998a: 27; 1998b: 13; 1999: 7; 2001b: 3). The Women's Workplace *Equity* Office, established to assist smaller employers in creating gender-equitable and family-friendly workplaces, was soon renamed the Centre for Workplace *Excellence* (MWE 2001b: 8). Finally, and more generally, cost effectiveness and accountability were assigned central importance as objectives guiding the work of Women's Equality and as values sought in the operation of the community-based agencies and services supported by the ministry (Teghtsoonian 2003: 39–41).

Although persuasively accomplished, these efforts to frame the ministry's work in terms of the fiscally prudential and accountability-oriented norms of the wider public service were not sufficient to save Women's Equality after the Liberals arrived in office, even though a similar adaptability to neoliberal administrative norms appears to have contributed to Women's Affairs' survival in Aotearoa/New Zealand. It is true that, even as these neoliberal orientations were seeping into the ministry's work in British Columbia under the NDP, Women's Equality continued to advocate for policies that were antithetical to the free enterprise agenda articulated by the provincial Liberal Party. Among other things, the ministry encouraged the expansion of pay equity initiatives into the private sector, supported increases to the provincial minimum wage, and welcomed the NDP's plans to move toward universal access to affordable child care – all measures to which the incoming Liberal government was adamantly opposed. Could it have been the ministry's advocacy of these policy directions under the NDP that sealed its fate?

This seems less likely when we consider the fact that Women's Affairs was also an enthusiastic advocate for women-positive policy directions that were anathema to the incoming New Zealand National government (and which were, in some cases, also highly unpopular with key figures in the Fourth Labour Government). For example, the ministry had offered strong support for employment equity legislation which, despite opposition from Labour's own Finance and Labour ministers, was passed in the dying days of the Fourth Labour Government's term in office and repealed by National soon after being elected. Women's Affairs also played a crucial role in deflecting attempts by the Labour government to transform the universal family allowance into a targeted benefit, another policy 'win' that was undone under National (Curtin 1992; Curtin and Sawer 1996). Moreover, the ministry's 1990 *Briefing to the Incoming Government* presented a carefully worded critique of neoliberal assumptions and policy directions in a number of areas, including labour market deregulation, state sector restructuring and social policy (MWA 1990a).

It is clear that Women's Affairs' adjustment to neoliberal norms while the Labour government was in office made a significant contribution to its survival under National, but that this adaptation by no means involved a capitulation to neoliberal policy preferences (see Curtin 1992). A similar combination of adaptation *and* opposition to various aspects of neoliberalism marked the experience of the Ministry of Women's Equality in British Columbia prior to the 2001 provincial election. Since both women's policy agencies displayed a pattern of partial adjustment to neoliberal orientations under the governments that established them, it is necessary to look beyond their capacity to adapt to the ideological contexts within which they were operating in order to understand why their institutional trajectories diverged once governments of the right took office.

Ministry mandates and neoliberal spending cuts

Women's policy agencies vary tremendously along a number of institutional dimensions, including the scope and nature of their responsibilities and their budgets and staff complements (Stetson and Mazur 1995). Some analyses of these agencies, and of horizontal policy agencies more generally, have suggested that programme responsibilities and the budgetary resources associated with them enhance considerably the political 'clout' that such agencies enjoy. As Jonathan Malloy has argued, '[t]he chief failure of earlier horizontal ministries [within the Canadian federal government] was seen to be their excessive reliance on knowledge and "information production" alone to produce policy influence, without budgetary and statutory resources or powerful ministers' (1999: 272–3). These lessons were reflected in the belief among staff in Women's Equality that the programme responsibilities attached to the ministry at various points over the years were 'critical because they entail a substantial budget and hence give the department some status on budgetary grounds, and because they give the ministry access to various forums of decision making that are important for women's issues' (Erickson 1996: 119). However, programme responsibilities and budgets may also have negative consequences for the women's policy agencies to which they are attached. In addition to stimulating or aggravating 'turf wars' with other departments (Malloy 1999), these involvements may also draw the hostile gaze of governments with a neoliberal commitment to reducing public spending on, and involvement in, the delivery of programmes and services.

Most discussions of the relationship between neoliberal policy directions and the interests of diverse groups of women have emphasized the negative impact of the former on the latter (for example, Brodie 1995; Kingfisher 2002). This troubled relationship flows, in many respects, from neoliberalism's antipathy toward the state and its strong normative preference for market-based allocation of resources and provision of goods and services, including those historically provided through welfare state structures. Where governments espousing neoliberal principles have taken office, they have sought to reduce the role of the state by, among other strategies, cutting government spending on social programmes and relocating responsibility for caregiving into the private realm of 'communities' (assumed to operate in a relatively unproblematic fashion) and 'families' (framed and understood in gender neutral terms). Activists and scholars alike have noted the gendered burden this creates as, in practice, women in communities and families are expected to take up the slack resulting from the underfunding or elimination of hitherto state supported services, frequently on an unpaid basis or in low wage, insecure jobs (Brodie 1995, 2002; Kingfisher 2002).

These general policy directions were pursued with great vigour by both the National Party government in Aotearoa/New Zealand after 1990 and the provincial Liberal government elected in British Columbia in 2001. National launched an ambitious assault on the welfare state that included significant reductions in social assistance benefits, the replacement of universal eligibility with tighter targeting of a number of benefits and services, and the introduction of market principles into the provision of health and housing (Boston 1999: 10–18). In British Columbia, the Liberals have made deep cuts to social programmes and services in a broad range of policy areas while at the same time implementing cuts to income and corporate tax totalling more than $2 billion along with increases to a variety of regressive taxes, including the provincial sales tax and Medical Services Plan (MSP) premiums (BC CEDAW Group 2003; Fuller and Stephens 2002).

These similar policy agendas had different implications for Women's Affairs in Aotearoa/New Zealand than for Women's Equality in British Columbia because of key differences in the mandate and budget priorities of the two ministries. Unlike Women's Equality, the Ministry of Women's Affairs' mandate did not include responsibilities for programme or service delivery and it provided only very limited funding to support the activities of community-based women. The work of its staff revolved instead around the development of policy advice for the Minister of Women's Affairs, including the analysis of policy proposals originating elsewhere in government. As a result, none of the government's cuts to programmes and services were targeted specifically at Women's Affairs because none were housed within the ministry.

Its lack of programme responsibilities also meant that the New Zealand Ministry did not appear as vulnerable to 'capture' as did other departments of government. 'Capture' presented itself to theorists of the new public management as a particular problem flowing from the absence of institutional boundaries between responsibilities for policy development, service provision and service funding. Where these various activities were located within a common organizational framework, there was a perceived risk that the 'narrow interests' of service providers, rather than the broader interests of the community they were serving or a disinterested analysis of policy options, would shape decisions (Boston *et al.* 1996: 93–4). These concerns led, among other developments, to a significant restructuring of the health care system under National through which service provision was established on a competitive, 'semi-commercial' basis, separated from government funding and purchasing agencies, with a view to decreasing costs and improving efficiency (Boston 1999: 14). With no role in the delivery of programmes and services to women, and only a minimal proportion of its budget allocated to grants to women's organizations in the community, Women's Affairs escaped similar restructuring initiatives of which it might otherwise have been the target. Ironically, then, the absence of these key components of 'clout' – programme responsibilities and associated budgets – and the restriction of its mandate to 'information production alone' may have contributed to the ministry's survival under National.

The Ministry of Women's Equality in British Columbia, by contrast, was implicated in a number of funding and service delivery programmes that arguably made it a target for an incoming Liberal government intent on reducing government involvement in, and financial support for, social services. During the 2000/2001 fiscal year these included funding for the province's network of transition houses; other support services for women fleeing abusive partners, including employment-oriented bridging programmes; and programmes for children who have witnessed violence. The ministry also provided funding for 37 women's centres that served as community-based resources for women throughout the province (MWE 2001b: 15). Spending on these programmes and services far outstripped spending on the ministry's policy and planning functions: in 2000/2001, $49.9 million was allocated to 'Stopping the Violence and Regional Programs', which constituted 92 per cent of a total ministry budget of $54.4 million (Finance 2001: 212). This was consistent with the general profile of Women's Equality's budgets during the NDP's second term in office: the percentage of the ministry's budget dedicated to programmes and services ranged from a low of 87 per cent in 1997/1998 to a high of 96 per cent in 1996/1997, the year preceding the transfer of child care services from Women's Equality to the Ministry for Children and Families.[10]

The institutional dismantling of the ministry facilitated spending cuts and other changes to programmes and services associated with it that the incoming government was intent on making. These included the elimination of funding allocated by the ministry to support the province's women's centres (discussed in greater detail below) and reviewing and reducing the funding basis for bridging programmes. In addition, the Liberals had a number of objectives in the area of child care services which entailed modifying or eliminating policies adopted under the previous administration. For example, one of the new government's first acts was to repeal the NDP's Child Care Act that had, as a first step toward universal access to child care services, provided funding that reduced to $7 the maximum daily cost of after school child care for children up to the age of twelve. The Liberals also reduced spending on subsidies available to low-income parents to assist with the costs of child care services, and cancelled a wage subsidy programme aimed at child care workers that the NDP government had developed during the late 1990s (Teghtsoonian 2003).

Interestingly, the government assigned responsibility for child care services to the Minister of State for Women's Equality, Lynn Stephens, who enthusiastically endorsed the new policy directions. Child care was thus reattached to a gender-based unit within government after several years in other ministries following its transfer out of Women's Equality in 1997. Moving child care services back to Women's Services contributed to two key political goals. First, eliminating Women's Equality as a free-standing ministry while at the same time attaching responsibility for child care services to its weakened successor served to reduce the visibility of the Liberals' spending cuts and policy changes in this area, and to minimize the political resources and clout that Women's Services – as a potential advocate for child care services – might bring to bear in attempting to oppose or modify the new government's policy directions in this area. Second, the reassignment of child care to a women's policy agency otherwise diminished in stature and political resources undermined the gender-specific focus of the ministry by making it as much about children as about women.[11] Finally, as the section below will demonstrate, the elimination of financial support for the province's women's centres gave expression to the Liberals' opposition to 'special interests' in addition to furthering the budget cutting goals flowing from its ideological agenda. Thus programme and spending responsibilities, which may well have enhanced the ministry's clout under the NDP, arguably contributed to its demise under the Liberals.

Relationships with community-based women and 'special interests' discourse

Both scholarly research and the accounts of activists within and outside of government have emphasized the ways in which a positive working relationship between a vibrant women's community and feminists working within a women's policy agency can contribute to the successful pursuit of feminist policy goals (Eisenstein 1996; McKinlay 1990; Sawer 1996). As Dorothy Stetson and Amy Mazur have noted, 'many have argued that it is only through the joint action of well-placed insiders and outsiders with certain levels of organizational capabilities that women's equality policies will rise on the political agenda' (1995: 276; see also Sawer 1996). The mobilization of community activists in support of policies that will benefit diverse groups of women can serve as a political resource for feminists within government. Community-based groups are able to advocate for policies in ways that may not be possible for feminist bureaucrats, but that can be referenced by the latter as they build a case for women-positive policy choices. Similarly, women's policy agencies can serve as a source of financial and other resources for women's groups in the community, and as a channel through which the views and voices of women in the community are brought into policy discussions within government circles (Stephen 2000; Stetson and Mazur 1995).

However, a collaborative and mutually reinforcing relationship between feminist activists in the community and the staff of women's policy agencies can serve as a target for neoliberal critique. Indeed, a key source of tension between neoliberalism and the interests of diverse groups of women is the normative and practical privileging of the individual that lies at the heart of neoliberal ideology. This philosophical stance is antithetical to feminism's focus on women's collective social and political disadvantage and has become aligned, in several jurisdictions, with a discourse of 'special interests'. This discourse has been mobilized to delegitimate political activism among women and other marginalized groups that seek to participate politically on the basis of one or more dimensions of a shared identity; it has also been directed against government programmes and services intended to address the needs of such groups (Brodie 1995; Sawer 2002, 2003). Thus, in addition to undermining the legitimacy of equity-seeking groups, a discourse of 'special interests' supports the wider anti-statist agenda of neoliberalism in the name of 'ordinary citizens' whose interests are understood to lie in a minimalist state and low levels of taxation (Harder 2003; Laycock 2002). On this view, women's policy agencies and their programmes constitute an unwarranted appropriation of public resources by politically powerful feminists who have little understanding of or interest in 'average women' but are, instead, bent on furthering their own narrow self-interest at the expense of 'taxpayers' (Teghtsoonian 2000).

A 'special interests' discourse reflecting such framings was not entirely absent in Aotearoa/New Zealand during the 1980s and 1990s, although it was not always articulated in precisely these terms. For example, there were regular outbreaks of letters to the editor questioning the extent to which the ministry was aware of, or capable of articulating, the interests and concerns of 'ordinary women'. There had been significant opposition to the establishment of the ministry among social conservatives (Abigail 1991: 144) and the National Party's initial position was that, if the ministry were to exist at all, it should be restructured as a Ministry of Family Affairs. However, National's official stance toward Women's Affairs softened during the 1980s and, in contrast to circumstances in British Columbia, an ideological opposition to the ministry's existence was not successfully entrenched in those sites within the National Party where authoritative decisions were taken. Indeed, Jenny Shipley, who went on to become Prime Minister in the latter part of the 1990s, spoke vigorously on behalf of the importance of Women's Affairs and its work while serving as its first minister under National. In responding to a vote by the Auckland divisional conference of the National Party calling for the elimination of the ministry, Shipley argued that Women's Affairs was 'a small but efficient policy unit which provides valuable contestable advice to the Government' and that it was 'working hard to give women a voice in Government policy'.[12]

In British Columbia 'special interests' discourse has occupied a more central place within the provincial Liberal Party. For example, its resonances were visible in the 'New Era' documents distributed by the party in preparation for the 2001 election which were intended to outline its vision for the province's future. The Liberals' plans for a 'New Era for Equality', which were presented toward the very end of the 33-page election package, emphasized the importance of addressing the needs of 'British Columbians' in terms that undermine the legitimacy of gender and other marginalized dimensions of identity as focal points for equity-oriented initiatives:

> The NDP have ... treated equality issues as so-called 'wedge issues', using women, aboriginals, seniors, gays and lesbians, multicultural groups and others as political pawns to try to gain partisan advantage. That's no way to build our future. We must start treating all citizens fairly, equally and with respect, regardless of where they live or who they are. A BC Liberal Government will be guided by the principle of equality ... Equality of opportunity, responsibility and rights is what our Constitution guarantees. And all British Columbians are entitled to no less.
>
> (BC Liberal Party 2001: 32)

As I have noted elsewhere, 'the ... commitments presented as avenues to "A New Era of Equality" discuss plans for "British Columbians", "Canadians", "rural communities", and "local government" – conceptual containers which render invisible the specific interests of identity-based groups, including (multiply-marginalized) women' (Teghtsoonian 2003: 37).

Within this discourse, as was the case when it had been deployed by the political right during the 1990s, a Ministry for Women's Equality appears deeply problematic (Teghtsoonian 2000: 113–14). And, in contrast to circumstances within the National Party, these views were well-established within the provincial Liberal Party rather than being confined to its periphery. Indeed, the Liberals had opposed the continued existence of Women's Equality as a free-standing ministry during the 1996 provincial election campaign, a position to which the party remained committed until January 2001 when it announced what turned out to be a transient commitment to retain the ministry if elected to office (Teghtsoonian 2003: 32).

These differences in the particular profile achieved by a 'special interests' discourse within the party of the right in each case have interacted in important ways with notable contrasts between the two ministries in terms of their relationship with community women's organizations. In Aotearoa/New Zealand only a small percentage (4–7 per cent) of Women's Affairs annual budget during the 1980s was directed to support women's activities in the community: from an annual ministry budget that ranged between $2 million and $3.3 million during the late 1980s, no more than $187,000 in total was ever allocated to women's groups in any given year.[13] Furthermore, much of this funding was one-off in nature and involved small amounts granted through a yearly competition to individual groups.[14] Even those opposed to the ministry had little to work with here in making the case that feminists were bleeding the state of scarce fiscal resources.

Combined with the reframing of Women's Affairs' relationship with community-based women's groups undertaken by Judith Aitken, the absence of significant funding from the ministry for these groups minimized its vulnerability to neoliberal criticism. Indeed, the ministry was able to mobilize neoliberal discourse to legitimate its community contacts. As we have seen, Women's Affairs argued that its ability to bring forward the views of community-based women constituted a critical contribution in providing the government with 'contestable policy advice', a key value within the civil service. In the marketplace of ideas, the views of community women were understood to have their own particular worth. Rather than a liability, then, the ministry's reformulated linkages with women's groups in the community were framed as a neoliberal 'good' that could be taken on board by the incoming National government in 1990 with relatively little difficulty.

By contrast, the relationship between Women's Equality and the provincial women's movement in British Columbia was configured in a way that arguably reduced substantially the odds of the ministry surviving the transition to Liberal rule in 2001. Women's Equality began providing core funding to women's centres in the province in 1992, financial support which became particularly important in light of the reduced amounts available through Status of Women Canada and the shift by the latter to project-based funding in 1998 (Burt and Hardman 2001: 205–6; Vancouver City Council 2003: 4–6). By 2000/2001, the NDP's final year in office, Women's Equality's budget included approximately $1.9 million to support the work of 37 women's centres located throughout the various regions of the province (MWE 2001b: 15).

In their first budget the Liberals announced that they would cut all provincial funding to women's centres effective 31 March 2004, a pledge which they subsequently implemented without blinking. Despite the best efforts of women's centres' staff and supporters to draw attention to the extensive volunteer time already being contributed to their operation by women in communities across British Columbia, and the increased demands on their services in the wake of the extensive cuts to innumerable public services, the government remained firm in its resolve. While partly a function of its budget-cutting agenda, the refusal to continue funding women's centres also expressed the government's broader ideological objectives. As the BC Coalition of Women's Centres has noted, their work involves systemic advocacy as well as the provision of much-needed services and support to women in their communities: 'Women's Centres are often the lone socio-political voice speaking out for the rights of women in our communities and in our province. If that voice is gone – if Women's Centres lose our agency and autonomy – many more women will lose their voices' (2003: 28).

By the time these cuts were implemented in the spring of 2004, Lynn Stephens had been replaced as Minister of State for Women's Equality by Ida Chong, who was promoted to the revised position of Minister of State for Women's and Seniors' Services in a January 2004 cabinet reshuffle. In justifying the withdrawal of financial support for women's centres, Chong noted that at the beginning of its term in office the government had decided that advocacy 'was not a core service' and so should no longer be funded. 'A determination was made that we wanted to ensure that direct, essential services would continue ... That means transition houses, second-stage housing, safe shelters and counselling' (Chong quoted in Clarke 2004: 3).[15] In this statement the services provided through women's centres, often to women with no other access to support, are effectively erased. In identifying women's centres solely with the advocacy that they undertake, and mobilizing this aspect of their work to justify the elimination of provincial government funding for them, Chong's comments offer an illustration of both the way in which 'special interests' discourse has informed the government's policies, and the material consequences of this discourse for women.

The cuts to government funding for women's centres have been easier to pursue in the absence of a free-standing Ministry of Women's Equality, the elimination of which has itself reflected and contributed to the Liberal's ideological agenda. As Laurel Weldon has argued:

> political support from external social movements is necessary to provide women's bureaus both the political pressure and input that is necessary to capitalize on improved institutional capacity ... Thus, a strong, autonomous women's movement improves the representative function performed by a women's policy agency. Conversely, women's policy agencies can strengthen women's movements. By providing financial support for organizing and independent research, women's policy machineries provide additional resources to women's organizations. In addition, by providing research support and opportunities for input on policy development, women's policy machineries can assist women's movement activists in publicly articulating women's perspective. *Thus, strong, autonomous women's movements and effective women's policy agencies reinforce one another in improving women's*

representation. This effect is interactive: Each factor magnifies the effect of the other.[16]

(Weldon 2002: 1160, 1162, original emphasis)

In British Columbia we have seen this dynamic play out in reverse, as the funding relationship between Women's Equality and the province's women's centres rendered both suspect in the eyes of the Liberal government. Buried deep within CAWS, led by Ministers of State indifferent to feminism and without prior Cabinet experience, 'Women's and Seniors' Services' lacks the visibility and other political resources that an independent ministry might be able to bring to bear in arguing against these cuts behind closed doors. And, with their very existence at stake, women's centres have more pressing issues on their plate than protesting the loss of the ministry.

Concluding comments

The analysis presented above suggests that in considering various institutional features of women's policy agencies, it may be useful to draw a distinction between their impact on *effectiveness* and their implications for the *capacity to survive* a partisan change in government intact. As we have seen, the programme responsibilities and financial links to community-based women's organizations developed by the Ministry of Women's Equality under the NDP, and conventionally understood to have enhanced its 'political clout', became liabilities when the provincial Liberal Party assumed office in 2001. The new government has been intent on reducing government spending on, and involvement in, the provision of services; in addition it has undermined the political expression of marginalized identities, including gender, targeted by 'special interests' discourse. This latter feature of the Liberals' ideological agenda was put into practice through mutually supportive policy choices: the elimination of the ministry and the withdrawal of government funding to women's centres. In addition, the spending cuts and changes the Liberals wanted to make in policy areas attached to Women's Equality were themselves facilitated by the Ministry's disestablishment and its reconfiguration as a minor sub-unit of CAWS. Through their interaction with the particular ways in which neoliberalism has been taken up by the provincial Liberal Party, key institutional features of the ministry rendered it more vulnerable than it might otherwise have been following the change of government in 2001.

Lacking the correlates of 'clout' with which its counterpart in British Columbia had been endowed, the Ministry of Women's Affairs nonetheless managed to survive intact as part of governments led by the National Party throughout the 1990s. While its capacity to adjust to neoliberal norms under the Fourth Labour Government undoubtedly contributed to its survival, the comparison with Women's Equality suggests that Women's

Affairs' status as a policy analysis unit without programme-related responsibilities and budgets served to insulate it from National's restructuring initiatives. Its odds of survival were further enhanced by the absence of extensive ministry funding for community-based women's groups and by the fact that the local version of a 'special interests' discourse targeting politicized gender was relatively marginalized within the National Party after 1990.

This last point takes on particular importance in light of the views articulated by Don Brash, who was selected as the new leader of the National Party in late 2003. Declining to appoint a spokesperson for Women's Affairs, Brash indicated his interest in eliminating the ministry altogether, stating that 'I don't frankly think there is any particular merit in having a Ministry of Women's Affairs any more than there is a ministry of men's affairs' (quoted in Young 2003). This renewed attack on the legitimacy of the ministry comes at a time when it is arguably at an especially vulnerable crossroads in its history, having been the subject of an intensely critical review by the State Services Commission earlier in 2003 (State Services Commission 2003; Teghtsoonian 2004). In this context, a resurgence of anti-ministry sentiment in leadership circles within the National Party, rather than at its periphery, may be a harbinger of change for Women's Affairs should National be returned to office at the next election.

These speculations about the ministry's future, as well as the comparative discussion presented in this chapter, leave open the question of whether the institutional structure of a women's policy agency is, in and of itself, of much consequence. The scope of this chapter does not permit a discussion of the consequences of the divergent institutional trajectories traced by Women's Affairs and Women's Equality after the arrival in office of parties of the right, nor a comparative assessment of their relative achievements prior to that development. I have argued elsewhere that, although it is unlikely that the survival of Women's Equality as a free-standing ministry would have had any significant impact on the policy directions pursued by the Liberal government, the elimination of the ministry has – in and of itself – had harmful consequences for women in the province of British Columbia. By undermining established working relationships and by reducing the visibility of, and thereby government's accountability for, the gendered impacts of its policy choices, the downsizing of Women's Equality has constituted a move in the wrong direction for women (Teghtsoonian 2003). With this analysis in mind, I suggest that although there may well have been significant limitations on the capacity of Women's Affairs to pursue effectively a feminist policy agenda serving the interests of diverse groups of women after the 1990 election, its institutional integrity as a free-standing ministry left it better placed to do so than the marginalized women's policy agency to which Women's Equality has been reduced in British Columbia. Exploring the extent to which this is, in fact, the case would be a fruitful avenue for further research.

Notes

1 This chapter is a slightly revised version of 'Disparate fates in challenging times: women's policy agencies and neoliberalism in Aotearoa/New Zealand and British Columbia', *Canadian Journal of Political Science*, Vol. 38, No. 2 (June 2005), pp. 307–33, © The Canadian Political Science Association, published by Cambridge University Press, reprinted with kind permission. My thanks to the anonymous reviewers for the *CJPS* for their helpful comments on my original submission. I would also like to thank the Social Sciences and Humanities Research Council of Canada for its financial support for the research on which this chapter is based; Pam Alcorn and Catherine van Mossel for research assistance; the Departments of Political Studies and Women's Studies and the Institute for Research on Gender at the University of Auckland for institutional support; and the staff of the Interlibrary Loans office in the McPherson Library at the University of Victoria for their unfailing assistance.

2 The analysis in this chapter is based on a close reading of two sets of primary source material: (1) official government documents produced by key government ministries in British Columbia and in Aotearoa/New Zealand; and (2) press coverage of the two women's ministries and of CAWS. My analysis is also informed by interviews and informal discussions with staff in both women's ministries during the late 1990s, although I do not draw explicitly on this material in developing my argument in this chapter.

3 Initially identified as 'Women's Equality and Social Programs', by the time CAWS's 2001/02 annual report was issued the name of the department had been changed to 'Women's *Services* and Child Care', although Lynn Stephens continued to be described as the Minister of State for Women's *Equality* (CAWS 2002). The department's name was changed again during the January 2004 cabinet shuffle, when it became 'Women's Services, Seniors and Child Care' and Stephens was replaced by Ida Chong, who was appointed as Minister of State for Women's and Seniors' Services (CAWS 2004).

4 Although I do not explore the influence of governing parties' electoral performance in this chapter, it is worth noting the success in this regard enjoyed by the BC Liberal Party compared with that of the National Party in Aotearoa/New Zealand. The Liberals occupied a commanding position in the BC legislature following the 2001 election, having won in all but two of the province's 79 constituencies, whereas National's tenure in office during the 1990s resulted from less comprehensive victories at the polls. The different electoral vulnerabilities of each government flowing from these results may well have contributed to the disparate institutional fates of the two women's ministries, reinforcing the impact of the institutional and ideological variables that constitute the focus for my analysis in this article.

5 In British Columbia Penny Priddy, the first Minister of Women's Equality, sat on a number of key Cabinet committees including Treasury Board (Erickson 1996: 119); the first Minister of Women's Affairs in Aotearoa/New Zealand, who simultaneously served as Minister for Social Welfare, 'had high political credibility and was able to push her agenda effectively in Cabinet' (Sawer 1996: 19).

6 This was particularly notable in British Columbia where the final years of the NDP administration were plagued by ongoing scandal and negative publicity. Sue Hammell, who had replaced Priddy as Minister of Women's Equality in 1996, resigned in mid-1999 in the context of Premier Glen Clark's refusal to step down in response to allegations of improper conduct that swirled around him. In the less than two years between Hammell's resignation and the 2001 election there were three different Ministers of Women's Equality who moved

in and out of the position as part of wider Cabinet reshuffles undertaken by Clark, as he sought to hang on to his position, and his successor Ujjal Dosanjh, as he tried to put his own stamp on the party in preparation for the looming election. None of the three Women's Equality Ministers during this period were key 'players' within the party (although Jenny Kwan, who briefly served as Minister between July 1999 and February 2000, was to be one of only two NDP candidates elected in May 2001). For Aotearoa/New Zealand see Sawer 1996: 16.

7 In 1996 the population of Aotearoa/New Zealand was 3,618,302 (MWA 1998: 1); in the same year, the population of the province of British Columbia was 3,855,140 (MWE 1998c: 1).

8 One further similarity is that the Ministries of Women's Affairs and Women's Equality were both established in the context of a wider institutional recognition of identity-based interests. Thus, the governments of which they have been a part have also included ministries focused on Aboriginal peoples (and, less consistently, organizational units intended to address disability issues). At the same time, there are important differences in the constitutional status and institutional profile of Aboriginal peoples and interests across the two cases that may well have influenced the shape, relative prominence and impact of the discourse of 'special interests' in each. While space does not permit an adequate exploration of these interactions in the present chapter, they could usefully be taken up in further research; my thanks to the anonymous reviewers of my initial submission to the *Canadian Journal of Political Science* for their thoughts on this issue.

9 For accounts of forums that took place in various locations around the country written by feminist participants see 'Forum Fever', *Broadsheet* (January/February 1985): 12–18. The ministry estimated that in total 24,000 women participated (MWA 1986: 5).

10 These calculations are based on figures presented for the Ministry of Women's Equality in the annual *Estimates* published by the Ministry of Finance and Corporate Relations for the years 1996/97–2000/01.

11 In this context, it is interesting to note that in mid-2004 the provincial government consolidated all child care services within the Ministry of Children and Family Development (MCFD), including the $184 million for child care subsidies previously housed within Women's and Seniors' Services (see Rud 2004). This move can be interpreted as consistent in a number of ways with the analysis presented above. Having implemented a series of significant cuts and changes in the child care policy arena while it was located in the murky backwaters of CAWS, the provincial government could afford to reattach responsibility for child care to a more visible part of government (i.e., MCFD). Insofar as the associated budget line had enhanced the 'clout' enjoyed by Women's and Seniors' Services, this shift will serve to undermine further the latter's status and influence. And finally, the 'gender-diluting' function that I argue was served by the attachment of child care policy to Women's Services in the early days of CAWS is now being performed by 'Seniors' Services'; child care policy could thus be relocated without risking an enhanced focus on gender per se in the institutional unit that remains.

12 These two quotes from Shipley appear in, respectively, 'Shipley defends Women's Affairs Ministry', *The Dominion*, 29 May 1991: 2 and 'Govt pledges to keep women's ministry', *New Zealand Herald*, 28 May 1991: 5.

13 These calculations are based on figures presented in the annual *Reports* prepared by the Ministry of Women's Affairs for the years 1987/88–1989/90.

14 For example, in 1987/88 the ministry's 'Project Fund' received 180 applications; 76 were funded from the available budget of $50,000 (MWA 1988a: 8).

Ministry funding was also made available through Putea Pounamu, which involved a series of community-based projects designed to foster participation in public decision-making processes among Maori women. In 1989/90, these two funding pools provided a total of $187,000 to women in various communities (MWA 1990b: 14 and 23).

15 The continued funding provided by Women's and Seniors' Services for transition houses and other programmes and services for women and children who have been the targets of violence is highlighted by the government as evidence of its commitment to advancing women's interests. This is consistent with developments in other jurisdictions where the marginalization of women's policy agencies has been accompanied by a narrowing of their effective scope to policy and programmes addressing violence against women (sometimes alongside an interest in supporting women as entrepreneurs) under neoliberal or 'third way' governments (see, for example, Benn 2000; Chappell 1995; Malloy 1999; Sawer 1996).

16 This pattern continued with the replacement of Ida Chong by Wendy McMahon as the new Minister of State for Women's and Seniors' Services in a December 2004 cabinet shuffle. Like her predecessors, McMahon lacked prior cabinet experience at the time of her appointment, and her biographical statement makes no reference to experience in, or connections with, community-based women's groups (British Columbia 2004).

References

Anon. (1985) 'Forum fever', *Broadsheet* (January/February): 12–18.

Anon. (1991a) 'Shipley defends Women's Affairs Ministry', *The Dominion*, 29 May: 2.

Anon. (1991b) 'Govt pledges to keep women's ministry', *New Zealand Herald*, 28 May: 5.

Abigail, J. (1991) 'Letter to a new friend', in M. Cahill and C. Dann (eds) *Changing Our Lives: Women Working in the Women's Liberation Movement, 1970–1990*, Wellington: Bridget Williams Books.

BC CEDAW Group (2003) *British Columbia Moves Backwards on Women's Equality*. Online. Available at: www.fafia-afai.org/Bplus5/bcCEDAWreport012103.pdf (accessed 28 February 2003).

BC Coalition of Women's Centres (2003) *The Herstory, Risk and Survival of BC Women's Centres*. Online. Available at: www3.telus.net/bcwomen/Archives.html (accessed 15 January 2004).

BC Liberal Party (2001) *A New Era for British Columbia*, Vancouver: BC Liberal Party.

Benn, M. (2000) 'A short march through the institutions: reflections on New Labour's gender machinery', in A. Coote (ed.) *New Gender Agenda: Why Women Still Want More*, London: Institute for Public Policy Research.

Boston, J. (1999) 'New Zealand's welfare state in transition', in J. Boston, P. Dalziel, and S. St John (eds) *Redesigning the Welfare State in New Zealand: Problems, Policies, Prospects*, Auckland: Oxford University Press.

——, Martin, J., Pallot, J., and Walsh, P. (1996) *Public Management: The New Zealand Model*, Auckland: Oxford University Press.

British Columbia (Government of British Columbia) (2004) 'Honourable Wendy McMahon'. Online. Available at: www.prov.gov.bc.ca/prem/popt/exec/ (accessed 8 April 2005).

Brodie, J. (1995) *Politics on the Margins: Restructuring and the Canadian Women's Movement*, Halifax: Fernwood.

—— (2002) 'The great undoing: state formation, gender politics, and social policy in Canada', in C. Kingfisher (ed.) *Western Welfare in Decline: Globalization and Women's Poverty*, Philadelphia: University of Pennsylvania Press.

Bunkle, P. (1993) 'How the level playing field levelled women', in S. Kedgley and M. Varnham (eds) *Heading Nowhere in a Navy Blue Suit*, Wellington: Daphne Brasell Associates.

Burt, S. and Hardman, S.L. (2001) 'The case of disappearing targets: the Liberals and gender equality', in L.A. Pal (ed.) *How Ottawa Spends 2001–2002: Power in Transition*, Don Mills, Ontario: Oxford University Press.

Campbell, G. (1988) 'Marketing the ministry', *NZ Listener*, 6 August: 32–4.

CAWS (Ministry of Community, Aboriginal and Women's Services, Government of British Columbia) (2002) *Service Plan 2002/2003–2004/2005*, Victoria: The Ministry.

—— (2004) *Service Plan 2004/2005–2006/2007*, Victoria: The Ministry.

Chappell, L. (1995) 'Women's policy', in M. Laffin and M. Painter (eds) *Reform and Reversal: Lessons From the Coalition Government in New South Wales 1988–1995*, Melbourne: Macmillan.

—— (2002) 'The "femocrat" strategy: Expanding the repertoire of feminist activists', *Parliamentary Affairs*, 55: 85–98.

Clark, D. (2002) 'Neoliberalism and public service reform: Canada in comparative perspective', *Canadian Journal of Political Science*, 35: 771–93.

Clarke, B. (2004) 'Women's group funding severed', *Saanich News*, 5 March: 1 and 3.

Curtin, J.C. (1992) 'The Ministry of Women's Affairs: where feminism and public policy meet', unpublished M.A. thesis, University of Waikato, New Zealand.

—— and Sawer, M. (1996) 'Gender equity in the shrinking state: women and the great experiment', in F.G. Castles, R. Gerritsen, and J. Vowles (eds) *The Great Experiment: Labour Parties and Public Policy Transformation in Australia and New Zealand*, Auckland: Auckland University Press.

Eisenstein, H. (1996) *Inside Agitators: Australian Femocrats and the State*, Philadelphia: Temple University Press.

Erickson, L. (1996) 'Women and political representation in British Columbia', in R.K. Carty (ed.) *Politics, Policy, and Government in British Columbia*, Vancouver: UBC Press.

Finance (Ministry of Finance and Corporate Relations, Government of British Columbia) (2000) *Estimates: Fiscal Year Ending March 31, 2001*, Victoria: The Ministry.

Fuller, S. and Stephens, L. (2002) *Cost Shift: How British Columbians are Paying for Their Tax Cut*, Vancouver: Canadian Centre for Policy Alternatives – BC Office.

Grace, J. (1997) 'Sending mixed messages: gender-based analysis and the "status of women"', *Canadian Public Administration*, 40: 582–98.

Harder, L. (2003) *State of Struggle: Feminism and Politics in Alberta*, Edmonton: University of Alberta Press.

Iannello, K. (1992) *Decisions Without Hierarchy: Feminist Interventions in Organization Theory and Practice*, New York: Routledge.

Kelsey, J. (1995) *The New Zealand Experiment: A World Model for Structural Adjustment?*, Auckland: Auckland University Press.

Kingfisher, C. (2002) *Western Welfare in Decline: Globalization and Women's Poverty*, Philadelphia: University of Pennsylvania Press.

Larner, W. (1996) 'The "New Boys": restructuring New Zealand 1984–94', *Social Politics*, 3(1): 32–56.

—— (1997) ' "A means to an end": neoliberalism and state processes in New Zealand', *Studies in Political Economy*, 52: 7–38.

—— (2000) 'Neo-liberalism: policy, ideology, governmentality', *Studies in Political Economy*, 63: 5–25.

Laycock, D. (2002) *The New Right and Democracy in Canada: Understanding Reform and the Canadian Alliance*, Don Mills, Ontario: Oxford University Press.

Malloy, J. (1999) 'What makes a state advocacy structure effective? Conflicts between bureaucratic and social movement criteria', *Governance*, 12: 267–88.

McKinlay, R. (1990) 'Feminists in the bureaucracy', *Women's Studies Journal*, November: 72–95.

MWA (Ministry of Women's Affairs, Government of New Zealand) (1986) *Report of the Ministry of Women's Affairs for the Year Ended 31 March 1986*, Wellington: The Ministry.

—— (1987) *Post-Election Briefing*, Wellington: The Ministry.

—— (1988a) *Report of the Ministry of Women's Affairs for the Year Ended 31 March 1988*, Wellington: The Ministry.

—— (1988b) *Statement of Intent: 30 September 1988*, Wellington: The Ministry.

—— (1990a) *Briefing to the Incoming Government: October 1990*, Wellington: The Ministry.

—— (1990b) *Report of the Ministry of Women's Affairs for the Transitional Quarter Ended 30 June 1989 and for the Year Ended 30 June 1990*, Wellington: The Ministry.

—— (1998) *Status of Women in New Zealand*, Wellington: The Ministry.

MWE (Ministry of Women's Equality, Government of British Columbia) (1995) *Business Plan 1995/96*, Victoria: The Ministry.

—— (1998a) *96/97 97/98 Annual Report*, Victoria: The Ministry.

—— (1998b) *98/99 Business Plan*, Victoria: The Ministry.

—— (1998c) *Women Count: A Statistical Profile of Women in British Columbia (3rd edition)*, Victoria: The Ministry.

—— (1999) *98/99 Annual Report*, Victoria: The Ministry.

—— (2001a) *2001/02–2003/04 Performance Plan*, Victoria: The Ministry.

—— (2001b) *Annual Performance Report 2000–2001*, Victoria: The Ministry.

Nathan, J. (1989) 'Establishment of the Ministry of Women's Affairs: a case study of the creation of a new organisation', unpublished M.A. thesis, Victoria University, Wellington.

O'Regan, M. and Varnham, M. (1992) 'Daring or deluded? A case study in feminist management', in R. Du Plessis (ed.) *Feminist Voices: Women's Studies Texts for Aotearoa/New Zealand*, Auckland: Oxford University Press.

Pearce, D. (1996) 'CEOs tame over-the-top workload by job-sharing', *Victoria Times-Colonist*, 17 December: C1.

Rose, N. (1999) *Powers of Freedom: Reframing Political Thought*, Cambridge: Cambridge University Press.

Rosier, P. (1989) 'Approaches to efficiency and effectiveness in government departments', *Broadsheet*, 169: 9.

Rud, J. (2004) 'Government to overhaul B.C. child-care services', *Victoria Times-Colonist*, 30 April, A5.

Sawer, M. (1996) *Femocrats and Ecorats: Women's Policy Machinery in Australia, Canada and New Zealand*, Geneva: United Nations Research Institute for Social Development.

—— (1999) 'The watchers within: women and the Australian state', in L. Hancock (ed.), *Women, Public Policy and the State*, South Yarra: Macmillan Education Australia.

—— (2002) 'Governing for the mainstream: implications for community representation', *Australian Journal of Public Administration*, 61(1): 39–49.

—— (2003) 'Populism and public choice: the construction of women as a "special interest"', paper presented at Australasian Political Studies Association Conference, Hobart, Australia, 2003.

Schwartz, H.M. (1997) 'Reinvention and retrenchment: lessons from the application of the New Zealand model to Alberta, Canada', *Journal of Policy Analysis and Management*, 16: 405–22.

Squires, J. and Wickham-Jones, M. (2002) 'Mainstreaming in Westminster and Whitehall: from Labour's Ministry for Women to the Women and Equality Unit', *Parliamentary Affairs*, 55: 57–70.

State Services Commission (2003) 'Capability reviews of the Ministry of Youth Affairs and the Ministry of Women's Affairs', paper presented to the Cabinet Policy Committee, 6 August 2003. Online. Available at: www.ssc.govt.nz/upload/downloadable_files/Capability_Reviews_MYA_and_MWA.pdf (accessed 12 September 2003).

Stephen, K. (2000) 'Catalysts for change? The effectiveness of state agencies in promoting equality', in F. Beveridge, S. Nott, and K. Stephen (eds) *Making Women Count: Integrating Gender into Law and Policy-making*, Aldershot: Dartmouth Publishing.

Stetson, D.M. and Mazur, A.G. (eds) (1995) *Comparative State Feminism*, Thousand Oaks: Sage Publications.

Teghtsoonian, K. (2000) 'Gendering policy analysis in the government of British Columbia: strategies, possibilities and constraints', *Studies in Political Economy*, 61: 105–27.

—— (2003) 'W(h)ither women's equality? Neoliberalism, institutional change and public policy in British Columbia', *Policy, Organisation and Society*, 22(1): 26–47.

—— (2004) 'Neoliberalism and gender analysis mainstreaming in Aotearoa/New Zealand', *Australian Journal of Political Science*, 39: 267–84.

Vancouver City Council (Director of Social Planning, Vancouver City Council) (2003) 'Administrative report: impact of provincial cuts on women's advocacy groups'. Online. Available at: www.city.vancouver.bc.ca/ctyclerk/cclerk/20030327/csb6.htm (accessed 20 April 2004).

Washington, S. (1988) 'Great expectations: the Ministry of Women's Affairs and Public Policy', *Race, Gender, Class*, July: 7–16.

Weldon, S.L. (2002) 'Beyond bodies: institutional sources of representation for women in democratic policymaking', *Journal of Politics*, 64: 1153–74.

Young, A. (2003) 'Brash drops women's affairs role', *New Zealand Herald Online*, 3 November. Online. Available at: www.nzherald.co.nz (accessed 9 December 2003).

8 Gender inequality and feminist activism in institutions

Challenges of marginalization and feminist 'fading'

Benita Roth

In this chapter, I address the question of what is likely to happen to feminist activists situated in male-dominated institutions through a review of selected previously published case studies by feminist scholars. I consider how the experiences of feminist activists challenge the perspective advanced in Roberto Michels' classic work on the co-option of activists within formal institutions and suggest that it is more useful to see their experiences as a process of 'feminist fading' rather than as co-option.

An understanding of gender is central to the arguments advanced in this chapter and here it is understood as a social institution predicated on inequality that permeates and organizes all aspects of social life (Lorber 1994). As a system of social ordering that generates inequalities, gender has specific manifestations in specific sites, and, given its character as an omnipresent 'background feature' (Ridgeway 2001) of social interaction, no site absolves actors of their obligation to 'do gender' in acceptable ways. Nonetheless, the obligation to perpetuate gender rules is often obscured; within concrete organizational and institutional settings there are 'gendered processes' whose unequal character is obscured through 'neutral, asexual discourse' (Acker 1990: 140). But feminists have notably challenged gender inequality in the male-dominated institutions and organizations in which they find themselves. Feminists in these institutions have organized on the basis of their rights as women and as citizens (West and Blumberg 1990; also Vickers in this volume) and have made claims based on being members of the particular institutions/organizations they inhabit. They may be situated within such settings because they share political identities, political statuses and/or a number of political interests with men. It is that which is not shared with men that generates feminist activism.[1]

As Vickers notes in Chapter 2 of this volume, the concept of 'a politics of women's interests' was at times dismissed by many feminists because of its universalistic underpinnings and its potential for erasing differences among groups of women. As I discuss the activism of women within institutions below, it should be borne in mind that women's being part of institutions mitigates to some degree worries about the construction of universalistic interests; institutions shape and particularize the interests of the women involved in them (although, of course, institutions' actions impact the lives of women beyond institutional boundaries in ways that institutional feminists may not be able to foresee). Feminists within institutions thread their way between commonality and difference. As I argue below, their 'outsider within' (Hill Collins 1998) status creates differences between them and other institutional actors, that is, men. At the same time, the similar positioning of women vis-à-vis men creates a locally situated commonality of interest. Vickers makes a second point about the word 'interests' itself connoting women's willingness to work within the system; many feminists have worried that such willingness would lead to the co-option of feminist politics and agendas. As I will argue, fears of co-option have been greatly exaggerated. Instead, I suggest that a process of what I call 'feminist fading' has occurred. This process continues to emphasize the importance of working toward a feminist agenda which is long-lasting and systematic. It suggests that if we wish to see large-scale shifts in the social organization of gender inequality, then we have to engage with existing institutions. Indeed, the fear of co-option of feminist politics on the part of some feminists might be blunted by the presence of 'inside agitators' (Eisenstein 1996) who have picked up the gauntlet and challenged male domination from within.

Although much sociological literature has focused on the co-option of activists by institutions, women and especially feminists within institutions have the inescapable status of being what Patricia Hill Collins has called 'outsiders within', individuals who find themselves 'in marginal locations between groups of varying power' (Hill Collins 1998: 5). As Hill Collins describes it, the experiences of outsiders within are riddled with contradictions; they may experience partial, sometimes only nominal, acceptance by institutions, all the while conscious of the provisionality of this acceptance. Outsiders within are further affected by having oppositional knowledge, an understanding of non-mainstream, even hidden, cultural realities and discourses. But as difficult as the outsider within position is, improvements in women's lives rest, for the most part, on engagement with and entrance into institutions. As the introduction and the chapters in this volume make clear, women's interests (however self-defined) cannot be exclusively pursued outside of established institutions, and I would further argue that all but the most male-dominated institutions gather together women who can then self-organize to challenge existing power arrangements of exclusion. In other words, institutions can create opportunities for similarly situated women to define localized women's interests and goals, goals that may include transforming the institutions themselves. The dilemma for women's and especially feminists' praxis within male-dominated institutions is that while such praxis is essential to improving women's lives, within these institutional settings, gender inequality and the specific obstacles it generates must be faced. Feminist activists within institutions may find themselves marginalized or they may find themselves accepted but see their agenda subject to 'fading'. In either case it is hard to see how feminists can safely abandon institutions.

The Michels debate: gender inequality as internal exclusion

The status of being an outsider within is, of course, not limited to feminist activists who enter institutions: it is also the classic position of the (non-gendered, and therefore assumed to be male) grass-roots activist who is allowed into institutionalized spaces. The institutionalization of grass-roots opposition has been a central concern of social movement scholarship, and the debate is most often centred on the problematics first posed by Roberto Michels' (1959) classic examination of the fate of the German Social Democratic Party in the early twentieth century. Michels suggested that outsiders who attain some measure of institutional power are co-opted by the institutions they inhabit, and they inevitably form oligarchies – concentrations of power among a select few members. These oligarchies then lose touch with the mass base that brought them to power in the first place. Growing conservativism and deradicalization of progressive agendas ensue. Following Michels, the question of the costs for social movement actors of institutionalizing is usually seen as an exchange of institutional power for the vitiation of movement actors' progressive agendas (see especially Piven and Cloward 1977).

Social movement scholars have broken down the dynamic that Michels described into analytically separable components; for the purposes of this essay, and for the purposes of establishing a gendered critique of Michels, I will stress only two of these. First, co-option itself is understood by Michels to be a voluntary process by which (male) former activists assent to a shift in loyalty from the grass-roots to the institution itself. Second, former activists' goals are displaced (Zald and Ash 1966) and replaced by goals more suitable to accommodation with the institution. This displacement of goals is what constitutes 'deradicalization' by activists and it is, in part, what distances them from the grass-roots (which presumably stays radical). This trajectory of co-option and deradicalization is assumed to be almost inevitable and deviation from it, when it occurs, is assumed to need explanation by scholars. Among activists, the Michels model is also assumed to be the norm. Cautionary tales may be told of once fiery agitators who had their edges blunted after 'selling out' to institutions. The 'sell-out' is a stock figure of protest politics, a defanged and sometimes dangerous player who is often seen as worse than the original adversary for having turned her or his back on compatriots in struggle.

Critics of Michels' model have taken issue with its assumptions of unilinearity of outcomes and with the inherent morality play at the centre of the institutionalization dynamic – that is, the assumed co-option, deradicalization of, and 'selling out' by former activists (see, among others, Clemens 1993; Jenkins 1977; Katzenstein 1998a, 1998b; Meyer and Tarrow 1998; Staggenborg 1988; Zald and Ash 1966).[2] But *gendered* critiques of Michels have looked beyond the issue of unilinearity of outcomes and further explored the *gendered* assumptions that lay behind Michels' model. Clemens (1993) and Katzenstein (1998a) have argued that women's activism, especially feminist activism, is not well described by Michels (or his critics) because of a failure to recognize women's social location of inequality. Clemens argued that Michels' vision of insurgent party activists seeking to maintain themselves in power in order to feed the members of their households was based on the model of a male breadwinner. In her work on 'first wave' US feminism, Clemens showed that nineteenth and early twentieth century middle-class suffragist women did not have such 'breadwinner' pressures and thus were 'insulated' from the co-option pressures that Michels envisioned. Clemens makes a further and even more fundamentally gendered critique of the unilinear Michels model, arguing that to the extent that women were excluded from formal political inclusion – to the extent that they were political outsiders – their adoption of mainstream forms of political organizing had potentially radical consequences. The adoption by women of seemingly conservative institutional forms, along with their inclusion in formerly all-male institutional preserves, had radical consequences because they had been excluded on the basis of being women. According to Clemens, Michels ignored the fact that the inclusion of the socially unequal 'other' had inevitably disruptive consequences.

The assertion of the inescapable effects of women's unequal social location is also key to Katzenstein's (1990, 1998a, 1998b) critiques of Michels in her work on institutional feminist protest in the US military and the US Catholic Church, about which more will be said below. Katzenstein maintained that the assumed dichotomy between inside and outsider forms of political challenge – that is, the assumed demarcation between institutional and extra-institutional politics – has not and does not describe women's activism. She argues that women's constrained social location has often led them away from confrontational extra-institutional political tactics (i.e. the strike, the mass demonstration), where the costs of confronting authority were very high. Women activists, because of their precarious social position, were much more likely to be found inside institutional spaces, chipping away at very specific kinds of male privilege. Michels' model has nothing to say about – has no way to explain, in fact – insurgent protest coming from *within* institutional spaces and, as Katzenstein has shown, insurgent feminist activism can come from outsiders within, from women who as women within institutions have been treated unfairly. Consequently, Michels' understanding of the institutional pressures on entering activists was devoid of a gendered understanding of women's (and consequently feminists') mobilizations within institutions.

Informed by the gendered critiques of Michels that take seriously the inescapable difference that women's unequal social location make for their institutional experiences, I argue below that in actual practice, institutional co-option may be the least of feminists' worries. Women's social position of inequality necessitates their engagement within institutional spaces, but structural gender inequality transcends institutional spaces and cannot help but impact the terms of interaction for outsiders within. Michels' feminist critics suggest that co-option and deradicalization may not be modal, or even very common, outcomes for institutionalized feminist protest. Other outcomes exist because institutions vary in their response to feminist agitation.

Institutional responses to feminist agitation within range from outright hostility, to the middle ground of 'post-feminism', where a 'depoliticized' kind of piecemeal feminist consciousness informs some aspects of praxis (Stacey 1990: 348), to 'feminist-friendliness', where members take 'a public stance of openness to feminist identities and ideas' (Roth 1998: 132–3).[3] Relative hostility and relative friendliness may be seen as resting on the degree of legitimacy that feminists are allowed within the institution/organization. While legitimacy is not the same thing as friendliness to feminism, friendly settings will legitimize feminist praxis more easily and quickly. Hostile institutions will either not accept the legitimacy of feminist praxis, or they will confer nominal legitimacy on feminist praxis without thorough commitments to a feminist agenda. I define legitimacy as the establishment of feminists' rights to make claims on other members' energies, with all that this entails – the right to use an organization's time, space, money and organs of communication – such that there is explicit acknowledgment of feminists' right to continue to be counted as members of the larger group. Legitimacy might really be thought of as *legitimization*, a contingent process that is normative and, generally speaking, explicitly acknowledged to be taking or to have taken place. But legitimization of the outsider within is always unstable; for example, institutions may confer partial or merely nominal legitimacy on feminists working within them, leading to dynamics of *marginalization* that limit effectiveness. In friendlier institutional spaces where feminists have gained some or a great deal of legitimacy as collective actors, co-option still poorly describes the structural, and thus far from volitional, processes to which feminists are subject. I call this second set of structural processes feminist *fading*, and distinguish it from both marginalization and Michels-style co-option, with the latter's implications of instrumentality on the part of both institutions and grass-roots actors.

In the discussion that follows, I contrast the problem of feminists' marginalization within hostile institutions – the impossibility of institutional assimilation – with feminist fading – a structural problem of the fading over time of a feminist political agenda that I argue exists especially in 'friendly' institutional spaces. Both marginalization and feminist fading follow from male domination of mainstream institutions, from the unacknowledged advantages that men have in institutions, and from the structural disadvantages women face as unequal outsiders within.

Marginalization within hostile institutions: the impossibility of co-option

In hostile institutions, where it is likely that legitimacy for feminist praxis has been hard-won and grudgingly granted, feminist activists and their agenda are often marginalized. This is not surprising but, as noted, it complicates the picture of the easy assimilation of activists into specific institutional contexts. Unlike Michels' assumptions of easily co-opted (male) activists, feminist praxis within hostile institutions is often generated from dynamics of gender marginalization experienced on the inside because gender inequality is part of the entire society within which the institutions exist.

It is hard to think of two less hospitable contexts for feminist organizing than the Catholic Church and the US military. These two long-standing, highly formalized, and politically conservative institutions have nonetheless seen feminist mobilizations from within that are the focus of Katzenstein's (1990, 1998a, 1998b) work. Katzenstein characterized the obstacles facing feminists in such unfriendly and highly institutionalized settings as 'momentous' (1990: 27, 36). Nonetheless, she found that Catholic feminists organized a discursive challenge to the Church from within the institution which fostered networks of insurgent feminist religious women and gave them spaces from which to practice their version of Catholicism. Katzenstein contrasted the challenges made by Catholic women in their institutional contexts to those made by US military feminists, who had been working since the early 1950s for parity for women in the armed forces. Military feminists saw their work supported by the outside legitimacy conveyed by federal government directives urging the military to pursue goals of gender equality and yet they were thwarted by the armed forces' masculinist structure and internal culture. In each case that Katzenstein studied feminist challengers experienced marginalization.

Within the Catholic Church, changes in the role of women instituted as a result of the Second Vatican Council in 1962, coupled with the rise in social movement activism of the 1960s, led to 'cross-fertilization' between feminist women in the church (especially activist nuns) and the feminist movement (1990: 37). In particular, church leaders' opposition to the call from Catholic feminists for the ordination of women was a catalyst leading to further calls for systemic change within the church.[4] Facing an entrenched patriarchal hierarchy, Catholic feminists debated the question of loyalty to the existing institution and formed an oppositional network/community within what became for them a redefined church. In the end, the church was redefined for the Catholic feminists, but not for the Catholic hierarchy. Feminists remained a distinct minority presence without much institutional power. The discursive nature of the challenge they mounted led them to channel their energy into a primary concern for women's issues and women's spirituality. Due to the discursive nature of the challenge – that is, the way that religious practice can continue among groups of women, even if the practice itself is not sanctioned by the institution – Catholic feminists were able to 'stay Catholic' but they were extremely marginalized within the greater Church.

Such a discursive 'exiting-within' was clearly not an option for US military feminists – not if they wanted to stay soldiers. Feminist activism within the feminist-unfriendly US military, where women activists sometimes even eschewed the label 'feminist', was nonetheless encouraged by federal law, which gave military feminists the legitimacy that they needed to organize (Katzenstein 1998b: Chapter 3). The hostility of the military elite to feminist protest was thus mitigated by its very conservative and rule-bound nature. Legally imposed mandates for equity and the legalistic traditions of the military played a role in fostering and then sustaining some level of feminist activism, which predated US second wave grass-roots feminist protest but was bolstered by it. Feminist challenges to the military were prefigured by the military's Defense Advisory Committee on Women in the Services (DACOWITS), formed in 1951 during the Korean War. DACOWITS was later used by feminists to challenge the military's relationship to the women within its midst. Within an institution structurally designed to channel any form of dissent into chains of command, feminists were able to form networks that highlighted problematic issues. DACOWITS became more outspoken, and '(t)he language of equality and discrimination started to appear repeatedly in the committee's proceedings' (Katzenstein 1998b: 59). For example, outspoken leadership in DACOWITS took up and criticized the culture of machismo in promoting women's lack of access to equal opportunity and susceptibility to harassment. But, as Katzenstein noted, military feminists have very much narrowed their demands in accordance both with federal directives and military intransigence, and they have made little headway in changing the 'meaning-making' around gender inequality within the institution (1998b: 171). With the narrowing of claims came a ceding of ground in meaning-making, and hence a diminution in effectiveness, making military feminists' activism more reactive rather than agenda-setting.[5]

The marginalization of feminist activists within institutions can occur immediately, or over time. The consequences of marginalization as an ongoing process are well-addressed in Dafna Izraeli's (1990) study of labour feminists in pre-state Israel's umbrella labour union, the *Histadrut*. In 1921, Jewish feminists in then-Palestine formed the Women Workers' Council (WWC) within the *Histadrut*. The WWC was to be an internal organizational entity that would work to represent women's interests. Never particularly popular with the male *Histadrut* leadership, and never universally supported by the few women in *Histadrut* leadership, the WWC came to be seen during the 1920s as a problem for the *Histadrut*, insofar as its very existence meant that the *Histadrut* was failing to successfully organize all workers. The WWC existed in a climate that became more and more hostile to it because it represented the *Histadrut*'s shortcomings.

The WWC won some concessions from the *Histadrut*, but changes in organizational structure, and the replacement of WWC leader Ada Maimon with (ironically) Golda Meir – who was approved by the male leadership and represented a different, non-feminist political generation within the *Histadrut* – led to the marginalization of the WWC, and the disappearance of women's issues from *Histadrut* convention agendas. Eventually, the WWC became a venue for the future marginalization of women who wanted to be active in the *Histadrut*; they were channelled into the WWC as it devolved into a more traditional 'women and children' social service organization. As Izraeli wrote, the existence of the WWC:

> reinforced the categorical treatment of women at the same time it monitored their public careers. Women in the Labor party ... were 'expected' to rise through the ranks of the WWC, while its leadership acted as gatekeepers between the female enclave and the male establishment, allowing only a selected few, sponsored by them, to pass.
>
> (Izraeli 1990: 155)

Thus, the WWC legacy in the increasingly hostile environment of the *Histadrut* was one of contributing not only to the marginalization of feminists but to that of *all* women in the organization. Here, we see an example of male institutional elites essentializing women's interests to their own advantage. The ease with which the male *Histradrut* elite transformed originally self-organized women's interests into something very different testifies to the inescapable otherness that feminist institutional actors face as a result of gender inequality.

Structural pressures versus voluntary deradicalization: feminist fading in friendly institutions

Although certainly to be preferred, even being in 'friendly' institutions does not remove all challenges to feminists in achieving their objectives. Institutionalized settings that are friendly to feminism create opportunities for the stabilization of a feminist agenda, but at some cost, and the origins of these costs are ill-described by the Michels model. The costs themselves are driven by the pervasive nature of society-wide gender inequality and by the longstanding character of institutions. Feminists coming from outside who use institutions to consolidate lasting social change may in fact be very conscious of the dangers of deradicalization, but may nonetheless face the problem of what I have described in previous work as feminist fading: the waning over time of a feminist agenda that stems from activists' shift in the locus of their work from the grass-roots to institutions (see Roth 2004).

As I see it, fading occurs for two main reasons. First, fading occurs because institutions and the offices within them simply outlast the people who fill them, and so grass-roots activists can be replaced, rendering once institutional feminist spaces less feminist. Second, activists who enter institutions will tend to substitute ties to the grass-roots with the institutional ties given by their new positions *in order to be effective on behalf of grass-roots constituencies.* On this second point, it is important to acknowledge that the imposition upon feminist activists of institutional lines of accountability become new structural – and not voluntary – features in the institutionally situated feminists' landscapes. Conflicts can be expected to ensue for new outsiders within. They face a structural and institutional landscape that changes their day-to-day practice of accountable politics.

Ethnographic looks at feminists working within friendly institutions show a complex picture of activists conscious of the risks of deradicalization that entering institutions engenders. The dynamics of feminist fading are shown in Eisenstein's (1995, 1996) study of Australian 'femocrats' (feminist bureaucrats), grass-roots feminists who became legitimized representatives of their movement within the Australian Labor government beginning in the 1970s and continuing to the present day. The feminist alliance with the state – or more accurately, with the Labor government that had captured the state – led to the implementation of policies that originated in the grass-roots feminist movement. According to Eisenstein, femocrats, who formed a reasonably tight network within multiple levels of the Australian state, were successful in four broad areas. First, they were able to establish a 'women's policy machinery, a network of women in the state and federal bureaucracies whose official duties were to bring the concerns of women and their needs to the attention of government for redress'. Second, the feminist foothold in the state allowed for close co-operation with grass-roots activists seeking funding for women's movement projects. Third, 'femocrats worked to stretch the limits of reform by redefining women's issues as mainstream issues' and fourth, femocrats 'won widespread acceptance for a feminist analysis of women's situation, and they established knowledge of women's issues as an important and respected form of expertise' (1996: 43).

Femocrats initially saw themselves as accountable to the grass-roots in setting an agenda on women's issues, and state openness to femocrats meant that they successfully represented these interests in various state arenas, creating 'an astonishing variety of women's projects across Australia' (Eisenstein 1995: 7). Eisenstein believes that femocrats to some extent weathered the mid-1990s state restructuring and shift in Australian politics from left/Labor to neoliberal governments at both the federal and state levels (see 1996: especially Chapters 13 and 14);[6] but she also found that in a stable bureaucracy, offices at first filled with the former grass-roots feminists become separate from the movement that worked to create them. In practical terms, what this meant was that the first occupant of an office was a feminist with movement experience and movement ties, but this was not necessarily true of those who followed her:

> The institutionalization of the femocracy meant also that there was a new generation of femocrats, some of them born within the bureaucracy, who lacked a background in feminist activism. Keeping in touch with the women's movement, then, became problematic.
>
> (Eisenstein 1996: 94)

Eisenstein noted that, at times, the vacating of a state or federal office occurred because the first femocrat occupant sought to broaden the mandate for women's issues, and moved from women's units into other spaces in the bureaucracy (see the discussion on pages 170–4). These moves were made by femocrats in part to avoid marginalization in women's units, but in moving to new positions, old ones came up for grabs. As Eisenstein pointed out, even the term 'femocrat' shifted in meaning from the 1970s to the 1990s. In the 1970s, the term was defined as 'a feminist woman who had entered the public service bureaucracy to advance the cause of women and whose responsibilities were defined in this manner by the male bureaucrats or politicians who appointed her'. In the 1980s it meant 'a powerful woman in government administration, with an ideological and political commitment to feminism' but by the 1990s, it referred to any powerful woman in state bureaucracy, regardless of her politics (Eisenstein 1996: 68).

Eisenstein's study also showed that Australian femocrats did increasingly supplant the logic of the bureaucracy for the logic of the street in order to be effective bureaucrats and that this dynamic played out chiefly in matters of institutional accountability. Formal lines of accountability for femocrats only existed between femocrats and the government, and this connection to the bureaucracy was made more intense by their positions chiefly being appointed ones. There were, of course, no comparable lines of accountability to the outside movement; femocrats were forced to improvise vis-à-vis accountability to the grass roots. The day-to-day experiences of actually doing the bureaucratic job exacerbated the accountability problem. Femocrats had to participate in closed-doors decision-making processes typical of bureaucracies and at odds with the participatory and democratic ethic of movements. In short, femocrats in the feminist-friendly Australian state found themselves within institutions where relationships were formalized and lines of accountability were clear. In contrast, the ties and accountability to an outside and weakening social movement were not formalized, and thus likely to be subordinated in practice.

The matter of the need to be accountable within institutions generated contradictions for institutionally situated feminists that do not stem from a will toward co-option and deradicalization. The femocrats Eisenstein interviewed feared 'losing touch' with the grass-roots movement (1995: 80), but 'losing touch' itself was grounded in institutional practice. As public servants, femocrats had to choose between being 'mandarins' or 'missionaries'; they could either act to win 'the confidence of their colleagues by playing by the bureaucratic rules' or they could act as 'missionaries' who 'fought publicly for the issues they believed in', and therefore endanger their relationships with colleagues and thus their effectiveness within bureaucracies (1996: 87). Femocrats recognized this choice as a structural one, and thus not about particular changes in their own personally held political ideologies.

Accountability to the state as such may in fact be *necessary* for institutionally based feminists, and although accountability to the grass-roots may be equally necessary, it is a separate process. In post-apartheid South Africa, state-based feminists confronted contradictions generated by the need to restructure lines of accountability to both the state and the grass-roots, as Gay Seidman (2003) argued. South African femocrats worked within the 'South African Commission on Gender Equality' (henceforth, the commission), which was founded in 1996. As part of the newly formed state's 'national machinery for women' (Seidman 2003: 544), the commission oversaw a series of spaces intended to inject gender issues into policy discussions; it was structured as a horizontal entity that would 'simultaneously monitor and stimulate transformation in South African society' (2003: 545). As in the Australian case, in South Africa one of the questions for femocrats within the state was 'to whom are we accountable?'

In contrast to the Australian case, the commission, as a horizontal entity, was not structurally accountable to anyone in particular within the state. Commissioners were handed considerable leeway in deciding whom they would represent and how they would define women's interests. Rather than use this leeway to maintain lines of communication with the organized grass-roots women's movement, Seidman showed that commissioners moved away from an existing grass-roots and largely urban-based feminist agenda; instead, they constructed new projects aimed at mobilizing poor rural women. According to Seidman, this turn to the mobilization of a new constituency of women over representing an already existing one, coupled with a lack of accountability within the state structure, led to the de-emphasis of work on controversial feminist issues (e.g. sex work) as commissioners tried to make feminism palatable to a new rural constituency. This newly sought constituency was in fact less likely – because it was poor and rural – to hold commissioners accountable for their actions. In this case, then, the relationship that femocrats had with the state was not bureaucratized as to lines of accountability; the state itself provided no mechanism for holding individual commissioners accountable for an overall agenda, or even for public statements. Commissioners were thus neither marginalized nor co-opted by the South African state, and it is debatable whether the substitution of a mandate for mobilization over representation constituted deradicalization; certainly commissioners did not think so. The feminist fading they experienced was arguably the result of too much responsibility, or, seen from another side, of badly structured power within the institution. Seidman noted that by 2001 the commission's latitude within the state did allow it to move back toward making a different set of connections with the organized and urbanized grass-roots women's movement; commissioners restructured their lines of accountability to the existing feminist constituency. This restructuring led to new appointments of 'strong feminist activists' (Seidman 2003: 560) who took firmer stances on controversial but established feminist issues. The commission may have reversed the effects of feminist fading engendered by its structural independence from both the state *and* grass-roots. Seidman is understandably cautious in her conclusions about the commission's ability to deal with conflicting mandates and argued that other state feminists may face similar conflicts generated by women's unequal social location.

Conclusion: institutional feminist projects and gender inequality in institutions

In the preceding discussion, I have focused on dynamics of feminist marginalization and fading within institutional spaces, neither of which were outcomes envisioned by Michels, or by his critics who lacked a gendered critique. By looking at a small number of cases, I hoped to make clear that gender inequality militates against any model that sees co-option and deradicalization as inevitable consequences of engagement with male-dominated institutions. As Vickers makes clear in Chapter 2 of this volume, questions remain about lines of accountability of institutionally situated feminists and those they supposedly represent; still, the presence of women in male-dominated institutions is crucial. I wish to extend this insight in order to suggest that: (1) feminist praxis in male-dominated institutions is essential and will continue; and (2) that gender inequality is inescapable in these settings and that this fact will always have an impact on feminists' success within male-dominated institutions.

Regarding feminist praxis in male-dominated institutions, it seems clear that institutions that accommodate feminist activism may do so in unfriendly, tokenistic, or genuinely inclusive ways. But there are few alternatives to entering institutional spaces when it comes to getting certain things done. As Chappell (2002: 3) noted in the beginning of her work on feminists in Australia and Canada, '[f]eminist activists cannot avoid the state', or indeed any other institutions that organize and/or provide services to large segments of society. Besides being resource-rich, longstanding institutions gather together interested parties who develop investments in them. Despite marginalization and fading, feminists have those investments as well, and need to feel entitled to enter and change institutions from within. Reality informs us that it does not always make sense – and may, in fact, rarely make sense – to exit male-dominated institutions in order to form autonomous feminist institutions. It is hard, for example, to envision a newly 'feminist' military – in fact many of us may not wish to, even if it were devoted solely to defence – but it is equally hard to build (feminist) schools, labour unions, or states from scratch.

Second, it is clear that some of the stories above of feminist activism in institutions are success stories. Feminists' goals in different institutions are of necessity institution-specific, as are challengers' definitions of 'success' (Katzenstein 1998b: see discussion on pages 16–22). Feminists, no less than other activists, are almost always dealing with half measures, compromises, and getting less than they want, and may not even agree among themselves about what they have won. But even in hostile circumstances, feminists have been able to make various degrees of headway in advancing their issues. For example, Catholic feminists may have been marginalized by the Church's hierarchy, but they have found each other and have been able to establish their own communities of religious practice. Feminists in the US military may have been stymied by military culture, but they have won the ability to legitimately self-organize, to represent other women within the institution and to take up a specific agenda of women's interests that is separable from the one defined for them by military hierarchy. Eisenstein's 'femocrats' have become a permanent part of the Australian political landscape, and while they regarded their struggles with mixed emotions, they charted many successes (see 1996: especially the conclusion). As Seidman noted, the space provided by the post-apartheid South African state for feminists may have been badly structured but the state provided enough room for the reconstruction of a feminist agenda in order to better balance conflicting mandates. In these latter two cases of 'state feminism', we see perhaps a greater measure of activists' success than in non-state institutions, but the reader is cautioned to consider the small, and therefore only suggestive, nature of my case selection.[7] In general, questions of 'what is success' need to be tempered with the recognition that even 'success' in male-dominated sites may engender other problems for feminist activists, given that gender inequality on a societal level will not have vanished.

Feminist activism in male-dominated institutional sites will also tend to be self-limiting because the institution will determine what kind of literal and figurative space will be provided. In the case of pre-state Israel, the *Histadrut* made less and less room for its Women's Workers' Council, ultimately emptying it of its feminist character and turning it into a social service agency (Izraeli 1990). In the United States, the future marginalization of military feminists is an open question; the US federal mandate for gender equality continues, but the military has historically wavered on equal rights under different presidential administrations, and many (male) members are still openly hostile to women's full participation. One crucial factor that can help overcome institutional limits on feminist success remains the pressure on institutions from those on the outside. Australian femocrats were keenly aware that their bureaucratic power was dependent on a vibrant grass-roots movement, and that their power was curtailed when the grass-roots grew quieter (for further discussion see Sawer, Chapter 6, this volume). As one femocrat put it, '[w]e still … haven't told anybody else there's not a women's movement yet' (Eisenstein 1996: 202).

Lastly, in returning to gendered critiques of Michels' expectations vis-à-vis the institutionalization of opposition, we can see that it is the gender system of inequality that constructs women as institutional outsiders within. The gendered critique developed by scholars and extended here shows that Michels' view of activists in institutions rests on the assumption that the *only* difference between activists and those inside is that of *class* power. Class as a social location is mutable in theory and in practice; the lower class status held by an individual male activist is subject to erasure by the very opportunities and compensation that are given by having the chance to come inside.[8] In contrast, outsiders within are not so easily digestible – the societal inequalities that make them different, such as gender (or race/ethnicity), are not mutable for the individuals entering institutions. It is the immutable otherness of gender that otherwise worthy sociological critiques of Michels' unilinearity miss, and that gendered critiques highlight. Gender status is not subject to easy modification. Feminist outsiders within remain outsiders – women stay women no matter how invisible they try to make themselves. Feminist women claiming rights as women and members of institutions make themselves all the more visible; they make themselves even more into *women,* that which is socially other and socially unequal. If they then use this indigestible 'otherness' to highlight an institution's contradictions (following Clemens' argument), this is more likely to lead to marginalization or fading than co-option or deradicalization. In short, the latter two processes are the 'privileges' that belong to those that the institution can easily digest.

Attention to these endemic challenges to feminists' and women's effectiveness within male-dominated institutions is salutary, and should not lead us to 'throwing in the towel' regarding the possibilities of structural change. In a political and social world which largely excludes women from institutions and restricts their self-organization, entrance into powerful institutions and access to 'male' forms of organizing can have transformative effects. As Chappell (2002: 177) has recently written, '[b]y intervening in institutions, feminists are involving themselves in a subversive act'. It was my aim in this discussion to provide some understanding of the challenges that face feminist activists in institutions so that we may think realistically about the institutional possibilities for feminist activism. Since institutions are at all points in time 'gendered', then, following Acker (1990: 146), it will continue to be true that 'advantage and disadvantage, exploitation and control, action and emotion, meaning and identity' will be arranged such that women will face obstacles to being full participants within them. This makes the existence of feminist praxis in institutions, hostile or friendly, 'an ongoing and unstable project' (Ostrander 1999: 641) which is nonetheless essential.

Notes

1 I use West and Blumberg's definition of feminist activism precisely because they emphasize the claiming of rights on the basis of being women *and* being citizens, that is, on the basis of that which is different about women's situation and that which is shared with men. I would only note that defining 'feminist' activism within institutions is a complicated project. First, some have argued that there are proto-feminist elements to women's participation in social protest and in public institutions generally, insofar as such participation widens women's 'traditional' roles in the private sphere (Kuumba 2001). Second, while women's claims as citizens are generally couched in terms of seeking equality with men, gendered citizenship claims can be made on the basis of difference; whether these claims are 'feminist' has been the subject of some debate (see Offen 1988; DuBois 1989; and Cott 1989). Third, feminist claims are often made in an 'intersectional' fashion, combining concerns about gender oppression with concerns about racial/ethnic, national, class, or sexual oppression since such interlocking oppressions are envisioned as mutually constitutive (Anzaldúa 1999 [1987]; Beal 1970; Crenshaw 1989, 1995; Hill Collins 2000 [1990]; King 1988; Naples 1998; Spelman 1982; Thorton Dill 1983).

2 Specifically, Zald and Ash (1966) challenged Michels' assumptions about the way that social movement organizations change by arguing for a variety of possible outcomes for the incorporation of grass-roots activists based on larger political contexts, and especially the relationships social movement organizations formed with other actors. Building on Zald and Ash, Jenkins (1977) and others have challenged Michels' assumption that oligarchies within organizations are necessarily more conservative than membership bases. Staggenborg (1988), in answer to the Piven and Cloward argument about the defusing of popular protest through the formalization and institutionalization of protest, argued that, at least in the US-based pro-choice movement, formalization and institutionalization of organizations facilitated participation with other groups in larger coalitions, and formalization itself sometimes prevented oligarchy by fostering concrete democratic practices. In short, Michels' critics have argued that the unilinearity of outcomes for activists in institutions predicted by Michels is belied by looking at the variety of activists' experiences (see Meyer and Tarrow 1998: especially pages 17–24).

3 I distinguish feminist-friendly organizations/institutions from explicitly feminist ones. In the latter, feminists do not have to make claims as *feminists* within organizations, although other subordinate statuses of race/ethnicity, class, sexual orientation and nationality may systematically affect feminist actors. For discussions of the dynamics involved in forming and running feminist organizations in the US in the 1980s and 1990s, see Marx Ferree and Yancey Martin (1995).

4 Despite serious opposition from the start, the issue of women's ordination was

not abandoned, but taken up with the Pope himself. Sister Theresa Kane addressed the Pope in a face-to-face meeting during a 1979 US visit, making history by linking women's ordination to other social justice struggles in the church, and asking that the Pope be mindful of those Catholic women who wanted to serve the church as 'fully participating members' (Katzenstein 1998b: 115).

5 Beyond the US military, other feminist scholars have noted that resistance within institutions, coupled with a grudging acceptance of internal feminist insurgency, can lead to the provision of a token space purportedly aimed at inclusion, but actually created to marginalize feminists and feminist issues. Gelb (1989) described just such immediate marginalization of feminist activists within political parties and trade unions in the US, Britain, and Sweden. Women's committees in these settings were kept far from the actual centres of policy decision-making and from party/union centres of power, while being charged with the responsibilities of overseeing the parties' policies on women. A woman's agenda was considered to be just another subset of interests to be attended to when and after 'main' party concerns were addressed. In short, feminists became organizational 'others'. As in the case of US military feminists, feminist withdrawal from the parties that Gelb examined was largely unthinkable; building new political parties was a huge task, with an attendant high risk of failure. For an assessment of the continued difficulties for women organizing within established parties in the context of recent struggles over constitutional change in the United Kingdom, see Dobrowolsky (2003).

6 For more on the issue of states' restructuring and women's movements in the 1980s and 1990s, see *Women's Movements Facing the Reconfigured State*, a collection recently edited by Banaszak *et al.* (2003).

7 While my case selection and discussion here seems to suggest that states are, in fact, friendlier venues for feminist organizing than non-state institutions, this remains a matter for investigation and, especially, for comparative analysis. States vary internally and cross-nationally, even when they seem to have fairly similar structures. Chappell's (2002) work comparing the institutional and normative structures found within the Australian and Canadian states underscores how different the terrain for feminist integration can be from setting to setting.

8 I distinguish class location from class consciousness here. Class and other kinds of oppositional consciousness, such as feminist consciousness, can persist in institutionalized settings, as several of the authors addressed in this chapter make clear. I only note that from a male-dominated institution's standpoint, male outsiders' class locations will shift by virtue of inclusion, as inclusion brings with it both higher compensation and higher occupational prestige.

References

Acker, J. (1990) 'Hierarchies, jobs, bodies: a theory of gendered organizations', *Gender and Society*, 4(2): 139–58.

Anzaldúa, G. (1999 [1987]) *Borderlands/La Frontera: The New Mestiza*, San Francisco: Aunt Lute Books.

Banaszak, L.A., Beckwith, K., and Rucht, D. (2003) *Women's Movements Facing the Reconfigured State*, New York and Cambridge: Cambridge University Press.

Beal, F. (1970) 'Double jeopardy: to be black and female', in T. Cade (ed.) *The Black Woman: An Anthology*, New York: New American Library.

Chappell, L. (2002) *Gendering Government: Feminist Engagement with the State in Australia and Canada*, Vancouver and Toronto: UBC Press.

Clemens, E.S. (1993) 'Organizational repertoires and institutional change: women's groups and the transformation of U.S. politics, 1890–1920', *The American Journal of Sociology*, 98(4): 755–98.

Cott, N. (1989) 'Comment on Karen Offen's "Defining feminism: a comparative historical approach"', *Signs*, 15(1): 203–5.

Crenshaw, K. (1989) 'Demarginalizing the intersection of race and sex', *University of Chicago Legal Forum*, 139: 139–67.

—— (1995) 'Mapping the margins: intersectionality, identity politics, and violence against women of color', in K. Crenshaw, N. Gotanda, G. Peller, and K. Thomas (eds) *Critical Race Theory: The Key Writings that Formed the Movement*, New York: The New York Press.

Dobrowolsky, A. (2003) 'Shifting states: women's constitutional organizing across time and space', in L.A. Banaszak, K. Beckwith, and D. Rucht (eds) *Women's Movements Facing the Reconfigured State*, New York: Cambridge University Press.

DuBois, E. (1989) 'Comment on Karen Offen's "Defining feminism: a comparative historical approach"', *Signs*, 15(1): 195–7.

Eisenstein, H. (1995) 'The Australian femocratic experiment: a feminist case for bureaucracy', in M. Marx Ferree and P. Yancey Martin (eds) *Feminist Organizations: Harvest of the New Women's Movement*, Philadelphia: Temple University Press.

—— (1996) *Inside Agitators: Australian Femocrats and the State*, Philadelphia: Temple University Press.

Gelb, J. (1989) *Feminism and Politics: A Comparative Perspective*, Berkeley, Los Angeles, and London: University of California Press.

Hill Collins, P. (1998) *Fighting Words: Black Women and the Search for Justice*, Minneapolis and London: University of Minnesota Press.

—— (2000 [1990]) *Black Feminist Thought: Knowledge, Consciousness, and the Politics of Empowerment*, New York and London: Routledge.

Izraeli, D. (1990) 'The women workers' movement: first-wave feminism in pre-state Israel', in G. West and R.L. Blumberg (eds) *Women and Social Protest*, New York and Oxford: Oxford University Press.

Jenkins, J.C. (1977) 'Radical transformation of organizational goals', *Administrative Science Quarterly*, 22(December): 568–86.

Katzenstein, M.F. (1990) 'Feminism within American institutions: unobtrusive mobilization in the 1980s', *Signs*, 16: 27–54.

—— (1998a) 'Stepsisters: Feminist movement activism in different institutional spaces', in D.S. Meyer and S. Tarrow (eds) *The Social Movement Society: Contentious Politics for a New Century*, Lanham: Rowman & Littlefield Publishers.

—— (1998b) *Faithful and Fearless: Moving Feminist Protest Inside the Church and Military*, Princeton: Princeton University Press.

King, D.H. (1988) 'Multiple jeopardy, multiple consciousness: the context of a black feminist ideology', *Signs*, 14: 1 88–111.

Kuumba, M.B. (2001) *Gender and Social Movements*, Walnut Creek: AltaMira Press.

Lorber, J. (1994) *Paradoxes of Gender*, New Haven and London: Yale University Press.

Marx Ferree, M. and Yancey Martin, P. (1995) *Feminist Organizations: Harvest of the New Women's Movement*, Philadelphia: Temple University Press.

Meyer, D.S. and Tarrow, S. (1998) *The Social Movement Society: Contentious Politics for a New Century*, Lanham: Rowman & Littlefield Publishers.

Michels, R. (1959 [1915]) *Political Parties: A Sociological Study of the Oligarchical Tendencies of Modern Democracy*, trans. E. Paul and C. Paul, New York: Dover.

Naples, N. (1998) *Community Activism and Feminist Politics: Organizing Across Race, Class, and Gender*, Philadelphia: Temple University Press.

Offen, K. (1988) 'Defining feminism: a comparative historical approach', *Signs*, 14(1): 119–57.

Ostrander, S.A. (1999) 'Gender and race in a pro-feminist, progressive, mixed-gender, mixed-race organization', *Gender and Society*, 13(5): 628–42.

Piven, F.F. and Cloward, R.A. (1977) *Poor People's Movements: Why They Succeed and How They Fail*, New York: Vintage Books.

Ridgeway, C. (2001) 'The persistence of gender inequality in employment settings', in J. O'Brien and K. Kollock (eds) *The Production of Reality: Essays and Readings on Social Interaction*, Thousand Oaks: Pine Forge Press.

Roth, B. (1998) 'Feminist boundaries in the feminist-friendly organization: the women's caucus of ACT UP/LA', *Gender and Society*, 12(2): 129–45.

—— (2004) 'Thinking about challenges/limits for feminist activism in extra-feminist settings', *Social Movement Studies*, 3(2): 147–66.

Seidman, G. (2003) 'Institutional dilemmas: representation versus mobilization in the South African Gender Commission', *Feminist Studies*, 29(3): 541–63.

Spelman, E.V. (1982) 'Theories of race and gender/the erasure of black women', *Quest: A Feminist Quarterly*, 5(4): 36–62.

Stacey, J. (1990) 'Sexism by a subtler name? Postindustrial conditions and postfeminist consciousness in Silicon Valley', in K.V. Hansen and I.J. Philipson (eds) *Women, Class, and the Feminist Imagination: A Socialist-Feminist Reader*, Philadelphia: Temple University Press.

Staggenborg, S. (1988) 'The consequences of professionalization and formalization in the pro-choice movement', *American Sociological Review*, 53: 585–606.

Thorton Dill, B. (1983) 'Race, class and gender: prospects for an all-inclusive sisterhood', *Feminist Studies*, 9(1): 131–50.

West, G. and Blumberg, R.L. (1990) *Women and Social Protest*, New York and Oxford: Oxford University Press.

Zald, M.N. and Ash, R. (1966) 'Social movement organizations: growth, decay and change', *Social Forces*, 44(3): 327–41.

9 Gender, interests, and constitutional matters in the EU

The case of the Charter of Fundamental Rights[1]

Roberta Guerrina

This chapter explores the impact of the European Union (EU) Charter of Fundamental Rights on the position of women in the EU. The context is current debates about women's rights and constitutionalism in Europe. The discussion outlines the development of EU women's rights, the introduction and development of Union citizenship within the Treaties and the proclamation of the Charter at the Nice Summit. The chapter thus explores the position of equality and women's rights in the Charter, with particular emphasis on the Commission and Treaties' commitments to gender mainstreaming. The chapter concludes with an evaluation of the power of gender mainstreaming as a theory and political strategy for the pursuit of substantive equality within the EU.

Recent developments in the process of European integration, namely the proclamation of the EU Charter of Fundamental Rights at the Nice Summit (2000) and the signing of the Constitutional Treaty (2004) are symbolic of the new challenges facing European politics in the twenty-first century. The EU and its institutions are now at an important juncture. It has been argued widely (Longo 2003; Skach 2005; Weatherhill 2002) that the future of European governance is at stake and that the result of the latest round of negotiations will define the parameters of European integration in years to come. In this context, the focus of current debates on democracy and institutional reform in Europe provides an important opportunity for reworking the values upon which the social contract and citizenship of the EU are based. It thus has the potential to bring about the introduction of what Jill Vickers called 'women's citizenship'.

In the negotiations that led to the signing of the Constitutional Treaty concerns over the impact of the latest round of the enlargement on the institutional framework of the EU and the overall thrust of the process of European integration dominated the negotiations. In this context, social issues and women's interests were marginalized, to the extent that the early drafts of the Constitutional Treaty downgraded the importance of the 'social' (Hoskyns 2003). Feminist assessments of women's position in contemporary European social and political structures further emphasize this division and distance between women's interests and the economic interests of the member states, and have argued that the process of European integration can serve to both advance and marginalize the cause of women's rights (Guerrina 2002; Hoskyns 1996). The challenge being set out for European institutions at the beginning of the twenty-first century is to make the Union relevant to the people of Europe. This means also making the Union a forum for the representation of women's interests beyond the sphere of employment. More importantly, it implies recognition of the fact that, although 'women/woman' is not a unified category, it is an important constituency whose needs and interests have to be addressed by political institutions.

The presentation of the Charter of Fundamental Rights at the Nice Summit (2000) and the signing of the Constitutional Treaty (2004) represent the most concrete steps thus far to bring citizens to the heart of the EU. It is thus essential to assess the extent to which the interests of women as workers and citizens were incorporated within the debates and negotiations that led to the signing of these two documents. The aim of this chapter is to assess how these developments contribute to the cause of expanding women's rights. The EU Charter of Fundamental Rights, in particular, is representative of current trends and discourses about making the Union more relevant to the people of Europe. As such, it constitutes a milestone in the development of a social Europe as it comes close to creating a bill of rights for the Union. The reach of this document, however, has come under increasing scrutiny and criticism from political and legal commentators, which resound all the more powerfully when gender structures and women are the starting point of analysis. Taking the latter approach to the analysis of European citizenship and governance as the theoretical background for this chapter, I will assess if and how the Charter has incorporated calls for a re-elaboration of the 'sexual contract' as defined by Western discourses on citizenship and participation in the public sphere (Pateman 1991). In this way, I will link gender discourses to contemporary debates about constitutionalism in Europe. Using the Charter as a 'case study' of EU politics, this chapter will ultimately seek to answer two interrelated questions. First, have the Commission's commitment to mainstreaming and the Treaties' obligations towards equality brought women, as a category, to the heart of the European project? Second, how does the EU 'tackle' the needs of women as workers and citizens in order to promote women's interests and substantive equality?

Positioning women in the Union

The evolution of European integration from the Treaty of Paris (1951) to the Treaty of Nice (2000)[2] and the advances in the field of women's rights brought about under the banner of the EU have been widely documented (on the EU see: Dinan 1999; Nugent 2003; Jones 2001; on women's rights in the EU see: Hantrais 2000; Hoskyns 1996). However, in order to under-stand the actual and potential role of this organization in promoting women's rights and interests, it is important to review how gender and equality between men and women entered the European policy agenda.

The first major development in the field of women's rights at the Euro-pean level was the introduction of Article 119 (equal pay for equal work) in the Treaty of Rome (1957). Although this article is a milestone in the development of women's policy, it should also be noted that the reason why this article was incorporated in the Treaty was to palliate French fears over social dumping.[3] More specifically, France had just introduced at the national level equal pay legislation, and was fearful that the absence of such legislation in the other member states would put the French market at a competitive disadvantage. Thus, economic interest rather than a real commitment to women's rights and the principle of equality drove the negotiations, and is reflected in the overall objectives of Article 119 (Hantrais 2000; Hoskyns 1996).

The next major developments came in the 1970s and 1980s. A variety of directives on equal pay and equal treatment were ratified in order to expand the principle of equality enshrined within European law. The time that lapsed between the signing of the Treaty of Rome (1957) and the rati-fication of the first equality directive (1975) is testament to the fact that Article 119 failed to engender a greater political commitment to the prin-ciple of equality. Moreover, the failure of member states' governments to comply with their obligations on equality two decades after signing the Treaty is further evidence of the biases and weaknesses of the Treaty foun-dation. Particularly telling in this context were the Defrenne cases.[4] These were the first court cases on the issue of equality brought before the Euro-pean Court of Justice. What the case of Gabrielle Defrenne shows is that member states had failed to implement within national legislation the equality provisions, thus finding themselves in violation of European law. The 1975 Equal Pay Directive (75/117/EEC) and the 1976 Equal Treat-ment Directive (76/207/EEC) fulfilled a dual purpose: first they expanded the scope of equality provisions at the European level; second, they brought back on the agenda the issue of equality between men and women, thereby prompting further developments in the field such as the 1979 Equal Treatment in Social Security Directive (79/7/EEC) and the 1986 Equal Treatment in Occupational Social Security Schemes (86/378/EEC) and Equal Treatment in Self-Employment (86/613/EEC) Directives. By the end of the 1980s the majority of member states had signed the Social Charter,[5] which provided a framework for the develop-ment of the social rights of workers in Europe, and confirmed the Community's commitment to equality (Hantrais 2000: 116; Hoskyns 1996).

The 1990s marked an important shift in the European equality agenda. The majority of directives ratified during this decade introduced a new concept that broadened the principle of equality to include reconciliation between work and family life. These policies include, amongst others, the 1992 Pregnant Worker Directive (92/85/EC), the 1993 Working Time Directive (93/104/EEC), the 1996 Parental Leave Directive (96/34/EC), and the 1992 Childcare Recommendations. The introduction of family-friendly policies at the European level represented an important change of direction in equality legislation, as it began to acknowledge the import-ance of the relationship between public roles and private duties in the achievement of equality and access to citizenship rights.

However, despite the importance of these developments and the gender neutrality of the language of family-friendly policies, they are, in reality, aimed at women. Nowhere in these policies is there a commitment to a thorough reassessment of the impact of gender dynamics on employ-ment structures. As such, these policies fail to challenge the male bias of the public sphere and ultimately reassert women's role as primary carers. The focus on the official labour market ultimately undermines their radical potential, and what ultimately transpires from their analysis is that reconciliation between work and family life does not seek to challenge gender divisions of labour in the private sphere. Therefore equality con-tinues to be tantamount to having an equal right to participate in the offi-cial labour market (Irving 1998). As such, the principles enshrined within family-friendly policies continue to support the attainment of formal equality at the expense of substantive equality. These policies should, therefore, be regarded only as an initial step towards a greater under-standing of the forces at play that prevent women from achieving substan-tive equality.

The main criticism raised by feminists against EU equal rights policies has focused on the pre-eminent place of employment as a catalyst for the introduction of the principle of equality at the European level. In other words, women acquired equality in Europe as workers rather than citizens. Women's interests have been defined in line with the liberal idea of promoting equality of opportunities and sameness. This assumption has led many feminist writers to conclude that the division between public rights and private duties continues to define gender relations and power hierarchies in national and EU legal structures (see Hantrais 2000; Hoskyns 1996; Hervey and Shaw 1998). The focus on employment can partly be explained by the primacy of economics in the process of Euro-pean integration. However, it is also clear that this bias has played an important part in the development of women's right in the EU. It is through this process that public rights and formal equality have become the norm, thus reinforcing the public–private dichotomy that many femin-ists have identified as being at the root of gender power hierarchies. As Lister's (1997) analysis of citizenship explains, the division between public and private, and the male bias inherent in the public/political sphere, serve to shape the relationship between family and employment structures, and contribute to women's continued exclusion from the full benefits of citizenship. Women's 'special' needs have been marginalized and little consideration given to the relationship between formal and informal politics, or women's roles in the public and private sphere.

By the mid-1990s, however, international discourses on gender had shifted towards the introduction of gender mainstreaming as a theory and strategy for equality. This principle engendered wide-reaching debates about the role and function of women's interests in politics and policy-making at large. The European Union's response and contribution to this change in discourse was outlined by Commission's 1996 Communication on *Incorporating Equal Opportunities for Women and Men into all Community Policies and Activities*. This document defines this new principle as follows:

> Gender mainstreaming involves not restricting efforts to promote equality to the implementation of specific measures to help women, but mobilizing all general policies and measures specifically for the purpose of achieving equality by actively and openly taking into account at the planning stage their possible effects on the respective situation of men and women (gender perspective). This means systematically examining measures and policies and taking into account such possible effects when defining and implementing them.
>
> (European Commission 1996)

In very simple terms, the principle of gender mainstreaming entails the recognition of the impact of gender on every aspect of political and economic life. For this reason, it advocates the introduction of a gender sensitive approach in all areas of policy-making rather than limiting such efforts to distinct women's rights policies. Theoretically this principle broadens the scope of EU policy action in this field, thus bringing the issue of gender to the heart of EU politics (Mazey 2001: 2; European Commission 1997: 2).

According to the Commission's (1997: 3) own assessment, 'mainstreaming, or "integrating equality", was seen as a way of meeting the needs of diverse groups equally and of ensuring good recruitment and employment practices, of encouraging equal participation in decision-making, and of achieving quality and cost effectiveness across all activities'. This statement reflects the expectation that mainstreaming will bring about the establishment of a comprehensive approach to equality, that will overcome the division between public and private, and thus challenge traditional gender hierarchies (Mazey 2001: 6; Pollack and Hafner-Burton 2000; Rees 1992).

The principle of mainstreaming was officially included in the Treaty on the European Union with the Amsterdam revisions. Articles 2, 3, and 13 of the Treaty of Amsterdam (ToA) were amended to include equality between men and women as one of the objectives of European integration (Hantrais 2000: 117; Shaw 2001: 3). As Shaw (2001: 3–4) explains, the

Amsterdam revisions can be 'said to "constitutionalize" the guarantee of proactive policy-making to eliminate inequality, a markedly different guarantee to that of bare equal treatment or non-discrimination'. This approach was thus supposed to produce a strategy for equal rights that moved beyond formal equality (Shaw 2001: 3–4).

However, a closer look at Articles 2 and 3 of the ToA highlight the weaknesses of the approach currently adopted by the EU. These articles appear in Part 1 of the Treaty, which is where member states' governments outline the main principles underpinning the future development of European integration. Taken together, Articles 2 and 3 summarize the aims of the Union and the position of equality within the organization. Article 2 specifically states:

> *The Community shall have as its task, by establishing a common market and an economic and monetary union and by implementing common policies or activities referred to in Articles 3 and 4,* to promote throughout the Community a harmonious, balanced and sustainable development of economic activities, a high level of employment and of social protection, *equality between men and women,* sustainable and non-inflationary growth.
>
> (Consolidated Version of the Treaty Establishing the European Community 1997, emphasis added)

Article 3, on the other hand, lists the areas of Community activity, thus establishing the parameters of EU policy action. It includes issues such as commercial and competition policy, free movement, economic and social cohesion, research and development, and education. Equal rights and equal opportunities are the focus of the second clause of the article which states: 'In all the activities referred to in this Article, the Community shall aim to eliminate inequalities, and to promote equality between men and women' (Art. 3 (2) Consolidated Version of the Treaty Establishing the European Community 1997).

Perhaps the most significant of all Treaty provisions on equality is Article 13, which reiterates this broad commitment to equality and reinforces the role of the Union as an important actor in creating a fairer European market. Specifically it states:

> Without prejudice to the other provisions of this Treaty and within the limits of the powers conferred by it upon the Community, the Council, acting unanimously on a proposal from the Commission and after consulting the European Parliament, may take appropriate action to combat discrimination based on sex, racial or ethnic origin, religion or belief, disability, age or sexual orientation.
>
> (Art. 13 Consolidated Version of the Treaty Establishing the European Community 1997)

Clearly, Article 3 (2) and Article 13 expand the remit of gender equality and fulfil the Commission's commitment to mainstreaming outlined in the 1996 Communication.

The inclusion of the principle of equality between men and women as one of the aims of the Union is an important development. However, it does not overcome the economic bias built into all Community policy which constrains the scope of EU action in the field of equal rights. It is important to note that such economic bias extends to all social provisions embedded within the treaties. Social policies are thus included in order to ensure the functioning of the single market, rather than as a way of fostering a more cohesive society. Thus the rationale for the inclusion of such policies within the broad remit of European integration has been primarily economic. Education, freedom of movement, and social cohesion have been developed only in as far as they can help to ensure the long-term success of the single market. Hantrais (2000: 118) draws attention to the limits of this approach, which assumes that the foundations of social rights are to be found in the relationship of an individual with the employment market. In her words, the 'analysis of European law as it affects women shows clearly how attention has been paid almost exclusively to their rights as workers' (Hantrais 2000: 128). This focus on the market significantly restricts the scope and potential of equal rights legislation by reasserting the link between equality and participation in the public sphere. Thus, the concept of equality that has become 'constitutionalized' through the EU treaties is that of formal equality. The justification for such a development is women's participation in the official labour market (Hantrais 2000: 135; Hervey and Shaw 1998).

Given the weaknesses of the equality provisions in the Treaty of Amsterdam it is debatable whether the principle of gender mainstreaming as incorporated within this document has lived up to its potential. As Mazey (2001: 2) points out, 'notwithstanding the proliferation of guidelines, there is at present no single blueprint for gender mainstreaming, and debate over what constitutes best practices is considerable'. More importantly, the principle of gender mainstreaming, as incorporated into the treaties, does not have the power to disrupt the social and economic structures that currently prevent women from taking full advantage of their rights as workers and citizens. The persistence of a link between employment and citizenship ultimately serves to limit the scope of mainstreaming to economic policy. It would thus appear that the introduction of this principle in the treaties has not been accompanied by a greater understanding of the role of gender structures in defining power hierarchies and social exclusion. In this context, it has been used to integrate women into existing policies rather than allowing gender discourses to inform policy-making. It is thus possible to conclude that, far from creating the necessary conditions for substantive equality, gender mainstreaming can serve to silence women and remove gender from the political agenda. The absence of a 'gender' voice is a constant concern of the analysis of the position of women's rights in the EU; however, it becomes all the more significant at a time when the debate is shifting towards citizenship and human rights (Mazey 2001: 3; Pollack and Hafner-Burton 2000: 33–4).

Two preliminary conclusions emerge from the discussion presented in this section: first, there is a hierarchy of interests at the heart of the process of European integration, whereby economic growth and competitiveness drive the process; second, women have been portrayed as a homogenous and universal category. More importantly, in the context of Jill Vickers' analysis of the difference between the categories of 'woman/women' and 'gender', it is interesting to note that the two have become mutually interchangeable, whereby to develop a gender sensitive approach is tantamount to promoting women's needs and interests. Women's needs, however, continue to be defined by the interests of the EU and its constituent parts (namely, the member states). In this context, European institutions have assumed that women's interests are best served by advocating formal equality and women's participation in the employment market.

Citizenship in the EU: the state of the debate

The absence of a clearly articulated discourse on women's interests is even more obvious when looking at the development of citizenship rights in the EU. Here it is possible to extend Jill Vickers' analysis of the patriarchal nature of state structures to regional organizations. As women's rights were introduced at the European level to protect French economic interests, it is unlikely that the EU will pursue women's interests beyond what is clearly in the 'interest' of the most powerful parties, i.e. the member states. The logical conclusion of this analysis is that EU politics and policies are not likely to foster a comprehensive re-evaluation of democratic theory and practice, thus reinforcing the power of gender hierarchies in formal politics. The analysis of the evolution of EU citizenship as a legal construct, and the debate that has emerged surrounding this principle, highlight the failures of mainstream approaches in representing women's interests at the regional level.

European Union citizenship was created in 1991 with the ratification of the Treaty of Maastricht. More precisely, the Treaty included Article 8, which defined the scope of citizenship rights at the European level. Current developments in this policy area have provoked a number of academic debates on the present and future of national and post-national citizenship. One of the key issues addressed by much of the contemporary literature is the bias of European citizenship towards the worker citizen, or the process through which economic rights have become the basis for political rights in the EU.

The 1997 Amsterdam revisions to the Treaty on the European Union highlight the increasing importance of citizenship as a unifying factor for the Union. Article 17 defines the parameters of EU citizenship, whereas Articles 18–22 outline the rights conferred on EU citizens under Treaty provisions, which are: the freedom of movement of workers and students; the right to vote and stand for election; the extension of consular protection in third-countries; and the right to petition the ombudsman and the European Parliament. It is important to draw attention to the fact that the key to understanding EU citizenship is the right to freedom of movement of workers and students, which provides the foundation and/or justification for all subsequent developments. As in the case of social policies discussed in the previous section of this chapter, the ability of workers to move freely within the single market has been seen as vital for the long-term success of this project. As this particular right is defined by an individual's participation in the official labour market and/or a close relationship to the public sphere, it thus follows that, as far as EU citizenship is concerned, political rights have become subsidiary to economic rights. This is compounded by the limited scope of the social and political rights embedded within the principle of EU citizenship.

In terms of mainstream scholarly debates about European citizenship, the most notable absentees are gender discourses. Most scholars seem to concentrate on the ascendancy of post-national citizenship, and the debate that has ensued focuses on the shift of allegiances towards postmodern and post-national identities, with a particular interest in the impact of ethnicity and nationality on the forces of exclusion (see for instance: Bellamy 2000; Delanty 1995; Delanty 1996; Green 2000; Habermas 1998; Jary 1999; Tambini 2001). Whilst these are important contributions, they fail to acknowledge and/or engage with the impact of social, political, and economic exclusion on women's participation in traditional as well as new forms of citizenship. Perhaps such absence should not be surprising, as the politics and practice of citizenship are part of a patriarchal state system that seeks to differentiate women's interests in the public sphere from women's needs in the private sphere.

Feminist critiques of democracy and governance have thus sought to uncover the gender bias of traditional conceptualizations of citizenship. According to Prokhovnik:

> [C]itizenship in our political tradition can, and has meant many different things, not all of them compatible. It has involved an identification with the state, a sense of belonging to a whole, a definition of membership as equals or entitlement to make a claim against the state.
>
> (Prokhovnik 1998: 85)

Citizenship therefore defines the parameters for social and political relations between individuals and between an individual and the state. As representative of such relations, it is a concept invested with the same power hierarchies that define social structures and dynamics. For instance, as currently understood, citizenship focuses on public discourses and relations, and is based upon a 'masculine' understanding of political participation and social interaction. The rights defined by citizenship are thus public rights and fail to account for women's position and roles in the private sphere. What follows from such a definition is a conceptualization of politics that is based upon a narrowly constituted agenda, and which excludes those areas of life traditionally associated with women and/or femininity (Prokhovnik 1998: 85; Yuval-Davis 1997: 4).

A more positive account from a feminist perspective of the developments currently taking place within the Union has been put forward by Vogel-Polsky. She maintains that the EU has the ability to challenge power hierarchies enshrined within national political and social structures. As she elaborates, 'the recognition of an autonomous right to equality of women and men in the Treaty on the European Union would make it possible to overcome the hitherto insurmountable contradiction between formal and substantive equality' (Vogel-Polsky 2000: 81). However, this shift would require a new understanding of equality that presupposes the affirmation of positive rights. What Vogel-Polsky's analysis seems to overlook is the economic bias of the process of European integration. It is difficult to get away from the fact that EU citizenship is market citizenship. The bias in favour of the public sphere and economic participation, upon which national citizenship rights are based, has been transferred to the principle of European citizenship. This conclusion should not come as a surprise, particularly as it is national governments, and their economic and political interests, that drive the process of European integration.

This economic bias in the EU draws attention to the argument presented by Jill Vickers in Chapter 2 of this volume that there is a difference between formal and active citizenship. More specifically, it highlights her argument that the acquisition of formal rights is meaningless if it is not accompanied by active participation in the political and/or economic sphere. Such participation, however, cannot be defined solely in terms of male values and interests. It is in this context that the acknowledgement and pursuit of women's interests can lead to a deeper and more inclusive form of citizenship and democracy.

The introduction of the Charter of Fundamental Rights as part of the EU legal and political structure has introduced a new variable in the equality framework of the Union. It is therefore essential to consider the overall aims of the Charter in order to assess if and how this document may challenge the foundations of gender structures in Europe. The next section will turn to a discussion of the Charter, its legal foundations and its potential impact on political and social relations in Europe.

The EU Charter of Fundamental Rights

The onset of talks about the introduction of human rights within the EU treaties is another important stage in the development of social, political, and citizenship rights in general in the EU. The groundwork for such discussion was laid with the negotiations for the Amsterdam revisions in 1997. More specifically, Article 6 of the Treaty on the European Union outlines the Union's commitment to human rights and reiterates the importance of applying these principles in all areas of EU policy (Miller 2000: 10).

However, the debate that surrounds the development of a Charter of Fundamental Rights is, in many ways, more far-reaching than a simple discussion about the introduction of a specific context for human rights within the EU (particularly if we consider that all EU member states are signatories of the European Convention on Human Rights). The debate that has ensued with reference to the Charter must be located within contemporary discussions about European constitutionalism, governance, and democratic accountability (Duff 2001: 17; Miller 2000: 13).

The Charter draws upon various regional agreements, namely the European Convention on Human Rights (ECHR), the Social Charter, EU treaties and directives, rulings by the European Court of Justice and the Permanent Court of Human Rights, as well as national constitutional traditions.[6] It was ratified by the European Convention, a meeting of representatives of member states' governments and parliaments, the European Parliament and the Commission; its objective was to create a bill of rights for the citizens of the Union. As Miller (2000: 14) summarizes, 'the EU Charter could present an opportunity to modernize and extend the ECHR by bringing together universal rights, such as the right to life, and rights specific to the EU, such as the right to stand for and vote in European elections'. The adoption of the Charter could, in turn, close the gap between the EU and its citizens by making their rights visible and altogether more tangible. As a result, this process could provide a response to calls for constitutionalism and address some of the issues surrounding the persistence of a democratic deficit in the EU (Duff 2000: 17).

In terms of the position of the Charter vis-à-vis the rest of EU law, it is necessary to point out that it takes the form of a joint declaration by the president of the European Parliament, the presidency of the European Council and the president of the Commission. As such the Charter was appended to, but not included in, the Nice Treaty. Thus, despite the political importance of this document, it is not a legally binding instrument and so its impact remains uncertain. Although it is difficult to predict how the introduction of the Charter into the treaties might affect the development of the EU's policy-making agenda, the biases uncovered by feminist discourses on European citizenship highlight the dangers inherent in an organization so focused on economic progress (Fossum 2002; Miller 2000: 18–21; Regan 2002: 3–4; Vitorino 2000: 1).

Gender sensitive critique of the Charter of Rights: defining women's interests

Endorsement of the principle of equality is outlined in Chapter 3 of the Charter. This section of the Charter is entirely devoted to the issue of equality and seeks to tackle the various forms of discrimination currently at work in the European market. It includes seven articles dealing with various forms of inequality and establishes a broad foundation for the development of an egalitarian society. It includes a right to equality before the law (Article 20); non-discrimination; protection of cultural, religious, and linguistic diversity; the rights of the child; equality between men and women; the rights of the elderly and the disabled; as well as a general right to non-discrimination. Two articles were specifically formulated to address women's rights: Article 21 – 'non-discrimination'; and Article 23 – 'equality between men and women'. As with all provisions within the Charter, these articles draw upon current policies and legal texts such as the EU treaties, ECHR and the equality directives (Draft Charter 2000a: 23–4).

Most important for women's rights is Article 21 as it defines the context for equal opportunities, by way of instituting a general right to equality and non-discrimination. However, what is particularly interesting to note about this article is the decision by EU members to introduce a negative rather than positive right to equality (Regan 2002). As this article provides the basis for equality in the Charter, it is questionable whether this document goes far enough to engender a greater commitment to substantive equality. Although the introduction of a right to non-discrimination may prove to have greater legal authority than a general right to equality (as the presence of discriminatory practices is easier to establish than the absence of equality) it also suggests that a legal/formal rather than substantive approach to equality will drive any future development in the field of equal opportunities (Vogel-Polsky 2000: 81–2).

The principle of non-discrimination is further reinforced by the introduction of Article 23, which defines the principle of equality between men and women. More specifically, it states:

> Equality between men and women must be ensured in all areas, including employment, work and pay. The principle of equality shall not prevent the maintenance or adoption of measures providing for specific advantages in favour of the under-represented sex.
>
> (Art. 23 EU Charter of Fundamental Rights 2000)

Through this article, the Charter reiterates the treaties' commitment to equal rights and equal opportunities, but fails to expand the remit of current trends in European equal rights legislation (for example, the Parental Leave Directive and Working Time Directive). However, Article 33 addressing family and professional life does represent an initial step towards a widening participation in the public sphere. Unfortunately, though, the scope of this article is limited to protection against dismissal for absence from the workplace in case of maternity and/or parental leave. No mention is made of gender divisions of labour and the impact of gender power hierarchies on women's participation in the public sphere. Thus, Article 33 cannot be regarded as a significant contribution to the achievement of substantive equality (European Women's Lobby 2000a). What transpires from this analysis is that the equality provisions within the Charter suffer the same shortcomings as current EU equal rights policies. More importantly, it draws attention to a very narrow understanding of women's interests and needs, which continue to be equated with the domestic sphere and women's role as carers. In other words, the Charter assumes that women's interests are best pursued by allowing them to combine public roles and private duties, rather than promoting a comprehensive re-elaboration of gender roles and power structures.

The weaknesses of the equality provisions in the Charter reflect a narrow understanding of equality principles underpinning the developments that have taken place in the last ten years. The failure of EU treaties and legislation to acknowledge the role of the private sphere in defining social and economic relations severely limits the scope of equality and citizenship rights. Despite the superficial benefits of the Charter to the cause of women's rights, it fails to mainstream women's interests in EU politics. Gender equality is included in the text but does not permeate the whole document (European Women's Lobby 2000a, 2000b).

The equality provisions ultimately fall short of their stated objective on two counts. First, they fail to reinforce the link between citizenship and employment. Through this process citizenship becomes commodified, hence limiting its political effectiveness (Lewis 1992; Esping-Andersen 1990; Borchorst 1994; Bussemaker and van Kerbergen 1994; Hantrais 2000). The repercussions of this process are all the more important in the context of women's rights, as much of women's work occurs in private and thus is outside the remit of the Charter and citizenship rights at large. Second, they fail to implement the Commission's commitment to gender mainstreaming. Clearly, over the last fifty years there has been a great deal of progress in the field of legal equality. However, European institutions and policy-makers have been unsuccessful in integrating gender into wider questions about the future of European integration (Shaw 2001). A possible explanation for this blindness can be found in the perceived threat such an approach may pose for traditional or masculine conceptualizations of politics and citizenship. The analysis of the Charter supports this position and in many ways brings into question the effectiveness of mainstreaming as a political strategy for gender equality, as it fails to challenge gender power hierarchies at the heart of formal politics.

The ongoing debate on the future of the EU highlights the importance of feminist contributions to the analysis of the Charter and the marginal position of women's interests in this process. One of the main participants in this debate is the European Women's Lobby (EWL) which has proposed 'the introduction, into the preamble of the future Treaty and in article 6 of the TEU, of the right to equality of women and men as one of the ultimate aims of the European Union as a fundamental prerequisite for European democracy' (European Women's Lobby 2002). As the Charter is supposed to provide the foundation for an EU bill of rights, it should provide settings for ensuring greater inclusiveness of women's interests and for challenging the socio-political and economic structures that have thus far limited the scope of citizenship rights at the national level.

Concluding remarks

The analysis presented in this chapter leads to one key conclusion: gender mainstreaming has failed to produce a concrete move towards substantive equality in the EU. On the one hand, it was introduced as a strategy for the creation of a more egalitarian single market; on the other, it has strengthened the division between formal and substantive equality at the expense of the latter. The criticisms of the Charter on gender grounds highlight the weaknesses of an approach to social, political and economic rights that focuses on the public sphere and fails to acknowledge the impact of gender hierarchies in the private realm on women's access to the public sphere and citizenship rights. A gender-sensitive critique of the Charter thus confirms Shaw's analysis that:

> [G]ender mainstreaming is certainly not unproblematic either as a principle or a strategy for developing gender equality. It has a chequered history in neo-liberal international governance. It is under-theorized and under-specified and leads to mixed results.
>
> (Shaw 2001)

Despite its potential, gender mainstreaming, as currently deployed by European institutions, has failed to achieve a more sensitive representation of the diversity of women's interests within European policy-making circles. Unfortunately, the conclusions of the analysis presented here confirm the findings of previous work that acknowledged the persistence of a division between public and private, formal and substantive equality, and the bias of the process of European integration in favour of a liberal approach to equality that ultimately fails to challenge traditional gender hierarchies.

The power of gender hierarchies is evident in the overarching lack of representation of women's interests in European and national institutions. The continued dichotomization of high and low politics at the expense of the latter highlights the persistence of male norms at the heart of the European Union.

Notes

1 A different version of this argument first appeared in *Policy, Organization and Society*, as 'Gender, Mainstreaming and the EU Charter of Fundamental Rights', 22(1), 2003. The author would like to thank the journal for permission to reprint that article.

2 The European Union was created through an evolutionary process that began in 1951 with the signing of the Treaty of Paris. The 'founding fathers' of European integration (Jean Monnet and Robert Schuman) envisaged the development of a Europe united initially through economic co-operation and subsequently through political integration. The 1951 Treaty of Paris brought together six western European states (Belgium, France, Germany, Italy, Luxembourg, and the Netherlands) to launch the European Coal and Steel Community. The early success of this initiative encouraged the participating states to expand the remit of European integration. In 1957 the same states came together to sign the Treaties of Rome, which created the European Economic Community and Euratom (European Atomic Energy Community). These treaties set out the scope of European integration and the institutional framework of the organization. The next thirty years were characterized by the progressive enlargement of its membership. However, the next major development in the timeline of the EU was the signing of the Single European Act in 1986. This was the first major set of amendments to the original treaties and represented a turning point in the evolution of this organization. It marks the beginning of a greater political commitment for deeper integration, which culminated with the 1992 Programme and the signing of the 1992 Treaty of Maastricht (ToM). The ToM, also known as the Treaty on the European Union (TEU), is the most ambitious project for international co-operation to date. It created a new organization which brought the early communities under its broad remit; it represents the creation of the Single European Market, it entrusts the Union with a political as well as economic role, and, finally, it set the foundations for the single currency. Clearly, the negotiations leading to the Treaty of Maastricht were fraught with difficulties and disagreements. For these reasons the governments of the participating states (Belgium, Denmark, France, Germany, Greece, Ireland, Italy, Luxembourg, the Netherlands, Portugal, Spain, and the UK) agreed to allow for revisions of the treaty at more auspicious times. This has led to the ratification of the Treaty of Amsterdam and the Treaty of Nice, which amend the TEU, readying the Union for the challenge of enlargement which occurred in 2004.

3 Social dumping refers to the practice of companies moving production to countries within the common/single market where costs are lower, thus exploiting the freedom of movement principles.

4 The Defrenne cases were the first to be referred to the European Court of Justice on the issue of equal rights. They are important because they highlighted the shortcomings of the Treaty provision on equal rights, as established by Article 119. For further details see Hoskyns 1996.

5 The Social Charter, also known as the European Charter for the Fundamental

Rights of Workers, was signed by EU member states (with the exception of the UK) during the Maastricht negotiations. It is based upon the Council of Europe's European Social Charter and it is supposed to create a framework for the developments of workers' rights. The Social Charter was included in the TEU with the Amsterdam revisions following the UK's acceptance of the Charter in 1997.

6 The European Convention on Human Rights and the Permanent Court of Human Rights are part of the Council of Europe, a pan-European, intergovernmental organization that fosters cultural and political co-operation and dialogue between the nations of Europe. Its remit is much more limited compared to the EU.

References

Bellamy, R. (2000) 'Citizenship beyond the nation state: the case of Europe', in N. O'Sullivan (ed.) *Political Theory in Transition*, London and New York: Routledge.

Borchorst, A. (1994) 'Welfare state regimes, women's interests and the EC', in D. Sainsbury (ed.) *Gendering Welfare States*, London: Sage.

Bussemaker, J. and van Kerbergen, K. (1994) 'Welfare state regimes: some theoretical reflections', in D. Sainsbury (ed.) *Gendering Welfare States*, London: Sage.

Consolidated version of the Treaty Establishing the European Community. *Official Journal* C 340, 10.11.1997, pp. 173–308.

Delanty, G. (1995) *Inventing Europe: Idea, Identity and Reality*, Basingstoke and London: Macmillan.

—— (1996) 'Beyond the nation-state: national identity and citizenship in a multicultural society: A response to Rex', *Sociological Research Online*, 1(2). Online. Available at: www.socresonline.org.uk/socresonline/1/3/1.html (accessed 2 February 2005).

Dinan, D. (1999) *Ever Closer Union?* Basingstoke and New York: Palgrave.

Draft charter of fundamental rights of the European Union – text of the explanations relating to the complete text. CHARTER 4473/00, CONVENT 50

Draft charter of fundamental rights of the European Union. Brussels, 28 September 2000. CHART 4487/00, CONVENT 50 in K. Feus (ed.) *The EU Charter of Fundamental Rights: Text and Commentaries*, Federal Trust: London.

Duff, A. (2000) 'Towards a European federal society', in K. Feus (ed.) *The EU Charter of Fundamental Rights: Text and Commentaries*, London: Federal Trust.

Esping-Andersen G. (1990) *The Three Worlds of Welfare Capitalism*, Cambridge and Oxford: Polity Press.

European Commission (1996) *Incorporating Equal Opportunities for Women and Men into all Community Policies and Activities*, COM (96) 67 final.

—— (1997) *Mainstreaming Gender Equality in Local Government*, London: European Commission and the Equal Opportunities Commission (GB).

European Women's Lobby (2000a) 'EWL position on the Charter of Fundamental Rights of the EU'. Online. Available at: www.womenlobby.org/ (accessed 21 November 2000).

—— (2000b) 'Women excluded from the EU Charter: gender gap and sexist language'. Online. Available at: www.womenlobby.org/Document.asp?DocID= 62&tod=17211 (accessed 2 August 2000).

—— (2002) 'Future of Europe: first contribution of the European Women's Lobby for the Convention – Equality between men and women'. Online. Available at: www.europa.eu.int/futurum/forum_convention/documents/contrib/other/0019_c_en.pdf (accessed 21 March 2002).

Fossum, J.E. (2002) 'Charters and constitution-making: Comparing the Canadian Charter of Rights and Freedoms and the European Charter of Fundamental Rights', *Arena Working Papers* 02/08. Online. Available at: www.arena.uio.no/publicaitons/wp02_8.htm (accessed 10 June 2005).

Green, D.M. (2000) 'The end of identity? Implications of postmodernity for political identification', *Nationalism and Ethnic Politics*, 6(3): 68–90.

Guerrina, R. (2002) 'Mothering in Europe: a feminist critique of European policies on motherhood and employment', *The European Journal of Women's Studies*, 9(1): 49–68.

Habermas, J. (1998) 'The European nation-state: on the past and future of sovereignty and citizenship', *Public Culture*, 10(2): 397–416.

Hantrais, L. (2000) *Social Policy in the European Union (2nd edition)*, Basingstoke and London: Macmillan.

Hervey, T. and Shaw, J. (1998) 'Women, work and care: women's dual role and double burden in EC sex equality law', *Biblio Europe*, 2: 74–7.

Hoskyns, C. (1996) *Integrating Gender: Women, Law and Politics in the European Union*, London: Verso.

—— (2003) 'Gender equality and the Convention – A comment', *Federal Trust Online Papers*, 08/03. Online. Available at: www.fedtrust.co.uk/eu_constitution (accessed 10 June 2005).

Irving, Z. (1998) 'Women, self-employment and the impact of social policy: a comparison of Denmark, France and the UK', in R. Sykes and P. Alcock (eds) *Developments in Social Policy: Convergence and Diversity*, Bristol: Policy Press.

Jary, D. (1999) 'Citizenship and human rights: particular and universal worlds and the prospects for European Citizenship', in D. Smith and S. Wright (eds) *Whose Europe? The Turn Towards Democracy*, Oxford: Blackwell.

Jones, R. (2001) *The Politics and Economics of the European Union (2nd edition)*, Cheltenham, UK and Northampton, USA: Edward Elgar.

Lewis, J. (1992) 'Gender and the development of welfare regimes', *Journal of European Social Policy*, 2(3): 159–73.

Lister, R. (1997) *Citizenship: Feminist Perspectives*, Basingstoke and London: Macmillan.

Longo, M. (2003) 'European integration: between micro-regionalism and globalism', *Journal of Common Market Studies*, 41(3): 475–94.

Mazey, S. (2001) *Gender Mainstreaming in the EU: Principles and Practice*, London: Kogan Page.

Miller, V. (2000) 'Human rights in the EU: the Charter of Fundamental Rights', *House of Commons Research Papers* 00/32. Online. Available at: www.parliament.uk (accessed 10 June 2005).

Nugent, N. (2003) *Government and Politics of the EU (5th edition)*, Basingstoke and New York: Palgrave.

Pateman, C. (1991) *The Sexual Contract*, Cambridge and Oxford: Polity Press.

Pollack, M.A. and Hafner-Burton, E. (2000) 'Mainstreaming gender in the European Union', *Harvard Jean Monnet Working Paper* 2/00. Online. Available at: www.jeanmonnetprogram.org/papers/papers00.html (accessed 10 June 2005).

Prokhovnik, R. (1998) 'Public and private citizenship: From gender invisibility to feminist inclusiveness', *Feminist Review*, 60(Autumn): 84–104.

Rees, T. (1992) *Women and the Labour Market*, London: Routledge.

Regan, E. (2002) *The Charter of Fundamental Rights*, Dublin: Institute of European Affairs.

Shaw, J. (2001) 'European Union governance and the question of gender: a critical comment', *Responses to the European Commission's White Paper on Governance – Jean Monnet Papers*. Online. Available at: www.jeanmonnetprogram.org/01/010601.html (accessed 10 June 2005).

Skach, C. (2005) 'We, the peoples? Constitutionalizing the European Union', *Journal of Common Market Studies*, 43(1): 149–70.

Tambini, D. (2001) 'Post-national citizenship', *Ethnic and Racial Studies*, 24(2): 195–217.

Vitorino, A. (2000) 'The Charter of Fundamental Rights of the European Union: the point of view of the European Commission', *European Trade Union Yearbook, 2000*. Online. Available at: www.etuc.ETUI/Publications/Yearbook/Yearbook2000/Yearbook00.cgm (accessed 10 June 2005).

Vogel-Polsky, E. (2000) 'Parity democracy: Law and Europe', in M. Rossilli (ed.) *Gender Politics in the European Union*, New York: Peter Lang.

Weatherill, S. (2002) 'Is constitutional finality feasible or desirable? On the cases for European constitutionalism and a European Constitution', ConWEB, No. 7/2002. Online. Available at: www.les1.man.ac.uk/conweb/ (accessed 8 January 2006).

Yuval-Davis, N. (1997) 'Women, citizenship and difference', *Feminist Review*, 57(Autumn): 4–27.

10 International citizenship and women's interests

Merryn L. Smith

Citizenship has served as a powerful concept throughout the historical development of formal and informal politics, constructing individuals as members of a political community with shared rights and responsibilities, and legitimating governmental and civil society institutions that represent the shared interests of these citizens. A concept that originally applied only to elite members of small, highly stratified urban communities has expanded to encompass virtually all of humanity through universal citizenship of nation-states in a global state system. More recent developments in international and transnational political organization, including the evolution of supranational political organizations such as the European Union (EU), the proliferation of intergovernmental organizations (IGOs), particularly within the global United Nations (UN) system, and the emergence of global civil society organizations and networks, arguably expand the concept of citizenship further, introducing new levels of political community situated above and across national citizenship.

Feminists have been highly critical of the discourse and institutional practices of citizenship; however, citizenship can also be (re)appropriated for feminist projects without implying uncritical acceptance of its value (Lister 1997a: 3). A substantial body of feminist literature demonstrates that citizenship is an inherently gendered concept that has been historically predicated on the exclusion of women (Jones 1990; Lister 1997a; Mouffe 1992; Orloff 1993; Pateman 1988; Vogel 1991; Walby 1994; Yuval-Davis and Werbner 1999). As Jill Vickers argues in Chapter 2 of this volume, this history of male-defined citizenship has discouraged many feminists from engaging with formal state-based politics, seen as male-dominated and implicated in patriarchy, allowing men to continue to shape political institutions, and to construct 'women's' interests represented by these institutions, from their own standpoint. Yet, the normative power of the concept of citizenship, particularly when the emerging international dimensions are considered, provides feminist academics, activists and political actors with a potentially potent tool for furthering women's interests.

This chapter explores the potential value of the concept of international citizenship as a strategic tool for furthering the 'politics of women's interests', utilizing a modified version of T.H. Marshall's classic tripartite model of citizenship (1950). I want to explore whether and to what extent a reconstructed Marshallian model is viable; I conclude that its chances are mixed due to the presence of both constraints and opportunities within the supra-national environment. These enabling and constraining variables are laid out and assessed in the following discussion.

The initial section provides a theoretical framework for this project, outlining the utility of the concept of citizenship for feminist research, while also acknowledging feminist criticisms of the gendered nature of the liberal and republican traditions of citizenship. Marshall's model and its utility for feminist projects are discussed, justifying the addition of a further dimension of reproductive rights and the application of a model based on national citizenship at different levels of analysis. The following sections discuss the limitations of the concepts of European and global international citizenship, before applying the modified version of Marshall's model at these levels, analysing the civil, political, social and reproductive rights granted to citizens in these emerging political communities through a gendered lens. In conclusion, international and regional citizenship are shown to be powerful concepts that can be harnessed to the pursuit of women's interests despite the replication of national citizenship's gender bias towards more typically male experience and interests. The normative power of citizen equality and the formally equal citizenship rights that flow from European and global international law provide feminist activists and political actors within and outside formal politics with a weapon for progressively closing the remaining gaps of substantive gender inequality at all levels of political community.

The concept of citizenship

The concept of citizenship provides a very powerful and flexible framework with great potential for exploring and promoting women's interests in international politics. As an overall concept it acknowledges the complexity of the relationship between the individual, the state, and society, constructing citizens as individuals bearing rights and responsibilities, but also locating them within a particular community, where they share common interests and a stake in the common good. An awareness of the historical development of the politics of citizenship as a politics of exclusion (Pettman 1996: 15), with citizenship status originally restricted to a narrow elite within highly stratified societies and only gradually expanding to the contemporary norm of universal citizenship, allows analytical attention to focus on measuring the extent to which women (and other historically marginalized groups) are fully incorporated into political communities, and on investigating the broader political and social implications of incomplete incorporation.

This feminist (re)appropriation of the concept of citizenship does not imply uncritical acceptance of its value (Lister 1997a: 3), but derives its analytical and strategic power from acknowledgement and exploration of the gap between the aspiration of universal citizen equality and the reality of gendered inequality of citizenship status. Feminist theorists have been highly critical of citizenship as a political concept, clearly demonstrating its gendered nature (Jones 1990; Lister 1997a; Mouffe 1992; Orloff 1993; Pateman 1988; Vogel 1991; Walby 1994; Yuval-Davis and Werbner 1999). Although the citizen has been traditionally depicted as a universal gender-neutral category, closer examination of the characteristics associated with this supposedly genderless citizen reveals that *he* possesses qualities that women have been historically assumed not to possess, such as the ability to use reason to transcend passion, and/or have been systematically denied, including social autonomy, economic independence, headship of a patri-archal household with the benefit of associated domestic services, and the right to bear arms in defence of the state (Berkovitch 1999: 12; Connell 1990: 511; Vogel 1991: 59). Paradoxically the revolutionary extension of citizenship status in eighteenth century Europe simultaneously reinforced female exclusion from this newly 'universal' status, as women became the 'property' that allowed married men of all social classes to claim a status previously reserved for the propertied elite (Werbner and Yuval-Davis 1999: 6). The characteristics and interests of the hypothetical 'universal citizen' of western political tradition have been consistently constructed from the perspective of (white heterosexual) men.

The dominant liberal discourse of citizenship, which emphasizes cit-izenship as a status with associated rights, has excluded women's interests through its rigid conceptual separation of politics from domestic life, lack of consideration of difference, and disconnection of politics from its social context. Liberalism seeks to protect individual liberty from state interfer-ence through rigid separation of the public sphere of political participation and membership inhabited by citizens en masse from the private domestic sphere inhabited by individual citizens and their families, thereby restricting the legitimate scope of politics to the public sphere. This division depoliti-cizes gendered inequality and divergence of interests within the private sphere, equating the interests of a household with those of its members who are active in the public sphere, denying a political voice to citizens, usually women, whose time and attention are dominated by domestic responsibil-ities. The liberal tradition constructs the public sphere of citizenship as uni-versalist and homogenous, relegating differences such as gender, and any divergence in interests which flow from these differences, to the private sphere, where they are considered as apolitical and irrelevant to citizenship status. The liberal citizen is also constructed as an autonomous individual, pursuing individual rather than collective interests in a polity divorced from social context, which excludes social relationships, including those of care and dependency, from political consideration.

The alternative civic republican discourse of citizenship, which emphasizes citizenship as a practice encompassing political obligations, has similarly excluded women's experiences and interests from its key concepts of the common good and active political participation. This tradition rejects the liberal focus on an individual citizen's rights, focusing instead on citizens' shared responsibility to actively participate in their political community, working to promote the common good, which is seen to transcend individual desires and interests. This assumption of prior common interests fails to consider differences and structural inequalities among citizens, allowing the interests of the socially disadvantaged, including women, to be excluded from a 'common good' defined from the perspective of the more powerful members of society, once again constructing 'universal' citizenship in a narrow and male-dominated image. The high value that this tradition places on active participation also works to exclude women and their interests by defining participation from a male standard, disregarding the value of domestic service and care obligations disproportionately borne by women. Particularly in contemporary versions of the duties discourse, strong emphasis is placed on the value of participation in the formal economy.

Despite the shortcomings of these dominant discourses of citizenship, feminists have been able to harness the concept of citizenship to claim both 'universal' and differentiated rights for women, although not without limitation. Making claims for women using concepts that fit women's experience and interests so poorly, potentially catches women's claim to full citizenship status in what has been termed 'Wollstonecraft's dilemma' (Pateman quoted by Lombardo 2003: 159). This term refers to a forced choice between emphasizing equality, asking for the same rights that are available to male citizens to be extended to women, or emphasizing difference, asking for the specific capacities, interests and needs of women to be recognized via differentiated citizenship. This can offer an unsatisfactory choice of citizenship as 'inferior man' or inclusion *as women* rather than as full *citizens* (Pateman quoted by Lombardo 2003: 160), both options leading to second-class rather than full citizenship. However, although the 'universal' citizen has been defined from a male perspective, the normative power of the ideal of universal citizenship provides feminist activists and political actors with a lever to claim full citizenship status, and all associated rights, for female as well as male citizens, and to lobby for the rights attached to citizenship status to be more reflective of the experience and interests of the female half of the citizenship body.

Models of citizenship

The most influential model for analysing citizenship status remains that developed by T.H. Marshall (Kymlicka and Norman 1995: 285). Following the liberal tradition, Marshall defines citizenship as 'a status bestowed on those who are full members of a community, [where] all who possess the status are equal with respect to the rights and duties with which the status is endowed' (1950: 28–9). His model divides citizenship rights into three component parts – civil, political, and social; with civil rights specified as 'the rights necessary for individual freedom – liberty of the person, freedom of speech, thought and faith, the right to own property and to conclude valid contracts, and the right to justice'; political rights identified as 'the right to participate in the exercise of political power, as a member of a body invested with political authority or as an elector of members of such a body'; and social rights defined as

> the whole range from the right to a modicum of economic welfare and security to the right to share to the full in social heritage and to live the life of a civilized being according to the standards prevailing in the society.
>
> (Marshall 1950: 10–11)

Marshall used this tripartite model to describe a phased evolution of citizenship status, with distinct formative periods for the three component sets of citizenship rights. Civil rights are described as well developed by the eighteenth century, with political rights building on this foundation in the nineteenth century, supplemented by social rights in the twentieth century (Marshall 1950: 14).

Marshall's model offers sufficient flexibility to be meaningfully applied at levels of analysis other than the state. Its emphasis on citizenship as membership of a community rather than a state loosens the traditional association of citizenship and the nation-state, enabling discussion of citizenship as a multi-layered concept (Hall and Held 1989; Lister 1997b; Werbner and Yuval-Davis 1999: 5), where individuals are situated as members of coexisting nested local, national, regional, and global political communities.

Although Marshall's model remains in use, it has been subjected to a number of criticisms (Bulmer and Rees 1996; Kymlicka and Norman 1995; Rees 1996; Turner 1990). The most relevant to this chapter is its false universalism of an historical account drawn only from male experience of citizenship. While acknowledging in passing that 'the status of women, or at least of married women, was in some respects peculiar' (1950: 18), Marshall's model does not define or explore the implications of this 'peculiar' status; rather, it tends to render invisible women's very different historical experience of citizenship status and associated rights by making claims about 'citizens' that are clearly false when applied to women, such as the assertion that '[n]o sane and law-abiding citizen was debarred by personal status from acquiring and recording a vote' (Marshall 1950: 20), as well as the posited existence of a universal civil 'right to work where and at what you pleased under a contract of your own making' (Marshall 1950: 22). It is generally acknowledged that, if women were included, Marshall's account of the evolutionary development of citizenship rights would be different and less optimistic (Bulmer and Rees 1996: 275; Vogel 1991: 65).

However, despite this inattention to the saliency of gender and the limits placed on women's citizenship in the initial development and application of Marshall's model, it retains many qualities that fit well with a gendered analysis of citizenship status. The model is highly sensitive to social inequality between nominally equal citizens, as it was originally designed to analyse the paradox of citizenship status as a basic human equality that coexisted and was deemed compatible with the inequalities of social class, such that citizenship itself became 'in certain respects, the architect of legitimate social inequality' (Marshall 1950: 8–9). This model *potentially* enables analysis of the impact of other social inequalities, in this case gender, on the degree to which citizens are fully included in their political communities, and enables consideration of the broader implications of partial or second-class citizenship status for citizens from socially disadvantaged groups, in this case women. Marshall's description of ideal citizenship 'against which achievements can be measured and towards which aspirations can be directed' (1950: 29) allows divergence from this ideal to be identified and also opens up the question of whether the extension of citizenship is a realistic political means for resolving, or at least containing, the contradictions of citizen equality and gender inequality (Turner 1990: 191).

The applicability of Marshall's model to a gendered analysis of citizenship can be enhanced by the addition of a further category of rights – reproductive rights. As Jill Vickers argues in Chaper 2 of this volume, although not all women bear children their capacity to do so makes a significant difference to their relationship to their political communities. Reproductive rights are important to consider not only because they relate to the ability of women to control their own bodies (Correa and Petchesky 1994: 113) but also because in the context of this discussion they influence women's citizenship status. Political communities have always had an interest in women's power to physically (and culturally) reproduce society. Historically, this interest has resulted in social and political controls being placed on women's sexuality as well as constraints on the time, money and other resources that women have available for political participation.

International citizenship

Citizenship studies have traditionally focused on membership of national political communities, but the concept of citizenship is now arguably applicable both at the sub- and supra-national levels, at least in some world regions. Some, such as Hannah Arendt (quoted by Elshtain 1987: 245), would argue that '[n]obody can be a citizen of the world as he is a citizen of his own country [as a] citizen is by definition a citizen among citizens of a country among countries'. However, using Marshall's model of citizenship, the salient question is whether a meaningful political community can and does exist at levels above the nation-state.

At the regional level, the European Union (EU) can be considered to be such a supranational political community. The EU is formally constituted as a polity, with structures for political representation of the citizens of its member states through the directly elected European Parliament, and indirectly through nationally elected representatives in the Council of the European Union and appointed members of the European Commission. The European Court of Justice (ECJ) also provides EU citizens with the opportunity to satisfy and achieve their national citizenship rights, offering a critical bulwark against the erosion of rights within member states (Hall and Held 1989: 183; Turner 1993: 178).

European Union citizenship status, automatically deriving from citizenship of member states, was formally introduced in Article 8 of the Maastricht Treaty. This status explicitly confers citizens of the Union with the rights to move and reside freely within member states, to vote at municipal elections, to vote and to stand as a candidate in European Parliament elections, to enjoy diplomatic or consular protection from the representatives of other member states in non-Union countries, and to appeal to the European Ombudsman (European Union 2004a). These citizenship rights are balanced with rights derived from overlapping national and sub-national political communities. This is achieved through the principle of subsidiarity, which requires decisions to be taken as close to the citizen as possible, with the Union only empowered to act where it is more effective than action taken at national, regional, or local levels, and through the related principles of proportionality and necessity, which restrict Union action from going beyond what it necessary to achieve the objectives of the EU Treaty (European Union 2004a).

However, there are also significant differences between the European Union and a national political community that should not be ignored in this analysis. The socio-cultural dimension of the EU is considerably less well developed than within its member states, with formal EU citizenship status imposed from above with the intention of creating a common socio-cultural identity rather than reflecting popular demand for expression of a pre-existing pan-European communal identity. The political dimension is also under-developed at the EU level. Political participation holds far greater significance for European citizens within their national political communities, as participatory structures – such as political parties, trade unions, and social movements – continue to be organized at the national level and to engage with citizens through culturally isolated national public spheres (Habermas 1995: 271). As a result, voting in EU elections tends to reflect national rather than European issues. National citizenship rights also remain far more significant than the few, and relatively trivial, additional formal rights listed above, that have been granted to citizens through EU citizenship status.

The existence of a meaningful political community at the global level is more questionable. The United Nations (UN) and other global governance organizations clearly lack the formal structures of participation, representation, accountability and enforcement possessed by a typical nation-state, or even the EU. Global citizenship does not exist in any formal or legal sense. The social-cultural dimension of citizenship is also problematic, with the concept of global citizenship more readily associated with a homogenized global corporate elite, often seen as lacking a global civic sense of responsibility, than with all the inhabitants of the globe (Falk 1994: 134; Hoff 1996: 11; Tickner 2001: 129).

However, an argument can be made that the UN system, other intergovernmental organisations (IGOs), and global civil society collectively constitute a sufficiently meaningful political community for the application of Marshall's model, provided that it is acknowledged that this ideal of global citizenship is more applicable as a normative aspiration than as an extant standard located in a specific place and time. This emerging global political community is based on a new tier of popular, and arguably legitimate, governance that is emerging alongside the formal political communities of states and governments, made up of formal IGOs within and outside the UN system,[1] and a global civil society consisting of groups, networks and movements[2] through which individuals negotiate and renegotiate political bargains at a global level (Gills 2002: 168; Kaldor 2003: 77).

European citizenship

Applying the modified version of Marshall's model at the European level shows that the EU political community provides its citizens with some additional limited sources of civil rights, and new avenues for protecting and fulfilling civil rights previously gained at the national level. The Community treaties that provide the basis for the EU's legal order reflect the defining purpose of the European Community, to facilitate economic co-operation, and so give primacy to market principles (particularly enabling competition), the formation of common policy, and the five freedoms of the common market – free exchange of goods, free movement of labour, freedom of entrepreneurial domicile, freedom of service transactions, and freedom of currency movements, making no specific references to the fundamental rights of individuals. The limitations of EU legal and political supremacy, together with the underlying principles of subsidiarity, necessity, and proportionality, also offer major barriers to EU legal competence on civil rights issues that are not employment-related (Walby 2004: 15). However, fundamental rights for individuals have become entrenched in the EU legal system via the parallel development of the European Convention for the Protection of Human Rights and Fundamental Freedoms, to which all EU member states are High Contracting Parties, the development of the EU's Charter of Fundamental Rights in 2000,[3] and the preparation of a Draft EU Constitution (Duthiel de la Rochère 2004: 345–50).[4] The EU legal structures also provide citizens with an additional avenue of appeal to satisfy or achieve their nationally derived citizenship rights, which has served as a critical bulwark against the erosion of civil liberties within member states when national governments have sought to wind back citizen rights, as happened during the period of the Thatcher government in the United Kingdom (Hall and Held 1989: 183; Turner 1993: 178).

European civil citizenship rights are formally equal for men and women, but the strong market and employment focus within the EU undermines substantive equality by constructing the European citizen as a paid worker. Sex equality provisions have been included in the EU legal code since the Treaty of Rome, which granted equal pay for the same work in Article 119, augmented by additional protections guaranteeing equal pay for work of equal value, equal treatment in employment conditions and equal treatment in retirement. These rights have been reinforced by European Court decisions explicitly ruling that elimination of discrimination based on sex forms part of the fundamental human rights that are upheld as a general principle of Community law (Meehan 1991: 140; Guerrina, Chapter 9, this volume). However, these guarantees of formal equality have been based more on the economic principle of free movement of workers than a fundamental right of non-discrimination (Duthiel de la Rochère 2004: 347; Stratigaki 2004: 34). This focus on the rights of workers and on inequality only within the formal labour market constructs the interests of the European citizen as those of the paid worker, marginalizing those outside the formal labour market, who are disproportionately women (European Union 2004b: 10).

European feminists have been able to use European civil citizenship rights to further the interests of European women who are also paid workers, and who constitute a narrow majority of the adult female population (European Union 2004b: 10). The EU has usually been in advance of the majority of member states on employment-related equal opportunity issues (Walby 2004: 17), and a 'ping-pong' pattern of legal development can be identified, where national provisions have been progressively strengthened in response to direct changes in EU law and indirect political pressure from the transnational women's network that has emerged within the EU policy arena. This network includes the EU-funded European Women's Lobby (EWL), other Brussels-based interest groups, feminists within EU bureaucratic structures, and sympathetic members of the European Parliament and Commission, connected to national women's organizations and trade unions (Walby 2004: 15–16; Zippel 2004: 67–8). Within this restricted issue area, where the EU's limited legal supremacy applies, an effective EU-wide feminism has developed, utilizing a common political discourse based in the language of rights to legitimate feminist claims (Walby 2004: 15–16).

The EU also provides its citizens with new political rights, and additional mechanisms for exercising their national political rights. The European Parliament provides an additional level of political representation, which has evolved from a purely consultative assembly into a legislative parliament with similar powers to national parliaments, approving EU laws which have direct legal effect on EU citizens and override domestic legislation that has not been brought into line (European Union 2004b). EU citizenship also extends voting rights in local elections to those who are residents in a member state other than their state of nationality. In addition to this formal representation, the EU provides an open and flexible field of opportunities for influencing policy, at both the European level and nationally, as the formation and consolidation of new supranational institutions provides space for transnational advocacy networks and interest group coalitions to fill expertise gaps, a process actively supported by the EU, particularly in the gender equality issue area (Zippel 2004: 58).

European women face no greater disadvantage in using these European political rights to further their interests than they do at the national level. Formal EU voting rights are granted following the principle of universal suffrage, without gender discrimination, in all member states. In 2003, 31 per cent of all European Parliamentarians were women, with most member states having a higher proportion of female representatives at the EU than in their national parliaments (Inter-Parliamentary Union 2003, 2004).[5] Avenues for influencing gender policy, and advancing women's political interests more broadly, have been provided through administrative and consultative structures including the European Women's Lobby and the Women and Equality Unit of the EU Advisory Committee. Such networks have been effective in bringing forward proposals for policy development and building EU-wide consultative networks (Walby 2004: 15), particularly since the EU preparation for the 1995 Beijing Conference, which created networks, built capacities, and facilitated a more global orientation (Kenney 2004: 92).

The EU provides European citizens with additional sources of social rights, and new mechanisms for protecting and fulfilling their nationally derived rights. The Treaty of Amsterdam (1999) incorporated a Social Policy Agreement into the European Community (EC) Treaty to guarantee that certain social rights are respected in member states, building on the foundation of the 1989 Fundamental Social Rights of Workers Charter (Social Charter) (European Union 2004a). The social rights explicitly protected by the EU are primarily those falling within its areas of greatest legal competence, namely, those related to employment and the labour market with health, social welfare, and other policies left to member states to regulate (Pudrovska and Ferree 2004: 120). However, the ECJ has more broadly declared that it is its duty to enforce the 'fundamental rights of access to social security' (Meehan 1991: 125) and has gradually extended important social rights to economically inactive members of workers' families by broadly interpreting the principle of facilitating mobility of workers to ensure that freedom of residence can be exercised without loss of welfare (Ackers 1998: 314; Meehan 1991: 127).

The EU's focus on social rights for workers and their families, rather than for citizens more broadly, marginalizes the interests of those not within the formal labour market, who are disproportionately women. EU social rights are attached to narrow economic definitions of social contribution, which do not value the unpaid domestic and caring labour disproportionately performed by women, and are only available to economically inactive partners and family members of paid workers while their relationship of dependency continues (Ackers 1998: 315–16). The linking of benefits to apparently gender-neutral categories, such as insured persons, workers, and spouses, reinforces substantive inequality because men and women, particularly married women, are unequally situated in the labour market, from which access to and levels of benefits are derived (Meehan 1991: 141–2). Such a formal and narrow concept of equality takes little account of other relevant differences in social and material circumstances between men and women (Lombardo 2003: 166). The EU's consistent privileging of the social rights of economically active citizens implies that it is only economic contribution to the European community that qualifies its citizens as full members deserving all rights and benefits of citizenship (Thomas 2002: 336).

The EU does not explicitly guarantee its citizens reproductive rights, but broader civil and social rights at the EU level have a significant impact on reproductive freedom. The freedom to travel and to sell services within the EU constrains the ability of member state governments to prevent their national citizens from learning about and accessing contraception, abortion, and other reproductive health services (Walby 2004: 21). An exception was created in a protocol to the Maastricht Treaty, ceding supremacy over Article 40.3.3 of the Constitution of Ireland, which upholds the rights of the unborn. Although the Irish government has since sought to delete this protocol after a high-profile legal case involving a 14-year-old rape victim, an ECJ decision on that case ruled that abortion is a service qualifying for these freedoms (Ackers 1998: 256–7).

Global citizenship

At the global level, the nascent political community made up of the UN system and global civil society has been the source of significant new civil rights for all of humanity. The Universal Declaration of Human Rights (UDHR), adopted by the UN General Assembly (UNGA) in 1948, the binding International Covenant on Civil and Political Rights (ICCPR) of

1966, and the expanding body of international human rights law that has been built on these foundations aspire to provide all humanity with equal and inalienable individual human rights that transcend national boundaries. These inherent rights of individuals are considered to have *prima facie* priority over the interests and desires of society and the state, effectively 'trumping' other legitimate claims. Further, they are considered to be universal, indivisible, interdependent, and interrelated, such that promoting and protecting one category of right can not exempt or excuse states from the promotion and protection of other rights (Donnelly 1999: 613–14). International conventions based on this principle of universal human rights extend civil rights to individuals who are not citizens of the states in which they are resident, increasingly empowering those excluded from national citizenship to make claims on the state (Jacobson and Soysal cited in Boli and Thomas 1997: 182; Soysal cited in Thomas 2002: 339).

The UN provides mechanisms for holding states accountable to these human rights instruments through the UN Commission on Human Rights (UNCHR) and monitoring committees for the major human rights treaties – the ICCPR, the International Covenant on Economic, Social and Cultural Rights (ICESCR), Convention on the Rights of the Child (Child Convention), Convention against Torture and other Cruel, Inhuman or Degrading Treatment or Punishment (Torture Convention), the International Convention on the Elimination of all Forms of Racial Discrimination (Race Convention) and the Convention on the Elimination of all Forms of Discrimination against Women (CEDAW) – most of which are empowered to hear individual complaints against state abuses of their relevant rights. A number of global civil society organizations have participated in the development of international human rights law and assist individuals in making claims in these and other relevant supranational institutions (Boli and Thomas 1997: 182; Ku 2002: 542). Human rights NGOs, such as Amnesty International, Human Rights Watch and the International Commission of Jurists, monitor and report on state violations of international human rights law, providing supporting information to the UN monitoring process, and pressuring states to comply through direct lobbying and public campaigns.

The civil rights granted to global citizens through the UN system and global civil society are not entirely equal for men and women. The UN became the first institution for which the equal rights of men and women are both an objective and an obligation, as specified in the UN Charter Preamble, and in Articles 1, 8, 13, 55, and 76 (Reanda 1999: 50). International conventions have been ratified to ensure women's rights in the public sphere, including equal pay for equal value in 1953, equal political rights in 1954, maternity protection in 1955, equality in employment in 1960, equality in education in 1962, and equality of marriage rights in 1962 (Ramirez *et al.* 1997). However, the UN Charter also privileges men as household heads, and many human rights mechanisms focus exclusively on the public side of the public/private divide, excluding consideration of 'private' issues of concern to women, particularly family violence (Tickner 2001: 113).

Mechanisms created specifically to enforce rights for women have not been granted the same status and resources as other human rights instruments. The major UN treaty to specifically address women's rights, CEDAW, lacks a mechanism for individuals to make complaints, although this provision was included in the earlier ICCPR, Torture Convention, and Race Convention (UN Division for the Advancement of Women 2005b). Although this has been remedied by CEDAW's 2000 Optional Protocol (which allows individuals to make claims against nation states), this protocol has fewer than half the signatories of the parent treaty, currently 71 compared with 180 (UN Division for the Advancement of Women 2005d, 2005c). CEDAW also allows state parties unprecedented scope for making reservations to the treaty, which exclude specified treaty provisions from their domestic implementation. The negotiating process for CEDAW considered and rejected the model of the Race Convention, which requires reservations to be approved as consistent with the intention of the treaty by two-thirds of state parties (Riddle 2002: 635–6). As a result, state parties to CEDAW have registered large numbers of reservations, including cases where the exclusions are clearly incompatible with the object and purpose of the convention, such as objections to Articles 2 and 16, the core provisions of the treaty relating to equality in legislation and married life respectively (UN Division for the Advancement of Women 2005a). States have registered reservations to CEDAW in cases where analogous reservations have not been made to other human rights treaties, and where such exclusions are inconsistent with their national constitutions (UN Division for the Advancement of Women 2005a). The treaty body for CEDAW is also geographically and organizationally isolated from the mainstream human rights treaty bodies, which are located in Geneva and serviced by the Secretariat of UNCHR, by its location in New York and attachment to the UN's Division for the Advancement of Women (DAW) (Gallagher 1997: 296).

However, the normative power of gender equality promoted at the global level by the UN, and supported by global civil society, has had a strong mitigating effect on the gendering of national civil citizenship rights. The previously contested idea that women are indeed persons and rights-bearing citizens is, at least, now taken for granted in global political discourse, and linked to other legitimizing norms including human equality, democracy, national independence, and national development (Ramirez *et al.* 1997: 742). Global political discourse no longer narrowly constructs women's interests based on their difference from men, their roles as wives of citizens and mothers of further citizens, and their perceived need for special protection rather than equal rights, but has recast women as full and equal citizens (Boli and Thomas 1997: 186). This world model of equal citizenship and rights for women has the potential to exert a substantial impact on policy options open to governments wishing to be perceived as legitimate since alternative models which deny women personhood and citizenship are marked as deviant cases typical of 'backward societies' (Berkovitch 1999: 10). This normative pressure is reinforced by the availability of material and technological assistance from the UN and global civil society structures, to assist states to implement the necessary legal, political, economic, and social reforms required to conform to these global rights norms.

The global political community does not provide individuals with new formal political rights, but offers a myriad of new possibilities for organized representation of political interests within international politics. The political structures of the UN represent member states, rather than their citizens, with representatives appointed by governments, rather than directly elected by citizens. However, global civil society organizations offer a basic form of popular representation, guaranteeing the political legitimacy of intergovernmental organizations (IGOs) through their participation in international relations (Boutros-Ghali, quoted by Baker 2002: 934). Most IGOs are heavily influenced by civil society organizations, which provide information, expertise, and policy alternatives (Boli and Thomas 1997: 179).

Women and women's interests have been poorly represented within the formal structures of IGOs within and outside of the UN system. Few women were involved in the formation of the UN system, with those present steered to committees on women's and social issues, setting a pattern of isolation in under-resourced, specialized sectors, and absence from areas considered most important that has persisted, although with some recent improvement (Reanda 1999: 52–4; Tickner 2001: 111). Women's interests have been easily marginalized in a male-dominated, highly sectorialized institutional setting; the Commission on the Status of Women, established in 1947 as the main structure to ensure a voice for women, has been constrained by a limited mandate, few resources and little communication or co-operation with other parts of the system (Reanda 1999: 51). Women comprised only 5 per cent of the UN's member state delegates in 1946, and their level of representation within the UN and other IGOs continues to lag behind national levels (Tickner 2001: 111). Women are also under-represented in UN senior policy-making positions, despite General Assembly mandated targets of equal gender distribution, making up 17.5 per cent of Under Secretary-General level positions and 22.2 per cent of Assistant Secretary-General level positions as at the end of 2004 (Office of the Special Adviser on Gender Issues and Advancement of Women 2005).

Women have more successfully used civil society organizations to represent their interests within the global political community. There is a long history of women's involvement in international NGOs, starting with nineteenth century organizations dedicated to various causes including anti-slavery, peace, temperance, and women's suffrage; and formal international NGOs specifically dedicated to women's interests have existed since the International Congress of Women was founded in 1888, proliferating rapidly since the UN's Decade for Women starting in 1975 (Tickner 2001: 117). These organizations have played a substantial role in incorporating women's interests into international law, particularly through the series of UN conferences on women's, population, and development issues. The Third World Conference on Women at Nairobi in 1985 marked a turning point for women's influence on general international policy-making, laying the groundwork for the UN to adopt a gender mainstreaming policy (Reanda 1999: 54), and mobilizing women around the world in local communities, states, and transnational networks to seek and gain access to international policy-making arenas. This international women's movement was consolidated at the 1995 Beijing Fourth World Conference on Women (FWCW), dedicated to the economic, social, cultural, civil, and political rights of women, and continues to pressure IGOs and their member governments to ensure that women's interests are adequately reflected in international and national law and political practice.

Norms of gender equality developed in this global political community have also reinforced the national political citizenship rights of women. Women's political equality and right to suffrage, once a controversial domestic demand within a small minority of countries, is now such a strong global norm that not one of the many countries that have become independent during the UN era have chosen to extend 'universal' suffrage rights to men only (Finnemore and Sikkink 1998; Ramirez *et al.* 1997).[6] The United Nations actively reinforces this norm through the Electoral Assistance Division of the Department of Political Affairs, which provides states with legal, technical, administrative, and human rights assistance to organize and conduct democratic elections 'in accordance with internationally recognized criteria established in universal and regional human rights instruments' (United Nations Department of Political Affairs 2003). This Division makes specific efforts to address women's political rights when carrying out electoral assistance, by providing expert advice on gender mainstreaming issues, researching techniques for enhancing women's participation in elections as voters and candidates, and applying research findings through specific projects (United Nations General Assembly 2003: 8).

International norms of equal citizenship rights have been of particular strategic value to feminist activists and political actors in states where space is opening for democratic participation. This has been particularly evident in states undergoing drastic political reconstruction, such as post-apartheid South Africa, where demands for women were enabled on the normatively powerful grounds of democracy (Hassim 2002: 694–5). Women previously separated by race and other differences adopted a strategic essentialist approach to pursue a range of issues seen as relevant to all South African women. Successful coalitions were built by acknowledging and respecting differences between their members, such as the Women's National Coalition (WNC), which was formed in 1992 to allow 70 diverse women's organizations to cooperatively identify women's needs, priorities, and aspirations and present a Women's Charter to the South African Parliament, a goal achieved in 1994 (Cock and Bernstein 2001: 138–9). The growing strength and influence of the global gender equality discourse in the early 1990s legitimated claims based on women's common interests, ensuring that gender inequality was taken seriously when new political structures, including the parliament and constitutions, were being constructed (Seidman 1999: 295). The gender equality clause in the new constitution grants formal equality to South African women, which can be leveraged as a 'weapon in the struggle against women's insubordination' (Hassim 2002: 709).

International gender equality norms have also helped to promote the spread of government bureaucratic structures dedicated to women's interests. Institutional models incorporating mechanisms for ensuring women's equality and political participation have proliferated since the UN Decade for Women in the 1970s, with almost all countries establishing official bodies responsible for representing women's particular political interests. These international institutional models of 'national gender machineries' are of particular value to feminists in transitional states, assisting them to ensure that women's interests are institutionalized into the reconfigured political structures of their state (Hassim 2003: 508; see also Sawer, Chapter 6, this volume).

The nascent global political community has also provided new sources of universal social rights, and new mechanisms for protecting and fulfilling national social rights. The Universal Declaration of Human Rights (UDHR) explicitly includes the rights to social security (Article 22), to work at freely chosen employment with equal pay, just and favourable remuneration, and trade union protections (Articles 4 and 23), to rest and leisure (Article 24), to an adequate standard of living (Article 25), to education (Article 26), and to cultural participation (Article 27) as fundamental human rights. The International Covenant on Economic, Social and Cultural Rights (ICESCR) further elaborates the social rights of citizens of state parties, reinforcing the non-binding hortorary provisions of the UDHR with the stronger legal status of a formal treaty, although lacking enforcement mechanisms. However, the UN system's large body of international law guaranteeing civil rights has not been replicated in the area of social rights, reflecting a strong bias towards so-called 'first generation' civil and political rights rather than 'second generation' social and economic rights; this bias was exacerbated by Cold War politics which associated support for economic and social rights with communism (Robinson 2003: 85).

Yet, it is important to bear in mind that these global social rights are predicated on a male standard, limiting their capacity to reflect women's interests. Although the UNDHR (Article 2) and the ICESCR (Article 3) explicitly extend all specified rights equally to both men and women, the language in both documents slides between gender-neutral and gendered terminology, with a number of specific references to 'himself and his family' revealing an underlying assumption that the rights-bearers of these treaties are male household heads. These documents also address economic rights exclusively from the perspective of the paid worker, excluding consideration of unpaid labour disproportionately performed by women.

Women's social rights have been similarly marginalized within global development projects, although this has been partially mitigated by the adoption of gender mainstreaming policies in the 1990s. Early UN efforts to promote economic and social development followed a gender-blind orientation, failing to consider the particular social needs of women. This policy direction changed in the 1970s to include explicit consideration of Women in Development (WID), prompted by the UN Decade for Women. However, the new WID programmes tended to construct women's interests very narrowly, focusing on child health and maternal projects which emphasize women's role in reproduction rather than production, leaving 'mainstream' projects untouched (Hafner-Burton and Pollack 2002: 348). The specific social and economic needs of women have since been more broadly addressed within UN development programmes, with a shift to a gender and development (GAD) approach, also known as gender mainstreaming, which requires the consideration of the impact of gender on every aspect of development policy. This more complete inclusion of women's specific development needs is reinforced by the dominant economic logic of national development, which seeks to fully exploit the under-utilized resource of women's labour (Berkovitch 1999: 17). At the same time, this approach to equality is simultaneously undermined by pressure from global institutions to structurally adjust national economies, transferring social costs from public to private sectors, eliminating public sector jobs, a major source of women's paid work, and increasing demand for unpaid household labour (Pettman 1996: 168).

It can be argued that the emerging global political community has also helped to expand the reproductive rights of all individuals. The UDHR (Articles 12 and 25) and ICESCR (Articles 10 and 12) include some aspects of reproductive rights in their guarantees of fundamental and social and economic rights, specifying specific rights to privacy, enjoyment of physical and mental health, special care and assistance for motherhood, economic protection for mothers before and after childbirth, and provision for the reduction of stillbirth and infant mortality. CEDAW more explicitly elaborates reproductive rights, including rights to freedom from discrimination based on women's procreative role (Preamble), maternity protection and child care (Article 4), family planning education (Article 10), reproductive health services (Article 12), and social services to allow the combining of family responsibilities with public life (Article 16) (Division for the Advancement of Women n.d.). UN conferences, particularly the 1994 International Conference on Population and Development in Cairo and the 1995 Beijing FWCW, have been utilized by global civil society organizations to promote a feminist understanding of reproductive rights, going beyond contraception and abortion rights to define reproductive and sexual rights in terms of power to make informed decisions and resources to carry out decisions safely and effectively (Pettman 1996: 181).

Despite these developments, such globally derived reproductive rights fail to provide women with genuine reproductive choice. The CEDAW document resolves the tension between equality and difference in a problematical way, using gender-neutral language to grant men and women *the same* reproductive rights, failing to acknowledge that women have a greater stake in the matter as child-bearers (and usually as child-rearers), and the limits to choice imposed by gendered power relations within the family (Correa and Petchesky 1994: 116). Many of the numerous reservations to CEDAW relate to sexual and reproductive rights (United Nations Treaty Collection n.d.). There has also been fierce resistance to the expanded feminist view of reproductive rights for women at the Cairo and Beijing conferences, led by the Vatican and Islamic states (Yuval-Davis 1997a: 35). International economic norms also continue to undermine the material basis of genuine reproductive choice through cuts to public health care and other government services.

Conclusion

This exploration of citizenship at the European and global supranational levels has demonstrated that the concept of international citizenship can be used strategically to further 'the politics of women's interests', even while it remains a strongly gendered concept that replicates much of the false universalism of male experience that has characterized national citizenship. The discourse and institutional practices of international citizenship have tended to resolve Wollstonecraft's dilemma in favour of promoting equality rather than acknowledging difference, granting women citizenship status that is formally equal to that of men without ensuring substantive equality which addresses both needs and formal rights. At the same time, the normative power of the concept of citizen equality has enabled feminist activists and political actors to use this formal equality as a point of leverage to advance strategically women's political interests at all levels of political organization, from local and national to regional and global.

Essentially, women have been incorporated into EU citizenship as inferior men, with a strong bias towards public rather than private rights and with their special needs and interests marginalized by a model of citizenship that tightly links rights to participation in the paid labour market. The European political community's origins as a mechanism for economic integration, and consequent limits to the legal and political competence of the EU, have resulted in a strong bias towards public sphere rights, particularly those relating to paid employment, granting significant new rights to women who follow a typically male life pattern of lifelong attachment to the paid labour market, but marginalizing the interests of those who are not active within the formal economy. In this area women's access to rights, particularly social rights, occurs through their relationship to a breadwinner, rather than autonomously. Reproductive rights have been barely addressed, as the decision to exempt Ireland's ban on abortion clearly demonstrates.

Not only have women been incorporated into global citizenship as inferior men but the degree to which women's specific needs are incorporated reduces as the degree of difference between women's and men's typical experience and interests increases. Civil rights are elaborated in a substantial body of international law, but additional specific rights that acknowledge women's difference are less fully protected than 'mainstream' rights. Equal political rights are guaranteed, but women are under-represented in formal global political structures; this has pushed them towards the informal politics of civil society organizations to participate in international politics. Social rights are considerably less well protected than the more public categories of rights, and women's needs and interests have only been belatedly incorporated into development efforts, while being simultaneously undermined by global structural adjustment policies. Reproductive rights have been elaborated, but with gender-neutral language obscuring highly relevant differences in this area, and without any meaningful implementation or enforcement mechanisms.

When European and global international citizenship status is used as a formal yardstick against which rights equality is measured, it is shown to follow the same gendered, and therefore limited, pattern of national citizenship. But the situation is more promising when the aspirational or normative aspect of Marshall's model of citizenship is considered. The citizenship rights elaborated by the EU and UN systems can be understood to function as regional and global norms that set the rules for legitimate internal state organization and national citizenship rights, promoted and reinforced by IGOs and civil society organizations that provide practical assistance to enable governments to conform. Following this pattern global norms of legal personhood and suffrage for women have become almost universal, and denial of social and reproductive rights to women is becoming increasingly difficult for national governments to justify. As we have seen, states undergoing political construction, such as post-apartheid South Africa, can be strongly influenced by these global norms and institutional models and material incentives to conform to them, offering local feminists a powerful lever for building women's interests into the political and institutional foundations of the new state. In this way the notion of citizenship, understood as a normative, multi-tiered concept wider than the relationship between an individual and the state, continues to provide those working to close the remaining gaps between men's and women's rights, whether at local, national, regional or global levels, with a potentially valuable tool for mobilization (Yuval-Davis 1997b: 22).

Notes

1 A multitude of IGOs exist to facilitate intergovernmental co-operation in a broad range of issue areas. The United Nations (UN) is almost universal in both membership and scope of issues covered, with significant component organizations including the UN General Assembly (UNGA), UN Security Council (UNSC), Economic and Social Council (ECOSOC), International Court of Justice (ICJ), UN Development Programme (UNDP), Office of the UN High Commissioner for Refugees (UNHCR), UN Children's Fund (UNICEF), UN Development Fund for Women (UNIFEM), and further specialized agencies associated through special agreements, such as UN Educational, Scientific and Cultural Organization (UNESCO), International Labour Organization (ILO), Food and Agriculture Organization (FAO), World Health Organization (WHO), and the World Bank Group. There are a number of other IGOs covering broad issue areas, and organized on a regional basis, such as the European Union (EU), Council of Europe, Organization of American States (OAS), African Union, Association of South East Asian Nations (ASEAN), and League of Arab States, or on the basis of other shared interests, such as the Commonwealth. Many IGOs have a narrower scope, including economically oriented organizations such as the World Trade Organization (WTO), Organization for Economic Cooperation and Development (OECD), and Organization of Petroleum Exporting Countries (OPEC), and those focused on other issue areas such as the International Criminal Police Commission (INTERPOL), International Organization for Migration (IOM), and World Conservation Union (IUCN). This list is far from exhaustive.

2 International civil society is made up of formally constituted international non-governmental organizations (NGOs) and informal networks of transnational contact between national civil society organizations and individuals. Although there is no central global organization equivalent to the UN, many NGOs are affiliated to the UN, enjoying observer or consultative status. NGOs exist in a large number of issue areas, including humanitarian organizations such as Care International, Oxfam, International Save the Children Alliance, Médecins Sans Frontières (MSF) and the International Federation of Red Cross/Crescent Societies, human rights groups such as Human Rights Watch, Amnesty International, and the International Commission of Jurists, and other groups such as the International Planned Parenthood Federation, International Confederation of Free Trade Unions, World Federation of Trade Unions, World Muslim Congress, International Chamber of Commerce, Rotary International and World Wide Fund for Nature. There are a large number of international civil society organizations claiming to represent women's interests collectively, constituting a

global women's movement; these include Womankind Worldwide, Associated Country Women of the World, Sisterhood is Global Institute, Global Fund for Women, Women's Peace Network, Women Law and Development International, International Council of Women, International Federation of Business/Professional Women, Pan-African Women's Organization, International Muslim Women's Union, and the European Women's Lobby (EWL). These lists are also far from exhaustive.

3 See also Guerrina, Chapter 9, this volume.

4 At the time of writing the draft constitution had been resoundingly rejected by both France and the Netherlands, making its passage into law highly unlikely and raising questions about the ongoing viability of the EU.

5 Exceptions are Sweden, with 40.9 per cent female parliamentarians at the EU and 45.3 per cent nationally, Denmark (37.5 and 38 per cent), and Spain (31.3 and 36 per cent). The largest gap is for France, with 12.2 per cent female representation nationally, and 42.5 per cent at the EU.

6 Although it should be noted that certain existing signatory states such as Saudi Arabia continue to refuse to enfranchise women.

References

Ackers, L. (1998) *Shifting Spaces: Women, Citizenship and Migration within the European Union*, Bristol: The Policy Press.

Baker, G. (2002) 'Problems in the theorisation of global civil society', *Political Studies*, 50(5): 928–43.

Berkovitch, N. (1999) *From Motherhood to Citizenship: Women's Rights and International Organizations*, Baltimore: Johns Hopkins University Press.

Boli, J. and Thomas, G.M. (1997) 'World culture in the world polity: a century of international non-governmental organization', *American Sociological Review*, 62(2): 171–90.

Bulmer, M. and Rees, A.M. (1996) 'Conclusion: citizenship in the twenty-first century', in M. Bulmer and A.M. Rees (eds) *Citizenship Today: The Contemporary Relevance of T.H. Marshall*, London: UCL Press.

Cock, J. and Bernstein, A. (2001) 'Gender differences: struggles around "needs" and "rights" in South Africa', *NWSA Journal*, 13(3): 138–52.

Connell, R.W. (1990) 'The state, gender and sexual politics: theory and appraisal', *Theory and Society*, 19: 507–44.

Correa, S. and Petchesky, R. (1994) 'Reproductive and sexual rights: a feminist perspective', in G. Sen, A. Germain, and L.C. Chen (eds) *Population Policies Reconsidered: Health, Empowerment and Rights*, Boston: Harvard Center for Population and Development Studies.

Division for the Advancement of Women (n.d.) *Convention on the Elimination of All Forms of Discrimination Against Women*. Online. Available at: www.un.org/womenwatch/daw/cedaw/econvention.htm (accessed 13 July 2004).

Donnelly, J. (1999) 'Human rights, democracy and development', *Human Rights Quarterly*, 21(3): 608–32.

Duthiel de la Rochère, J. (2004) 'The EU and the individual: fundamental rights in the draft constitution', *Common Market Law Review*, 41(2): 344–54.

Elshtain, J.B. (1987) *Women and War*, New York: Basic Books.

European Union (2004a) *Glossary*. Online. Available at: www.europa.eu.int/scadplus/leg/en/cig/g4000.htm (accessed 8 July 2004).

—— (2004b) *Employment in Europe 2004*, European Commission. Online. Available at: www.europa.eu.int/comm/employment_social/employment_analysis/eie/eie2004_forew_toc_sum_en.pdf (accessed 12 April 2005).

Falk, R. (1994) 'The making of global citizenship', in B. van Steenbergen (ed.) *The Condition of Citizenship*, London: Sage.

Finnemore, M. and Sikkink, K. (1998) 'International norm dynamics and political change', *International Organization*, 52(4): 887–917.

Gallagher, A. (1997) 'Ending the marginalization: strategies for incorporating women into the United Nations human rights system', *Human Rights Quarterly*, 19(2): 283–333.

Gills, B.K. (2002) 'Democraticizing globalization and globalizing democracy', *Annals of the American Academy of Political and Social Science*, 581: 158–71.

Habermas, J. (1995) 'Citizenship and national identity: some reflections on the future of Europe', in R. Beiner (ed.) *Theorising Citizenship*, Albany: State University of New York Press.

Hafner-Burton, E. and Pollack, M.A. (2002) 'Mainstreaming gender in global governance', *European Journal of International Relations*, 8(3): 339–73.

Hall, S. and Held, D. (1989) 'Citizens and citizenship', in S. Hall and M. Jacques (eds), *New Times*, London: Lawrence and Wishart.

Hassim, S. (2002) ' "A conspiracy of women": the women's movement in South Africa's transition to democracy', *Social Research*, 69(3): 693–732.

—— (2003) 'The gender pact and democratic consolidation: institutionalising gender equality in the South African state', *Feminist Studies*, 29(3): 504–28.

Hoff, J. (1996) 'Editors' note: citizenship and nationalism', *Journal of Women's History*, 8(1): 6–14.

Inter-Parliamentary Union (2003) *Women in Regional Parliaments*. Online. Available at: www.ipu.org/wmn-e/regions.htm (accessed 12 July 2004).

—— (2004) *Women in National Parliaments*. Online. Available at: www.ipu.org/wmn-e/classif.htm (accessed 12 July 2004).

Jones, K.B. (1990) 'Citizenship in a woman-friendly polity', *Signs*, 15(4): 781–812.

Kaldor, M. (2003) *Global Civil Society: An Answer to War*, Cambridge: Polity Press.

Kenney, S.J. (2004) 'Equal employment opportunity and representation: extending the frame to courts', *International Studies in Gender, State and Society*, 11(1): 86–116.

Ku, A.S. (2002) 'Beyond the paradoxical conception of "civil society without citizenship" ', *International Sociology*, 17(4): 529–48.

Kymlicka, W. and Norman, W. (1995) 'Return of the citizen: a survey of recent work on citizenship theory', in R. Beiner (ed.) *Theorising Citizenship*, Albany: State University of New York Press.

Lister, R. (1997a) *Citizenship: Feminist Perspectives*, Houndmills: Macmillan Press.

—— (1997b) 'Dialectics of citizenship', *Hypatia*, 12(4): 6–26.

Lombardo, E. (2003) 'Trapped in the "Wollstonecraft dilemma"?', *The European Journal of Women's Studies*, 10(2): 159–80.

Marshall, T.H. (1950) *Citizenship and Social Class*, Cambridge: Cambridge University Press.

Meehan, E. (1991) 'European citizenship and social policies', in U. Vogel and M. Moran (eds) *The Frontiers of Citizenship*, Houndmills: Macmillan.

Mouffe, C. (1992) 'Feminism, citizenship and radical democratic politics', in J. Butler and J.W. Scott (eds) *Feminists Theorize the Political*, New York: Routledge.

Office of the Special Adviser on Gender Issues and Advancement of Women

(2005) *Gender Balance Statistics: The Status of Women at the United Nations.* Online. Available at: www.un.org/womenwatch/osagi/fpgenderbalancestats.htm (accessed 27 May 2005).

Orloff, A.S. (1993) 'Gender and the social rights of citizenship: the comparative analysis of gender relations and welfare states', *American Sociological Review,* 58(3): 303–28.

Pateman, C. (1988) *The Sexual Contract,* Cambridge: Polity Press.

Pettman, J. (1996) *Worlding Women: A Feminist International Politics,* St Leonards, NSW: Allen & Unwin.

Pudrovska, T. and Ferree, M.M. (2004) 'Global activism in "virtual space": the European Women's Lobby in the network of transnational women's NGOs on the Web', *Social Politics,* 11(1): 117–43.

Ramirez, F.O., Soysal, Y., and Shanahan, S. (1997) 'The changing logic of political citizenship: cross-national acquisition of women's suffrage rights, 1890 to 1990', *American Sociological Review,* 62(5): 735–45.

Reanda, L. (1999) 'Engendering the United Nations: the changing international agenda', *European Journal of Women's Studies,* 6(1): 49–69.

Rees, A.M. (1996) 'T.H. Marshall and the progress of citizenship', in M. Bulmer and A.M. Rees (eds) *Citizenship Today: The Contemporary Relevance of T.H. Marshall,* London: UCL Press.

Riddle, J. (2002) 'Making CEDAW universal: a critique of CEDAW's reservation regime under Article 28 and the effectiveness of the reporting process', *The George Washington International Law Review,* 34(3): 605–38.

Robinson, F. (2003) 'NGOs and the advancement of economic and social rights: philosophical and practical controversies', *International Relations,* 17(1): 79–96.

Seidman, G.W. (1999) 'Gendered citizenship: South Africa's democratic transition and the construction of a gendered state', *Gender and Society,* 13(3): 287–307.

Stratigaki, M. (2004) 'The cooptation of gender concepts in EU policies: The case of "Reconciliation of work and family"', *Social Politics: International Studies in Gender, State and Society,* 11(1): 30–56.

Thomas, E.R. (2002) 'Who belongs? Competing conceptions of political membership', *European Journal of Social Theory,* 5(3): 323–49.

Tickner, J.A. (2001) *Gendering World Politics: Issues and Approaches in the Post-Cold War Era,* New York: Columbia University Press.

Turner, B.S. (1990) 'Outline of a theory of citizenship', *Sociology: The Journal of the British Sociological Association,* 24(2): 189–217.

—— (1993) 'Outline of a theory of human rights', in B.S. Turner (ed.) *Citizenship and Social Theory,* London: Sage.

UN Division for the Advancement of Women (2005a) *Reservations to CEDAW.* Online. Available at: www.un.org/womenwatch/daw/cedaw/reservations.htm (accessed 26 May 2005).

—— (2005b) *Optional Protocol to the Convention on the Elimination of All Forms of Discrimination against Women.* Online. Available at: www.un.org/womenwatch/daw/cedaw/protocol/ (accessed 26 May 2005).

—— (2005c) *State Parties.* Online. Available at: www.un.org/womenwatch/daw/cedaw/states.htm (accessed 26 May 2005).

—— (2005d) *Signatures to and Ratifications of the Optional Protocol.* Online. Available at: www.un.org/womenwatch/daw/cedaw/protocol/sigop.htm (accessed 26 May 2005).

United Nations Department of Political Affairs 2003, *United Nations Electoral Assistance*. Online. Available at: www.un.org/Depts/dpa/ead/ead-main-page.htm (accessed 27 May 2005).

United Nations General Assembly (2003) *Strengthening the Role of the United Nations in Enhancing the Effectiveness of the Principle of Periodic and Genuine Elections and the Promotion of Democratization – A/58/212*, United Nations General Assembly. Online. Available at: www.daccessdds.un.org/doc/UNDOC/GEN/NO3/451/82/PDF/NO345182.pdf?OpenElement (accessed 7 January 2005)

United Nations Treaty Collection (n.d.) *Convention on the Elimination of All Forms of Discrimination Against Women (Parties and Reservations)*. Online. Available at: www.un.org/womenwatch/daw/cedaw/econvention.htm (accessed 13 July 2004).

Vogel, U. (1991) 'Is citizenship gender-specific?', in U. Vogel and M. Moran (eds) *The Frontiers of Citizenship*, Houndmills: Macmillan.

Walby, S. (1994) 'Is citizenship gendered?', *Sociology: The Journal of the British Sociological Association*, 28(2): 379–95.

—— (2004) 'The European Union and gender equality: emergent varieties of gender regime', *Social Politics: International Studies in Gender, State and Society*, 11(1): 4–29.

Werbner, P. and Yuval-Davis, N. (1999) 'Introduction: women and the new discourse of citizenship', in N. Yuval-Davis and P. Werbner (eds) *Women, Citizenship and Difference*, London: Zed.

Yuval-Davis, N. (1997a) *Gender and Nation*, London and Thousand Oaks: Sage Publications.

—— (1997b) 'Women, citizenship and difference', *Feminist Review*, 57: 4–27.

—— and Werbner, P. (1999) *Women, citizenship and difference*, London: Zed.

Zippel, K. (2004) 'Transnational advocacy networks and policy cycles in the European Union: the case of sexual harassment', *Social Politics: International Studies in Gender, State and Society*, 11(1): 57–85.

11 'Women's interests' as 'women's rights'

Developments at the UN criminal tribunals and the International Criminal Court[1]

Louise Chappell

The creation of the International Criminal Court (ICC) in 2002, and the UN ad hoc tribunals for Yugoslavia and Rwanda, which were established in the early 1990s, provide a unique opportunity for exploring assumptions about the way in which women's interests are defined and constructed through international legal institutions. These international tribunals and the ICC offer women's activists an additional arena through which to challenge existing biases and redefine concepts related to women and gender, especially in times of war and conflict. This chapter considers the extent to which this opportunity has been realised. In doing so, it assesses whether the jurisprudence of the ad hoc tribunals and the ICC statute provide for the development of new and different constructions of 'women's interests', primarily in terms of 'women's rights'. A second objective is to consider the relationship between women activists and politico/legal institutions through the lens of the ICC. This chapter assesses the extent to which women's activists are able to shape these institutions and evaluates whether such institutions can be exploited to achieve just outcomes for women. The overall argument of the chapter is that, although there is still a long way to go, feminist activists have successfully engaged with these institutions to bring about a broader understanding of women's interests through employing the notion of women's rights.

Women's interests and institutions

This chapter grows out of a broader interest in the relationship between feminist activists and political institutions.[2] For many years there was a widely held view, at least within western feminist thought, that women were merely subjects of political and legal institutions and were unable to exercise agency in relation to the institutions that framed their lives (MacKinnon 1989; Brown 1995). From this perspective, institutions were perceived to be fixed and static entities reflecting the interests of men who dominated them in both a corporeal and normative sense. As Vickers points out in Chapter 2 of this volume, such a perspective led many women's activists to reject state-based strategies and, as a result, the men were left to determine what policies were in 'women's best interest'. In the past decade, many feminists have begun to rethink these assumptions and strategies. Through studies of legal, bureaucratic, and legislative institutions, scholars have begun to document instances where women activists have successfully revealed and disrupted inherent gender biases in order to use these institutions to advance women's equality and justice claims (Chappell 2002; Dobrowolsky 2000). At times activists, such as 'femocrats' in the Australian bureaucracy, have done this through working inside political institutions. At other times they have achieved success by working as 'outside' lobbyists and advocates for change.

Much of this new work focuses on the way in which activists have taken advantage of changes in the political opportunity structure within institutions to advance their claims (Katzenstein 1998; Banaszak 1996). At the national level, this can involve the election of a new government or the elevation to the bench of judges who are sympathetic to issues of gender discrimination. Opportunities can also arise from the creation of new institutions, such as the introduction of a bill of rights or women's policy agencies in the bureaucracy.[3] Opportunity structures also appear (and disappear) for activists at the international level, as the important work of Margaret Keck and Kathryn Sikkink (1998) on transnational advocacy networks clearly demonstrates. Whether the creation of the two ad hoc tribunals and International Criminal Court (ICC) are examples of such an opportunity structure at the international level is one of the central questions of this chapter.

While this more positive assessment of women's engagement with institutions is a better reflection of what occurs in practice, it does need to be tempered by two qualifications. First, with the acceptance that institutions are dynamic rather than static entities comes the concomitant understanding that any institutional inroads made by women's activists are not always secure. This does not imply that activists' gains are illusory; in unsettling the 'taken-for-grantedness' of previous institutional structures and norms it is often difficult for these entities to return to their previous operational modes. However, feminists wanting to use institutions to advance their aims are engaged in a process of incremental change and very often in the dance of 'one step forward and two steps back'.

A second qualification relates to the notion of how 'women's interests' are defined in relation to institutions. How do we know if institutional norms and structures are operating to advance or retard women's interests? What are these interests? Do all women share them equally? As Vickers demonstrates so clearly in Chapter 2 of this book, the feminist literature is alive with debates surrounding these questions. Women from diverse ethnic, regional, class, and sexual orientation backgrounds have challenged the previous conception of a global 'sisterhood' – within which women share common interests – by demonstrating the ways in which the definition of 'woman' underlying this notion has reflected a white, western, middle-class bias (Rai 1996; Mohanty 2003). As a result, feminists have become more circumspect about using universal categories for defining 'women's interests', preferring to focus on the ways in which institutions such as the law, bureaucracy, and legislature *construct* the category of woman through a process of gender differentiation. Such an approach to understanding 'women's interests' rejects the notion that because women share certain biological attributes, they share all other experiences. Rather, the focus is on the way in which gender stereotypes, based on assumptions about differences between men and women's behaviour and about similarities within each sex, evolve within institutions to include and exclude particular experiences and categories of women (and men). Understanding how both international actors and institutions, especially international criminal and humanitarian law, help to construct the notion of women's interests is a key concern of this chapter. This includes a discussion of how feminist actors strategically apply a human rights framework to advance 'women's interests' in the face of opposition from more conservative forces. Before considering developments in UN tribunals and the ICC, it is important first to consider how women have historically been treated under international law.

The historical construction of 'woman' under international law

It is not the case that women have been entirely excluded from international law. However, where they have been included, women have been narrowly defined in limited roles and always situated in terms of their relationship with others – especially men or children. Charlesworth and Chinkin summarise women's position thus:

> [W]omen's presence on the international stage is generally focussed in their reproductive and mothering roles that are accorded 'special' protection. The woman of international law is painted in heterosexual terms within a traditional family structure ... She is constructed as 'the other', the shadow complement to the man of decision and action.
>
> (Charlesworth and Chinkin 2000: 308)

International law has incorporated women primarily as victims of armed conflict and as mothers but never as independent actors. Women have not been entitled to the 'mainstream' protection afforded to men in similar circumstances, nor has the law taken into account their unique and varied experiences of and participation in armed conflict.

This construction of women as 'other' is obvious within the various key documents that have, until the International Criminal Court (ICC) Statute, formed the basis of international humanitarian and criminal law. A few examples will help illustrate this point. In all four 1949 Geneva Conventions as well as the 1977 First Protocol to the Conventions, women are accorded 'special consideration' on account of their sex. Each of these measures is based on an underlying assumption about the ways biological differences between women and men define their appropriate behaviour and roles. Special measures include: separate quarters for women internees and prisoners of war, protection of women from sexual assault, and protection for pregnant women and mothers of young children. The latter category, which emphasised women's reproductive capacity, provides the rationale for many of the provisions relating to women. The extent to which women as individuals are subsumed in law by a mothering role is revealed by the fact that of the 42 provisions of the four Geneva Conventions that address women, 19 deal with women as mothers (Gardam and Jarvis 2001: 96).

Women have also been defined in international law through their relationship with men. Although the notion of what constitutes a 'special consideration' of women is left unstated in the conventions, official commentaries on this provision make the intention clearer: special consideration is 'no doubt that accorded in every civilized country to beings who are weaker than oneself and whose modesty and honour calls for respect' (in Gardam and Jarvis 2001: 63). In other words women are seen as the weaker sex and dependent upon men in situations of conflict. Moreover, they are assumed to possess the gender-specific, feminine virtues of an archaic (that is, chivalrous) and male-centred moral code.

This construction of women is especially obvious in existing provisions to protect women from sexual violence in armed conflict. Although sexual assault has been defined as a crime under international law,[4] until recently it has not been considered equivalent to other war crimes. Indeed, under the Geneva Conventions, rape along with other forms of sexual assault is explicitly categorised as a 'lesser crime' and not as a 'grave breach' of international law, subject to universal jurisdiction exercisable in national courts. Rape and sexual assault more broadly have been treated as a form of 'humiliating or degrading treatment' (in Geneva Convention I) or as an offence against a woman's honour. According to Article 27 of Geneva Convention IV, women must be 'especially protected against any attack of their honour, in particular against rape, forced prostitution or any form of sexual assault'. In neither the Geneva Conventions nor in international case law has rape been treated as a crime of violence (Boon 2001: 627).

The emphasis on rape as an attack against honour, rather than as a crime of violence, illustrates much about the way international law constructs gender identities. Honour is not a neutral term but, especially in this context, a highly gendered and dichotomised one. As Gardam and

Jarvis note, for men honour relates to bravery, fortitude, and self-reliance but for women it implies chastity, modesty, and dependence (2001: 11). By referring to rape as a breach of honour, international law has treated it as an act that is wrong because it brings shame upon a woman, to the men in her community, and, more widely, to her ethnic or national group. A woman who experiences rape is shamed because it is an offence against her chastity, while her male protector is also shamed because he has not defended her as a brave and chivalrous soldier should. Traditionally, international laws on rape are not about protecting individual women from an act of violence, but about the protection of dependent women by dependable men and even the protection of men from insults inflicted on dependent women by other men.

The key conventions and jurisprudence of existing international law have obviously helped to actively construct women as mothers and dependants. But they have also contributed to the process of defining women and their rights in a more subtle way; that is, through silences and omissions. There are many examples of how this occurs. The exclusion of any reference to gender specific crimes such as rape and sexual assault in the Genocide Convention is a case in point. The fact that the Refugee Convention does not include flight from continued sexual abuse as constituting a 'well founded fear of persecution' elides women's experience of armed conflict and leaves them without the ability to claim legitimate refugee status. Nowhere does international law address the fact that women are often as vulnerable to personal attack from 'friendly' as from 'hostile' forces. When women experience violence from within their community in times of armed conflict, it is too often treated as a 'private' matter, or seen as an acceptable feature of the spoils of war (see MacKinnon 1994). Moreover, international law does not address the economic and social hardships that are created for non-combatants by armed conflict (see Charlesworth and Chinkin 2000: 255). The notion of women as objects rather than subjects of war and armed conflict has also been emphasised through their historical exclusion from combat roles (and the expectation that men will fulfil these positions) as well as the lack of attention paid to women as the perpetrators of crimes. Whereas women's mothering roles have been embedded within international legal documents, there is a distinct absence of any reference to men's responsibility as fathers. Silence about many of the realities of women's lives in situations of armed conflict has served to reinforce a narrow view of women as victims, rather than active subjects in war, and has worked to render them invisible in international law.

Through acts of commission and omission, international criminal and humanitarian law has helped to define men and women in distinct, gendered roles. However, the law, as with other institutions, is not fixed but dynamic and open to challenge. Opportunities to contest assumptions about women and their interests can arise periodically either through the development of case law or from the creation of new institutions. When the two occur simultaneously – such as with the development of jurisprudence at the International Criminal Tribunals for Yugoslavia and for Rwanda and the creation of the ICC – a window of opportunity emerges and the chances of challenging existing assumptions appear all the greater. The possibility for making use of this window of opportunity has not been lost on feminist activists. They have worked hard at both the ad hoc tribunals and the Rome Conference and preparatory committees (prepcoms) to establish the ICC to contest assumptions and attitudes about women's place under international law.

Engaging with the war crimes tribunals for Yugoslavia and Rwanda

Throughout the 1990s, women's NGOs were active in a range of UN fora to push for new ways of framing women and their interests. In engaging with international institutions, feminist activists employed the language of rights and argued specifically for the recognition of 'women's rights as human rights'. This slogan suggested that, because of their historic position in the private realm, women experienced rights violations differently to men, and that the nature of violation, which was often of a sexual nature, was not treated as seriously under international law. Adopting this view of 'women's interests', activists pushed these claims in key UN conferences including the 1993 Vienna Conference on Human Rights, the 1994 Cairo Conference on Population and the 1995 Beijing World Conference on Women. Through these conferences, feminist activists concerned with women's experiences of war and conflict argued that sexually based crimes such as rape and enforced pregnancy needed to be seen as egregious violations of humanitarian law (Copelon 2000: 219; Freeman 1999). At the same time as working through these conferences, feminists were attentive to opportunities to pursue women's rights issues through the newly created UN International Criminal Tribunal for Yugoslavia (ICTY) (1993) and the International Criminal Tribunal for Rwanda (ICTR) (1994) that were established to prosecute war crimes arising from the conflicts in these countries.

Feminist activists were quick to engage with the ad hoc tribunals. Relying on extensive evidence of the use of mass rape as an instrument of war and genocide in the conflicts in Yugoslavia and Rwanda,[5] women's groups successfully undertook an extensive lobbying effort to have rape recognised as both a war crime and a crime against humanity in the statutes of the ICTY and ICTR (Freeman 1999). This first step did not mean that rape was automatically prosecuted in applicable cases at either tribunal. Indeed, ensuring the prosecution of such cases by the tribunals has been a constant challenge for feminist activists. Women's activists have had to work at a number of levels to pressure the tribunals to take on these cases. They have operated as lobbyists, through organisations such as the Women's Project of Human Rights Watch (IWHRC), and as lawyers in the preparation of *amicus curaie* briefs which have helped demonstrate to the tribunals the relevance of a gender perspective of the law (see Gardam and Jarvis 2001: 219). In a number of instances, demands for action from 'outside' feminist lobbyists have been facilitated by key female prosecutors and judges who have been willing to pursue sexual violence and other gender issues from inside the tribunals (Nahapetian 1999: 133).

The efforts of women's NGOs and lawyers have been rewarded with some significant developments in the jurisprudence of sexual violence in international law. At the ICTR, the case of *Prosecutor v. Jean Paul Akayesu* has been one particularly noteworthy case. Akayesu, who served as the equivalent of a mayor at the Taba commune, was tried and convicted of ordering, instigating, aiding and abetting crimes against humanity as well as acts of genocide against Tutsis during the 1994 Rwandan Civil War. The prosecution did not initially include charges of sexual violence in this case. However, this changed after the only female judge on the tribunal, Judge Navanethem Pillay, heard initial witness testimony of the use of rape and other forms of sexual violence by the accused. While Judge Pillay pursued the testimony of witnesses, women's NGOs, including IWHRC, developed an *amicus curaie* brief for the tribunal, outlining the need to include rape in charges against Akayesu (Copelon 2000: 225). When the tribunal handed down its judgement in 1998, it reflected some of the key arguments made by feminists involved in the case. The tribunal made three significant findings: first, that sexual violence was an integral part of the genocide in Rwanda; second, that rape and other forms of sexual violence were independent crimes constituting crimes against humanity; and third, that rape should be defined in a broad and progressive manner (Askin 1999).

The tribunal's decision that Akayesu had committed genocide through acts of sexual violence and rape was especially significant. For the first time, the law recognised that rape and sexual violence could:

> constitute genocide in the same way as any other act so long as they were committed with the specific intent to destroy in whole or in part, a particular group targeted as such. Indeed rape and sexual violence ... certainly constitute one of the worst ways of inflict[ing] harm on the victim as he or she suffers both bodily and mental harm ... Sexual violence was an integral part of the process of destruction targeting Tutsi women and specifically contributing to their destruction and to the destruction of the Tutsi group as a whole.
>
> (Akayesu judgment in Askin 1999)

This judgment moved a long way from the idea of rape as an injury against a woman's honour. First and foremost, it recognised the serious bodily and mental harm of rape on individual women. Moreover, it linked these acts to the destruction of the group, thus demonstrating an awareness of the connection between gender and ethnic identity. In other words, it accepted that these acts could be used specifically to destroy the women members of the community – that they were gender-based. It also found that the physical and mental damage suffered by women experiencing these acts was such that they were intended to prevent births within the group (Gardam and Jarvis 2001: 195). Through this judgment, women were recognised as individuals, as members of a group as well as having a reproductive role. For once, the woman of international law was seen as being multi-dimensional.

The tribunal's definition of rape in the Akayesu case also represented a breakthrough in terms of recognising women's experience of this form of violence. The tribunal found that rape was 'a physical invasion of a sexual nature, committed on a person under circumstances which are coercive'. In January 2000, the ICTR upheld this definition in the case of *Prosecutor* v. *Musema*, stating that 'the essence of rape is not the particular details of the body parts and objects involved, but rather the aggression that is expressed in a sexual manner under conditions of coercion' (in Boon 2001: 649). The definition was an advance on the existing international legal definition that had failed to recognise the violent and individual aspects of rape. It is also an improvement on most common law definitions in that it removes the focus on acts of penetration, which views rape from the perpetrator's point of view, and replaces it with 'invasion', which takes a victim's perspective (Boon 2001: 650). The emphasis on coercion rather than the more problematic notion of consent used in most common law definitions of rape further shifts the definition towards a victim's perspective of the crime. While it is probable that adopting this perspective reinforces the notion of women as 'victims', it does, at the same time, construct women as subjects, rather than just the objects of the law.

Trials at the ICTY have also brought about some important developments in jurisprudence related to women and international law. The tribunal has convicted several people on charges of rape as a form of torture which, in this context, is considered a war crime and thus a 'grave breach' of the Geneva Conventions (Nahapetian 1999: 131). In 2001, in the case against *Kunarac, Kovac and Vukovic*, the ICTY convicted the accused on charges of rape as a war crime and rape as a crime against humanity (ICTY 2001).[6] In sentencing Kunarac at the ICTY, Judge Florence Mumba stated:

> By the totality of these acts you have shown the most glaring disrespect for the women's dignity *and their fundamental right to sexual self-determination,* on a scale that far surpasses even what one might call, for want of a better expression, the 'average seriousness' of rapes during wartime.
>
> (International Criminal Tribunal for Yugoslavia 2001: 5, emphasis added)

Mumba's reference to women's right to sexual self-determination is a radical shift in international law as it rejects the notion that women are naturally submissive to men. Her statement demonstrates that there is a growing understanding on the part of some judges that women are not merely the dependants of men or mothers of children under the law, but individuals who have the right to control their own bodies. This judgment underlines further the importance of having judges sympathetic to gender issues within these institutions.

New opportunities at the ICC

The ICTY and the ICTR established the background against which the ICC was developed. The precedence set by the tribunals offered both the framers of the ICC and activists wanting to challenge existing norms of international law a range of new opportunities. Before analysing the ways in which women's activists have sought to further advance 'women's interests' under the ICC, it is necessary to outline the origins and significance of the court.

Although an international criminal court had been mooted since 1937, the proposal was not given serious attention until the early 1990s. When, in 1993, the proposal to establish the ICC was put on the table at the General Assembly of the UN it was developed remarkably quickly, at least in terms of international institution-building. The ICC statute was adopted in Rome on 17 July 1998 and the court came into being on 1 July 2002 after 60 countries ratified the statute.[7] The process of devising and ratifying the statute was facilitated by the end of the Cold War – which enabled greater consensus within the UN including the Security Council – as well as growing international pressure from a range of NGOs to bring an end to immunity for perpetrators of international criminal law (for a discussion see Dieng 2002: 690–3). The creation in the early 1990s of two ad hoc tribunals to prosecute war criminals also led to demands for the development of a permanent international body to uphold international criminal law.

The ICC is a unique institution, different to other international legal bodies such as the International Court of Justice (ICJ) as well as other previous and existing ad hoc international criminal law tribunals. One of the features which differentiates it from the ICJ, is its ability to hold *individuals* (and not just states) accountable for criminal acts under international law. Unlike the ad hoc tribunals, the court is a permanent, treaty-based organisation. It has jurisdiction over crimes committed within the territory of a ratifying state or by a national of a signatory state operating in other countries.[8] The statute also gives the UN Security Council the ability, under certain circumstances, to refer a crime to the court that involves a non-state national or occurs on the territory of a non-signatory state. An important feature of the ICC statute is that it attempts to balance state sovereignty with a system of international justice through the notion of complementarity. As outlined in Articles 17 to 19 of the statute, the ICC cannot exercise jurisdiction over a case if a national court addresses it. The ICC can only intervene to prosecute an alleged criminal when a state has demonstrated its *inability* or *unwillingness* to carry out an investigation (see Robertson 2000: 350). The ICC statute upholds the principle of double jeopardy, which means that once a national court has heard a case, so long as the proceedings were legitimate, it cannot be re-heard by the ICC.

The offences over which the ICC has jurisdiction fall into four main categories: genocide, crimes against humanity, war crimes, and aggression.[9] Some of these crimes have been previously codified under international law within such instruments as the Geneva Conventions and Protocols, the Convention on Genocide and the Convention against Torture.[10] However, these instruments have been difficult to enforce, allowing violators to escape justice. The ICC therefore provides the first permanent court with the capacity to enforce penalties against these execrable crimes. Also, under the Rome Statue and its two subsidiary documents – the Elements of Crimes (EOC) and the Rules of Procedures and Evidence (RPE) – these crimes have been restated to give them greater currency and up-to-date expression (Lee 2002: 751). At least in relation to the first three categories of crime, the ICC statute also reflects important recent developments in international criminal jurisprudence, especially those arising from the ICTY and ICTR. As the following discussion illustrates, the elaboration of these categories of crimes in the ad hoc tribunals and their codification in the Rome Statute have provided an important opportunity structure for the reconfiguration of 'women' and their rights under international law.

Drawing on their experience with the two ad hoc tribunals, women's activists have been persistent in their efforts to have a gender perspective incorporated into the ICC statute. One organisation, the Women's Caucus for Gender Justice (WCGJ), was particularly active in this regard. Created in 1997, it included over 300 women's organisations and 500 individuals, and had a mandate to 'ensure that the International Criminal Court will be able to effectively investigate and prosecute crimes of sexual and gender violence' (WCGJ 2000). In order to achieve its objectives, the WCGJ played an active role at the 1998 Rome Conference and the numerous subsequent prepcoms to establish the EOC and RPE for the ICC. Since the ICC came into being in July 2002, the WCGJ was disbanded, but the Women's Initiatives for Gender Justice (WIGJ) has continued to monitor developments. The WCGJ/WIGJ has used a variety of tactics to influence proceedings, including the preparation and presentation of briefs to delegates, direct lobbying of delegates and governments through the use of open letters and petitions, and through press releases. Both organisations have made good use of the internet, creating an e-newsletter to inform interested parties around the world about developments at the prepcoms and to call on them to lobby national governments to support particular initiatives. Since the ICC became a reality, the WIGJ has lobbied hard to ensure that the senior personnel of the court, including its judges and prosecutorial staff, are sensitive to women's rights issues (see WCGJ 2002a).

The WCGJ and other like-minded activists have had some success, inserting into the ICC statute as well as the EOC and RPE documents an expanded conception of women and their interests to that which existed in earlier international law statutes. This broader view is obvious not only in terms of the nature of crimes included in the Rome Statute but also in procedural and structural matters. In relation to the crime aspect, the ICC statute has come to reflect the demands of women's activists in two of its main articles. Due in part to their efforts, Article 7, relating to crimes against humanity and Article 8, concerning war crimes, include reference to sexual violence as acts constituting such crimes. These articles remove the moral element of these offences – which, in earlier international law statutes, linked such acts to insults against 'honour' and the lesser crime of 'humiliating and degrading treatment' – and place them in the category of grave breaches of international law. Further, to emphasise the gravity of sexually based crimes against humanity, women's NGOs were successful in having these crimes enumerated in a separate sub-paragraph (Moshan 1998: 177).

Feminist activists were also successful in securing a broad-based definition of types of sexual violence constituting war crimes and crimes against humanity. In relation to war crimes these include:

> Rape, sexual slavery, enforced prostitution, forced pregnancy, enforced sterilization, or any other form of sexual violence of comparable gravity.
>
> (International Criminal Court 2002: Article 7 (h))

Similar crimes are enumerated under the category of crimes against humanity (see Article 8 (b) (xxii)). The codification for the first time of the offences of sexual slavery and forced pregnancy[11] as an element of war crimes and crimes against humanity represents a significant shift toward international law, better reflecting women's experience of armed conflict. As witnesses had testified at both the ICTY and ICTR, these crimes were used extensively in both the Yugoslavian and Rwandan conflicts (for a full discussion see Boon 2001: 656–67). Before the crime of forced pregnancy was adopted into the statute, feminist activists had to battle with lobbyists from the Vatican as well as Islamic representatives and American anti-abortion groups who feared that the enumeration of this crime would interfere with national anti-abortion laws and were in favour of limiting women's reproductive rights (Stanley 1998; WCGJ 1998; Chappell forthcoming). The eventual inclusion of forced pregnancy represents a major victory for the WCGJ who were pursuing an expanded understanding of women's interests, through a rights framework, in the face of strong opposition supporting the status quo.

The influence of feminist activists can also be seen in the way gender has been 'mainstreamed' in sections of the statute. For instance, Article 7 (h) includes gender as a ground for persecution, alongside political, racial, religious and other such categories. The mention of gender as a form of persecution is important not least because of its potential use in other contexts, including women's claims to refugee status on the basis of gender persecution, which, except in a few jurisdictions such as Canada, the US, and Australia, has seldom been accepted as legitimate (Charlesworth and Chinkin 2000: 320). It is possible that this article will also prove helpful in the prosecution of war criminals who rape or otherwise violate women as an expression of their misogyny, rather than as a means of persecuting a particular ethnic or religious group (Moshan 1998: 182). Similarly, Article 21, which prohibits discrimination based on gender in the application and interpretation of the statute, reflects an attempt to ensure gender concerns are considered in interpretations of the statute. It is hoped that this article will be applied in cases where state parties may prove to be 'unwilling or unable' to investigate and prosecute gender-based crimes. The incorporation of these broader gender articles were again hard-won victories for the Women's Caucus against the Vatican and Arab League countries. Opposition to the articles was based on a fear that replacing the terms men and women with 'gender' would challenge the traditional roles and expectations of the two sexes in various cultures and would also open the door to claims of persecution based on homosexuality and transexuality (Copelon 2000: 236). Due to the intervention of these latter groups, a narrower and somewhat more muddled definition of gender[12] than that proposed by women's activists was accepted in the statute. Nevertheless, its inclusion was an important advance given gender had never before been defined in any international legal statute. Moreover, it comes with the prospect of being subject to further refinement through future feminist intervention in the law (see Facio 1999).

Women's NGOs have also had some success at influencing the structural aspects of the court. After much lobbying from the WCGJ, some effort has been made to ensure that the staff of the ICC is representative of women and gender interests more broadly. The statute includes a statement that there should be '[a] fair representation of female and male judges' (Article 36 (8) (a) (iii)) and notes that in nominating judges, state parties 'shall also take into account the need to include judges with legal expertise on specific issues including ... violence against women or children' (Article 36 (8) (b)). Article 42 determines that the prosecutor will appoint advisers with expertise in sexual and gender violence while Article 43 states that the registrar of the court shall provide a victims unit which shall 'include staff with expertise in trauma, including trauma related to crimes of sexual violence'.

The seriousness with which state parties treat these representative issues was tested with the call for nomination for, and election of judges to, the first bench of the ICC. When nominations closed on 30 November 2002, ten women had been nominated out of 45 candidates. The rules governing the elections identify gender, region, and field of expertise as minimum eligibility requirements for ICC judges. They also specify that at least six men and six women are to be elected to the ICC bench. The WCGJ was very active around the nomination and election period, calling on state parties to nominate and elect women to these positions. They conducted a survey of views of all nominees in relation to women's human rights in an effort to ensure that those judges who were selected had a knowledge of gender issues (WCGJ 2002b). In a sign of the influence of the organisation, in January 2003 female judicial nominees agreed to take part in panel discussions organised by the WCGJ (WCGJ 2003a).

Elections for the first bench of the ICC were held between 3 and 7 February 2003. In the event, seven women and eleven men were elected as judges in a long and drawn out process that took five days and 33 rounds of voting. When six female judges were elected in the first round of voting, the results were met with spontaneous applause from the floor. Representatives from the WCGJ were also elated but not completely satisfied. They continued to lobby delegates and state parties to ensure that the election of women judges was not limited to the minimum gender representation requirements (WCGJ 2003b). Many of the female judges that have been elected to the ICC (including Navanethem Pillay (South Africa), Maureen Clark (Ireland), Elizabeth Odio Benito (Costa Rica), and Anita Usacka (Latvia)) have an extensive background in women's human rights issues. Moreover, some of the male judges, such as Adrian Fulford, the first openly homosexual judge to be appointed to the High Court in Britain, also have a background in issues related to violence against women (ICC 2002). Although there is no guarantee that these results will produce better outcomes for women, they are certainly a step in the right direction and go further than any other international legal tribunal in terms of ensuring female representation and representation of gender issues.

Concerns about the representation of women have also been evident in the efforts of the first ICC prosecutor, Luis Morento Ocampo, to ensure women are appointed to senior roles in the office. In 2004, the prosecutor nominated three women for the second post of deputy prosecutor to ensure the Assembly of State Parties would elect a woman (Schense 2004: 3). Ocampo's efforts were backed up, if not influenced, by a strong campaign led by the WIGJ to encourage female applications for the position. The WIGJ compiled information on the experience and skills of the applicants and held panels for candidates to address delegates to the Assembly

(Inder 2004: 4). When the Assembly met in September 2004, it elected Fatou Bensouda from Gambia, who has a strong background in gender issues and the law, to take on the position of deputy prosecutor, head of prosecutions.

A final area where feminist concerns have been reflected in the ICC statute is in relation to procedural matters. Drawing on (mostly negative) experiences from the ad hoc tribunals, feminists, through the WCGJ, have pushed to ensure that the prosecutor is obligated to address gender issues. As a result, the prosecutor is charged with investigating and prosecuting crimes in a way that 'respect[s] the interests and personal circumstances of victims and witnesses, including . . . gender'. He or she is also required to 'take into account the nature of the crime, in particular where it involves sexual violence, gender violence or violence against children' (Article 54 (1) (b)). Article 68 of the statute, which gives the court the authority to protect victims and witnesses, specifies the need to give due attention to victims of sexual violence, which may include the use of *in camera* evidence to shield victims from confronting their aggressors in the court room.

The WCGJ/WIGJ and other feminist activists have obviously made some important advances in shaping both the crime and procedural aspects of the ICC statute. However, it would be wrong to assume that activists have achieved all their aims or that the ICC resolves every problem relating to women and gender issues under international law. One of the major disappointments for women's activists in relation to influencing crimes under the statute is the absence of any reference to sexual violence in Article 6 pertaining to the crime of genocide. In part, its absence can be explained by the fact that the *Akayesu* judgment of the ICTR, which created new jurisprudence on the issue, was handed down after the issue of genocide was settled at the Rome Conference. Having missed the opportunity to influence the statute itself, and armed with the judgment of the ICTR, women's activists then turned their attention to having the matter clarified in the Elements of Crimes document. The WCGJ prepared a detailed submission on the issue for the February 1999 prepcom. Its submission used similar reasoning to the ICTR to argue for the inclusion in the EOC of sexual violence as a feature of this offence.[13] In the event, the coalition was unsuccessful in having a general statement to this effect included in the EOC, but had to be satisfied with a footnote stating that genocide may include 'acts of torture, rape, sexual violence or inhuman treatment' (Copelon 2000: 235). More optimistic observers, such as Warbrick and McGoldrick (2001: 421), hope that the omission of sexual violence from the body of the EOC text on genocide was main- tained 'only because it was felt unnecessary to expressly state something that clearly represented current law'. Whether their view is correct will be an important test of how far gender issues have been 'mainstreamed' into international criminal law.

Other problems are also inherent in the existing statute and supporting documents. Feminists have expressed concern that the ICC Statute qualifies crimes of sexual violence and gender-based persecution in such a way that they are not *automatically* considered to be as grave as other war crimes and crimes against humanity but will have to be proven to be so (Moshan 1998: 182–3). Moreover, the rules relating to crimes against humanity state that such crimes must be part of a 'widespread and systematic attack', committed with the knowledge of the attack. This legal language could create problems for addressing women's experiences of armed conflict because attacks on them are often isolated events and, at least in the case of the crime of forced pregnancy, a perpetrator can use a defence of not having knowledge of actually impregnating the victim (Moshan 1998: 183).

For Charlesworth and Chinkin (2000: 334), problems with developments at the ad hoc tribunals and the development of the ICC are more generalised. First, they note that violence against women in situations of armed conflict and peace time is 'part of the same spectrum of behaviour'. By focusing on violence in times of conflict, recent developments do little to challenge the 'acceptability of violence and . . . the private order of the domination of women' at other times. Second, in their view, international criminal law continues to employ a very limited understanding of women by emphasising their sexual and reproductive identities. The emphasis on sexual violence, including acts of forced pregnancy, keeps women in the role of 'other' – identified only through their relationship with men and children. Finally, the social burden that falls on women in armed conflict remains unacknowledged and women continue to be cast as passive victims rather than as survivors or agents of change. Gardam and Jarvis agree that recent advances do little to alter the social, economic and health aspects women experience as a result of armed conflict (2001: 229).

Women and international law institutions: an assessment

These critiques point to ongoing challenges for feminist activists and the international community as a whole. However, as Durham notes, in making these assessments critics may be asking too much of international law (2002: 657). The institutions and norms of this area of the law 'make no claim to deal with the basis of social structure in general'. To be fair, any assessment of recent developments needs to concentrate on measuring what has been achieved within the restricted ambit of what international humanitarian and criminal legal institutions are established to do – that is, ensure the survival of as many people as possible during the most extreme circumstances and to bring to account those who break the rules relating to established norms of behaviour under these circumstances.

On these grounds, it can be argued that some important inroads have been made to expand the notion of women's interests under international law. Feminist activists, working through organisations such as the IWHRC and WCGJ have had some degree of success both in terms of influencing the nature of crimes and the representative nature of international legal institutions. In terms of crimes, activists have been limited to working within the bounds of an existing international law that continues to emphasise women's sexual and reproductive identities. Nevertheless, within these confines, they have been able to make sure that the law's construction of these identities is more subtle than ever before. Women are no longer understood solely as mothers or as the dependants of men, but as individuals who have the right to sexual autonomy and who can be harmed both mentally and physically through acts of violence such as rape. Crimes previously ignored in international law, such as forced pregnancy, have been given due recognition. Moreover, to some degree, gender is 'mainstreamed' in the ICC statute, which should make it more difficult to ignore these concerns in future prosecutions and judgments. It is important to note that these developments did not occur without significant opposition, and therefore they represent important victories for feminist activists such as those working through the WCGJ.

Learning from the experience of the ad hoc tribunals, where women's voices have been muted but nonetheless influential, feminists have also been determined to see gender justice in terms of representation within the ICC. Securing a place for women on the ICC bench, coupled with signs of an increasing sensitivity to gender issues in the procedures of the court, have been significant advances on previous practice. Feminists now face the task of ensuring that these changes are more than just tokenistic and symbolic. The WCGJ campaign around the election of judges is a strong indication that the issue of gender representation is set to remain on the agenda for the foreseeable future.

A final but important point in assessing these developments relates to the potential influence that changes wrought by these international institutions can bring to law-making at the national level. As noted earlier, the ICC statute can only hear cases not prosecuted by national courts. Thus much of the onus for bringing war criminals to justice remains with domestic-level institutions. It is the hope and expectation of those seeking legal reform that in hearing cases related to war crimes and crimes against humanity these institutions will apply the latest international legal norms and jurisprudence (Warbrick and McGoldrick 2001: 428). If and when this occurs, it will not only enable a better acknowledgment at the national level of the experiences of women during armed conflict, but may also help to expand an understanding of women's lives in peacetime. For instance, one step forward would be the application at the national level of the expanded definition of rape that is being developed through international jurisprudence; namely one which emphasises the violation from a victim's rather than a perpetrator's point of view. Indeed, such a development may assist in bringing to light the spectrum of women's experiences of violence, as noted by Charlesworth and Chinkin (2000) and others (see MacKinnon 1994), but hitherto ignored in international law.

Conclusion

In recent years, feminists have challenged the way in which international criminal and humanitarian law constructs 'women' and understands gender. Whilst women and their interests are still defined within gendered confines, a more nuanced and diverse understanding of women's experiences is starting to emerge. Feminists have been able to unsettle existing conceptions of 'women' by taking advantage of opportunities arising from the development of new institutions such as the ad hoc tribunals and the ICC, as well as the evolution in jurisprudence relating to women, gender, and the law. Once the newly elected bench of the ICC starts hearing cases, further opportunities for challenging gender norms may arise. There is no guarantee that activists' demands will be met in future, especially given the (growing) strength of opposition to changes to the gender status quo. Nor will any future development toward a more complex and diverse construction of women in international law come about of its own accord. The gradual replacement of the one-dimensional female figure of international law with a multi-dimensional woman will only be developed through the ongoing vigilance and efforts of women's activists operating at both the international and national level.

Notes

1 A different version of this argument first appeared in *Policy, Organization and Society*, as 'Women, gender and international institutions: exploring new opportunities at the International Criminal Court', 22 (1), 2003. The author gratefully acknowledges their permission to reproduce substantial portions of that article here.

2 In this analysis political institutions are understood in their widest sense and include domestic level parliamentary, political party, bureaucratic, and legal institutions as well as international political institutions including the UN and its cognate bodies such as the ICC.

3 As Teghtsoonian points out in Chapter 7 of this volume, these opportunities at the bureaucratic level can also disappear with the election of new governments.

4 Although rape has not been given serious attention under international law it has been prohibited by the law of war since the time of Richard II in 1385. It was treated as an infringement of the Lieber Code of 1863 during the American Civil War. More recently, it was prosecuted as a war crime under the Tokyo Tribunal after the Second World War, and included in the Geneva Conventions (Meron 1993: 425).

5 The UN estimates that upwards of 20,000 women were raped between 1992 and 1994 in the former Yugoslavia (quoted in Nahapetian 1999: 127). Figures for Rwanda are difficult to find, but estimates indicate that hundreds of

thousands of women experienced some form of sexual violence during this conflict (Nahapetian 1999)

6 Crimes against humanity are defined as 'inhumane acts of a very serious nature committed as part of a widespread or systematic attack against a civilian population on political, ethnic or religious grounds. They may be committed in times of peace or war' (in Robertson 2000: 295).

7 It should be noted, however, that the USA has refused to sign the statute for fear of frivolous or politically motivated prosecutions of its nationals. This is despite the fact that under the Clinton administration the USA played a prominent role at the Rome Conference and significantly influenced the court's rules and structures (for a discussion see Robertson 2000: 325–7). Under the Bush Administration the USA has, controversially, used its dominance in world affairs in 2002 and 2003 to pressure the UN Security Council to grant US military personnel immunity from the court under Section 98 of the ICC statute. It has also entered into bilateral agreements with some signatory states for the same purpose.

8 In other words, 'crimes committed by a national of a non-State party on the territory of a State Party are subject to the Court's jurisdiction' (Dieng 2002: 683). Moreover, crimes committed by a national of a state party on the territory of a non-state party are also subject to the court's rules.

9 This latter category is yet to be defined under international law, and will not come under the jurisdiction of the court until state parties to the ICC can agree on its meaning.

10 The full title of these treaties are: *The Convention of the Prevention and Punishment of the Crime of Genocide*, 9 December 1948, 78 UNTS 277; *Geneva Conventions I–IV*, 12 August 1949 and the *Protocol I and II to the Geneva Conventions of 12 August 1949*, June 1977; *Convention against Torture and Other Cruel, Inhuman or Degrading Treatment or Punishment* 10 December 1984, 1465 UNTS 85.

11 Article 7 (2) (e) defines forced pregnancy as: 'the unlawful confinement of a woman forcibly made pregnant, with the intent of affecting the ethnic composition of any population or carrying out other grave violations of international law'. To satisfy conservative delegates an additional rider was added: 'This definition shall not in any way be interpreted as affecting national laws relating to pregnancy'.

12 Article 7 (3) states 'that the term "gender" refers to the two sexes, male and female, within the context of society. The term "gender" does not indicate any meaning different from the above'. By including mention of the two sexes anti-gender delegates were hoping to exclude sexual orientation from the definition of gender persecution (Copelon 2000: 237). Whether they will be successful in their aims is yet to be tested.

13 In its submission the WCGJ carefully documented how sexual violence is an instrument or means of committing genocide in respect to each of the five enumerated acts of genocide including: genocide by killing, genocide by inflicting serious bodily or mental harm, genocide by inflicting conditions of life calculated to bring about the physical destruction of the group, genocide by imposing measures intended to prevent birth, and genocide by forcibly transferring children of the group. The Akayesu judgment considered sexual violence to constitute the first four of these (see WCGJ 1999).

References

Askin, K. (1999) 'Sexual violence in decisions and indictments of the Yugoslav and Rwandan tribunals: current status', *The American Journal of International Law*, 93(1): 97–123.

Banaszak, L. (1996) *Why Movements Succeed or Fail: Opportunity Culture, and the struggle for Woman Suffrage*, Princeton: Princeton University Press.

Boon, K. (2001) 'Rape and forced pregnancy under the ICC statute: human dignity, autonomy, and consent', *Columbia Human Rights Law Review*, 32: 624–75.

Brown, W. (1995) *States of Injury: Power and Freedom in Late Modernity*, Princeton: Princeton University Press.

Chappell, L. (2002) *Gendering Government: Feminist Engagement with the State in Australia and Canada*, Vancouver: University of British Columbia Press.

—— (forthcoming) 'Women's rights and religious opposition: the politics of gender at the International Criminal Court, in Y. Abu-Laban (ed.) *Gendering the Nation State: Canadian and Comparative Perspectives*, Vancouver: UBC Press.

Charlesworth, H. and Chinkin, C. (2000) *The Boundaries of International Law: A Feminist Analysis*, Manchester: Manchester University Press.

Copelon, R. (2000) 'Gender crimes as war crimes: integrating crimes against women into international criminal law', *McGill Law Journal*, 46: 217–40.

Dieng, A. (2002) 'International criminal justice: from paper to practice – a contribution from the International Criminal Tribunal for Rwanda to the establishment of the International Criminal Court', *Fordham International Law Journal*, 25: 688–707.

Dobrowolsky, A. (2000) *The Politics of Pragmatism: Women, Representation and Constitutionalism in Canada*, Oxford: Oxford University Press.

Durham, H. (2002) 'Women, armed conflict and international law', Current Issues and Comments, *IRRC*, 84: 847: 655–9.

Facio, A. (1999) 'Integrating gender into the world's first permanent criminal court'. Online. Available at: www.iccwomen.org/archive/resources/bplus5/part1.htm (accessed 9 November 2004).

Freeman, M. (1999) 'International institutions and gendered justice', *Journal of International Affairs*, 52(2): 513.

Gardam, J.G. and Jarvis, M.J. (2001) *Women, Armed Conflict and International Law*, The Hague: Kluwer Law International.

Inder, B. (2004) 'Short-changing global justice', *The International Criminal Court Monitor*, November.

International Criminal Court (2002) *ICC Judges, Facts and Background, Resumes*. Online. Available at: www.iccnow.org/building the court/judges/statusofnominations/resumes.html (accessed 6 January 2003).

International Criminal Tribunal for Yugoslavia (2001) *Press Release. Judgement of Trial Chamber II in the Kunarac, Kovac and Vukovic case*. Online. Available at: www.un.org/icty/pressreal/p566–e.html (accessed 6 January 2003).

Katzenstein M.F. (1998) *Faithless and Fearless: Moving Feminist Protest Inside the Church and Military*, Princeton: Princeton University Press.

Keck, M. and Sikkink, K. (1998) *Activists Beyond Borders: Advocacy Networks in International Politics*, Ithaca: Cornell University Press.

Lee, R.S. (2002) 'An assessment of the ICC statute', *Fordham International Law Journal*, 25: 750–66.

MacKinnon, C. (1989) *Toward a Feminist Theory of the State*, Cambridge, MA: Harvard University Press.

—— (1994) 'Rape, genocide, and women's human rights', *Harvard Women's Law Journal*, 17: 5–16.

Meron, T. (1993) 'Rape as a crime under international humanitarian Law', *The American Journal of International Law*, 87: 424–8.

Mohanty, C.T. (2003) ' "Under western eyes" revisited: feminist solidarity through anticapitalist struggles', *SIGNs: Journal of Culture and Society*, 28: 499–538.

Moshan, B.S. (1998) 'Women, war, and words: the gender component in the permanent International Criminal Court's definition of crimes against humanity', *Fordham International Law Journal*, 22: 154–84.

Nahapetian, K. (1999) 'Selective justice: prosecuting rape in the International Criminal Tribunals for the former Yugoslavia and Rwanda', *Berkeley Women's Law Journal*, 14: 126–35.

Rai, S.M. (1996) 'Women and the state in the third world: some issues for debate', in S.M. Rai and G. Lievesley (eds) *Women and the State: International Perspectives*, London: Taylor & Francis.

Robertson, G. (2000) *Crimes Against Humanity: The Struggle for Global Justice*, Melbourne: Penguin.

Rome Statute for the International Criminal Court. 1998. UN Doc. A/Conf. 183/9.

Schense, J. (2004) 'Prosecutor's office gears up for investigations', *The International Criminal Court Monitor*, February.

Stanley, A. (1998) 'Semantics stalls pact labeling rape as a war crime', *New York Times*, 9 July, A3.

Vickers, J. (1997) 'Toward a feminist understanding of representation', in J. Arscott and L. Trimble (eds) *In the Presence of Women: Representation in Canadian Governments*, Canada: Harcourt Brace and Co.

Warbrick, C. and McGoldrick, D. (2001) 'The Preparatory Commission for the International Criminal Court: Current Developments – Public International Law', *International and Comparative Law Quarterly*, 50: 420–35.

Women's Caucus for Gender Justice (1998) *The Crime of Forced Pregnancy*. Online. Available at: www.iccwomen.org/icc/iccpc/rome/forcedpreg.html (accessed 2 October 2002).

—— (1999) *Genocide: Sexual Violence as Acts of Genocide*, submitted to 16–26 February Preparatory Committee for the International Criminal Court. Online. Available at: www.iccwomen.org/icc/iccpc/0219999pc/genocide.html (accessed 2 October 2002).

—— (2000) *Recommendations and Commentary to the Elements Annex and Rules of Procedure and Evidence*, submitted to the 12–30 June Preparatory Committee for the International Criminal Court. Online. Available at: www.iccwomen.org/icc/iccpc062000pc/elementsannex.html (accessed 2 October 2002).

—— (2002a) 'ICC women news: 3:4'. Email (received 7 January 2003).

—— (2002b) 'Women on the court now!' Campaign Communiqué No. 3. Email (received 17 December 2002).

—— (2003a) 'ICC Elections – Panel Discussions with Women Candidates'. Email (received 29 January 2003).

—— (2003b) 'Update – action alert: 6 women elected after first round: Keep advocating for parity on the court'. Email (received 6 February 2003).

Index

www.ingramcontent.com/pod-product-compliance
Ingram Content Group UK Ltd.
Pitfield, Milton Keynes, MK11 3LW, UK
UKHW020357010325
455677UK00021B/498